TRUST IN MEDICINE

Over the past decades, public trust in medical professionals has steadily declined. This decline of trust and its replacement by ever tighter regulations are increasingly frustrating physicians. However, most discussions of trust are either abstract philosophical discussions or social science investigations not easily accessible to clinicians. The authors, one a surgeon-turned-philosopher and the other an analytical philosopher working in medical ethics, combined their expertise to write a book that straddles the gap between the practical and theoretical.

Using an approach grounded in the methods of conceptual analysis found in analytical philosophy which also draws from approaches to medical diagnosis, the authors have conceived an internally coherent and comprehensive definition of trust to help elucidate the concept and explain its decline in the medical context.

This book should appeal to all interested in the ongoing debate about the decline of trust – be it as medical professionals, medical ethicists, medical lawyers, or philosophers.

MARKUS WOLFENSBERGER is Emeritus Professor of Otorhinolaryngology at the University of Basel. Until his retirement in 2010, he was head of the Department of Otorhinolaryngology, Head and Neck Surgery, as well as director of the Head and Neck Tumour Centre at the University Hospital of Basel. He also holds a doctorate in medical ethics and was, for many years, chair of the Clinical Ethics Advisory Board at the University Hospital of Basel. His particular interest, both as a surgeon and as a researcher, was in cancer of the head and neck. As a clinical ethicist one of his major interests was in preventing unnecessary and over-aggressive cancer treatment.

ANTHONY WRIGLEY is Professor of Ethics at the Centre for Professional Ethics (PEAK), School of Law, Keele University, UK. He is a philosopher with a special interest in issues in biomedical ethics. His particular area of interest is the analysis of key concepts in bioethics, including vulnerability, hope, harm, personhood, mental illness, consent for others, moral authority, and the nature of moral expertise. His many publications include *The European Textbook on Ethics in Research* (with Jonathan Hughes et al., European Union, 2010), *Ethics, Law and Society Volume V* (edited with Nicky Priaulx, Ashgate, 2013), and *Loss, Dying and Bereavement in the Criminal Justice System* (edited with Sue Read and Sotirios Santatzoglou, Routledge, 2018).

CAMBRIDGE BIOETHICS AND LAW

This series of books – formerly called Cambridge Law, Medicine and Ethics – was founded by Cambridge University Press with Alexander McCall Smith as its first editor in 2003. It focuses on the law's complex and troubled relationship with medicine across both the developed and the developing world. In the past twenty years, we have seen, in many countries, increasing resort to the courts by dissatisfied patients and a growing use of the courts to attempt to resolve intractable ethical dilemmas. At the same time, legislatures across the world have struggled to address the questions posed by both the successes and the failures of modern medicine, while international organisations such as the WHO and UNESCO now regularly address issues of medical law.

It follows that we would expect ethical and policy questions to be integral to the analysis of the legal issues discussed in this series. The series responds to the high profile of medical law in universities, in legal and medical practice, as well as in public and political affairs. We seek to reflect the evidence that many major health-related policy debates in the UK, Europe and the international community over the past two decades have involved a strong medical law dimension. With that in mind, we seek to address how legal analysis might have a trans-jurisdictional and international relevance. Organ retention, embryonic stem cell research, physician assisted suicide and the allocation of resources to fund health care are but a few examples among many. The emphasis of this series is thus on matters of public concern and/or practical significance. We look for books that could make a difference to the development of medical law and enhance the role of medico-legal debate in policy circles. That is not to say that we lack interest in the important theoretical dimensions of the subject, but we aim to ensure that theoretical debate is grounded in the realities of how the law does and should interact with medicine and health care.

Series Editors
Professor Graeme Laurie, *University of Edinburgh*
Professor Richard Ashcroft, *Queen Mary University of London*

TRUST IN MEDICINE

Its Nature, Justification, Significance, and Decline

MARKUS WOLFENSBERGER

University of Basel

ANTHONY WRIGLEY

Keele University

CAMBRIDGE
UNIVERSITY PRESS

CAMBRIDGE
UNIVERSITY PRESS

University Printing House, Cambridge CB2 8BS, United Kingdom

One Liberty Plaza, 20th Floor, New York, NY 10006, USA

477 Williamstown Road, Port Melbourne, VIC 3207, Australia

314-321, 3rd Floor, Plot 3, Splendor Forum, Jasola District Centre, New Delhi - 110025, India

79 Anson Road, #06-04/06, Singapore 079906

Cambridge University Press is part of the University of Cambridge.

It furthers the University's mission by disseminating knowledge in the pursuit of
education, learning and research at the highest international levels of excellence.

www.cambridge.org
Information on this title: www.cambridge.org/9781108732734
DOI: 10.1017/9781108763479

© Markus Wolfensberger and Anthony Wrigley 2019

First published 2019
First paperback edition 2021

A catalogue record for this publication is available from the British Library

Library of Congress Cataloging in Publication data
Names: Wolfensberger, Markus, 1948– author. | Wrigley, Anthony, author.
Title: Trust in medicine : its nature, justifi cation, significance and decline / Markus
Wolfensberger, Universitat Basel, Switzerland and Anthony Wrigley, Keele University.
Description: New York, NY : Cambridge University Press, 2019. | Series: Cambridge
bioethics and law | Includes bibliographical references and index.
Identifiers: LCCN 2019014862 | ISBN 9781108487191 (alk. paper)
Subjects: LCSH: Medical ethics.
Classification: LCC R724 .W585 2019 | DDC 174.2–dc23
LC record available at https://lccn.loc.gov/2019014862

ISBN 978-1-108-48719-1 Hardback
ISBN 978-1-108-73273-4 Paperback

To my wife Erika in gratitude for her unwavering love, trust, companionship, and support

and

to Mags for her love, support, and trust

CONTENTS

FIGURES

TABLES

PREFACE

Anyone picking up this book will probably wonder what motivated us to write a book on trust in medicine and who should consider reading it. We can definitely answer the first question and will certainly try to answer the second.

Let us start with a few words about the genesis of this book. The foundations for this brief monograph were originally part of a research project on medical ethics undertaken by Markus Wolfensberger (M.W.) and supervised by Anthony Wrigley (A.W.). We decided to join the expertise of the surgeon-turned-philosopher (M.W.) with that of the professional academic analytical philosopher with a special interest in medical ethics (A.W.). Keeping this in mind, it should be obvious that the main focus of the book lies on trust in the context of medicine (or, more particularly, on the role of trust in the patient–physician relationship). We will, however, explain how much of what we say is equally applicable to other medical professions. As a caveat, we would like to make it clear that, although we repeatedly refer to legal implications of trust, we do not engage in any detailed analysis on issues of the law.[1]

The initial motivation to work on trust in medicine in the first place arose from reflection upon the more than thirty years during which M. W. practised head and neck cancer surgery. During this time, medical practice changed considerably (most importantly from the 'paternalistic' to the 'shared decision-making' patient–physician relationship model). The one change that he found increasingly haunting was the decline of trust in the patient–physician relationship and its replacement by controls, regulations, and other formal measures. Some people, such as

---

[1] First, because we are medical ethicists, this is primarily a book dealing with the ethical and conceptual issues rather than legal ones, and, second, because any such comment would have to address the difference between the legal systems in the United Kingdom, Europe, and the United States, with which we are primarily concerned. This should not, however, imply that law scholars may not benefit from becoming acquainted with the medical and philosophical perspective.

health-economists and managers of for-profit health institutions, wel-
comed these changes. This is hardly surprising, since such formal measures have a tendency to increase their power and influence. However,
this left M.W. (like many other physicians) puzzled, worried, and feeling
somewhat humiliated. This generated the initial step towards motivating
this entire project by raising the question, 'why should physicians be left
feeling like this at all?' Here, M.W.'s initial description of the problem he
faced might strike a resonant note with many:

> I am *puzzled* because I do not understand why patients, who
> only a few years ago trusted paternalistic physicians, today
> mistrust doctors who listen to them and who are willing to
> discuss possible treatment options. Moreover, I find it hard to
> understand why patients seem so little concerned about this
> development. After all, the patient–physician relationship is
> not just any encounter. It is a special, intimate relationship. In
> almost no other relationship are we equally vulnerable, do we
> have to reveal similarly intimate details, and do we have to let
> ourselves be touched as in the patient–physician relationship.
> In this situation, it would appear to be in the patient's interest
> to trust his doctor. I am *worried* because the vacuum created
> by the disappearance of trust is filled by bureaucratic regula-
> tions and controls and because I know from experience how
> much easier it is to treat a trusting patient. Finally, I *feel
> humiliated* because unsubstantiated mistrust is an offence to
> anyone who does his best to justify the other's trust.

So, years of personal experience as a surgeon in oncology combined
with the many philosophical issues that underpinned these concerns
motivated both authors to look further and deeper into the problem of
the decline of trust in medicine. While many aspects of answering this
question were relatively straightforward, as the reader will doubtless
perceive, this still leaves the more difficult question as to why anyone
should read it. We think that most people will instinctively agree that
trust is important in relationships, especially in such an intimate relationship as the one between patient and physician. Yet, the concept of trust
has found rather little attention in the medical ethics literature, with a few
notable exceptions:

> Autonomy has been a leading idea in philosophical writing on
> bioethics; *trust has been marginal* ... Trust is surely more

important, and particularly so for any ethically adequate
practice of medicine, science, and biotechnology ... Why
then has ... trust secured no more than a walk-on part?[2]

Indeed, although there is no dearth of publications on trust per se,
there is no coherent, robust theory of trust *in medicine*. Moreover, none
of the available definitions of 'trust' enables us to explain what 'trust'
means in the patient–physician relationship; whether (and how) trust can
be justified; why trust has declined; and why (to use O'Neill's words) trust
is important for an ethically adequate practice of medicine.

Using an approach grounded in the methods of conceptual analysis
found in analytical philosophy and bioethics, we have conceived
a definition of trust which (we believe) is internally coherent and comprehensive; which is adaptable to different situations; which can be
applied to individual physicians as well as to the institutions they work
in; and which, most importantly and contrary to the definitions found in
the literature, helps us understand and explain why trust has declined.
We therefore hope this book will appeal to all those who are actively
involved in the ongoing debate about the decline of trust – be it as
medical ethicists, philosophers, medical professionals, including physicians, nurses, healthcare managers, and hospital administrators, as well
as policy makers and legal scholars or, indeed, to anyone who simply has
an interest in the nature of trust in medicine. Furthermore, the discussion
is not intended to be geographically bound but draws upon examples
from the United Kingdom, the United States, and a range of European
countries. As such, our discussion of trust covers aspects one may find in
the National Health Service or in private medicine.

---

[2] O'Neill 2002a, p. ix, our emphasis.

ACKNOWLEDGEMENTS

Although, inevitably, it isn't possible to acknowledge everyone who has commented or provided feedback on the many different elements that have gone into this book, we would like to offer special thanks to those who have made specific or important contributions along the way, be it in the form of detailed comments on draft work, debate, and discussion over particular aspects of argument, or through their support and encouragement. Of these, our sincere thanks to Bobbie Farsides and Jonathan Hughes, who provided extensive comments, questions, and suggestions for possible refinements on Markus's research thesis on the topic of trust. Their generous and detailed feedback helped to motivate and develop many aspects of this book. Our thanks must also go to those individuals and audiences who engaged in some extremely fruitful discussion and feedback on a somewhat eclectic mix of approaches to conceptual analysis and the practical application of such analysis in the field of bioethics. Of these, our special thanks go to Mikey Dunn, Eve Garrard, Neil Manson, Ainsley Newson, Mark Sheehan, and Stephen Wilkinson, as well as colleagues and audiences at Keele University's '30 Years of Medical Ethics and Law: Looking Back, Moving Forward' conference and at the ETHOX Centre at the University of Oxford. Anthony Wrigley would also like to gratefully acknowledge the support he received from Keele University in allowing him research leave to finish writing this book, and the support of colleagues who helped to cover some of his teaching duties while on leave. We would also like to thank the editors, staff, and reviewers at Cambridge University Press for their very useful comments on the initial manuscript and their support during the publication process. Of course, we owe our greatest debts of gratitude to our respective partners, Erika and Mags, who have helped and encouraged us through the project and lent us their unfailing support.

A NOTE ON USAGE

Throughout the book, we seek to add clarity wherever possible by distinguishing between when we are referring directly to a concept and when we are simply using a concept by the use of *single quotation marks*. Thus:

> We provide a pattern-based definition of 'trust'

and

> There are seven characteristic features of 'trust'

are examples of cases where we are referring to the concept of trust itself, in order to offer an analysis of that concept. Whereas:

> Patients are losing trust in physicians

and

> A competent physician has earned the trust of his patients

are examples of cases where we are using the expression.

Moreover, we use *double quotation marks* to identify verbatim quotations from the literature (except in those cases of longer quotations which have been indented instead).

PART I

Introduction

1

Introduction

1.1 Everyday Use of 'Trust'

In her Presidential Address at the Scientific Session of the American Heart Association of 2004, entitled 'Rebuilding an Enduring Trust – A Global Mandate', Alice K. Jacobs said that "one of the most critical issues facing our profession today is the erosion of trust".[1]

We do not doubt that Professor Jacobs got a thundering applause at the end of her address. After all, the decline of trust is something about which everyone might worry. Yet, it is likely that few in the auditorium would have been able to say what exactly they meant by 'trust', why they were worried about the decline of trust (apart from the fact that 'doctoring' had become more difficult lately), and what were the reasons for the alleged decline.

This statement may sound surprising, but it is not. It sounds surprising because we all use the word 'trust' and we all think we know what it is and when its use is appropriate. Yet closer inspection of the way people use 'trust' reveals that the term is often used in a range of different contexts. Here are just a few examples of 'what people trust'. They trust that the weather will be good at the weekend. They trust the brakes on their motorbike. They trust that their car will keep going for another year. They trust that their partner will be faithful. Some people even say that they trust in homeopathy.[2] What these examples illustrate is that this everyday usage or 'folk' understanding of 'trust' is very broad. As we will discuss later, it would probably be more appropriate when considering issues of clarity and accuracy to replace many instances of 'trust' with some other term. To continue with the examples just mentioned as illustration, it would be more appropriate to say that we *hope* that the weather will be good; that we *rely* on the brakes; that we are *confident* that the car will keep going; that some people *believe in* homeopathy. In these

---

[1] Jacobs 2005, p. 3494.
[2] Of course, people also trust in God. We will leave this aside, because it belongs to the discourse of religion and faith – two topics that are outside the scope of this book.

instances, the use of the term 'trust' should ideally be limited only to the case of the faithfulness of our partners. As long as 'trust' is used so imprecisely and in so many different ways, discussion about the meaning, the decline, and the value of trust must border on the futile. Yet, not only the folk understanding but even the definitions of 'trust' we find in the literature are, on the whole, rather vague and (as we will discuss in Chapter 3) neither sufficient to explain the decline of trust nor adequate to explain why we should worry about the decline of trust. It therefore follows that our first and foremost need is an expedient definition of 'trust'. To present such a definition is one of our goals. To avoid any misunderstanding, we do not aspire to present a definition of 'trust' in general but only a definition of 'trust in medicine' or even more particularly of 'trust in physicians' (and other healthcare professionals).[3]

1.2   Two Model Case Histories

Throughout this book, we will try not to argue in the void but to illustrate our arguments with examples (whenever possible from the field of medicine). To set the stage for what is to follow, let us start by presenting *two short model case histories.*[4] Their purpose is to show why we believe that trust has declined and to point to some of the consequences of this decline. The beginning is common to both histories: one day a woman notices a small lump in front of her ear. Since it is painless, she is not overly worried, but when it does not go away after a few months, she consults a physician.

1.2.1   First Case History

After listening to her history, asking a few pertinent questions, and palpating the lump, the doctor tells the patient that this is almost certainly a so-called pleomorphic adenoma of the preauricular salivary gland (the parotid gland).[5] He[6] tells her that this is a benign tumour but that he

---

[3] Although, given the particular expertise of the authors, our primary focus is clearly on trust in the patient–physician relationship, the concept of trust we are offering here we take to be equally applicable to other healthcare professions.

[4] The two case histories are modelled on real cases from the practice of M.W. but are slightly idealised for didactic purposes.

[5] Pleomorphic adenomas are the most common tumours of the parotid gland.

[6] Whenever possible, we have attempted to establish gender balance in our examples through regular use of the female pronoun 'she' or 'her'. However, in cases where we

would nevertheless recommend removing it. After briefly reflecting upon the diagnosis and recommendation, and after consulting with her family, the patient agrees and goes ahead with the recommended surgery.

1.2.2 Second Case History

After listening to her history, asking a few pertinent questions, and briefly examining the patient, the doctor performs an ultrasound exam of the lump and recommends taking a fine-needle aspiration biopsy. After he has reassured the patient that this is a harmless and almost painless procedure, she agrees to it. The aspirate is sent to a pathologist and, a few days later, the patient is told that the cytology (i.e. the result of the needle biopsy) is compatible[7] with a pleomorphic adenoma of the parotid salivary gland. She is informed that (in all likelihood) this is a benign tumour but that, since no biopsy can ever completely rule out a malignant tumour (because a few percent of all pleomorphic adenomas have a malignant component that may have been missed by the aspiration biopsy) and since about 5 per cent of all pleomorphic adenomas will eventually turn malignant if left in place for ten or more years, he would advise her to have the tumour removed. Chances are that ('just to make sure') the doctor will also send her for a computerised tomography (CT) and/or a magnetic resonance imaging (MRI) exam. Of course, he tells her all about the side effects and potential risks of the surgery. Finally, the conscientious physician tells her that there is no alternative treatment option and that even after properly performed surgery there is a 5 per cent risk of a later tumour recurrence. Yet, although this is comprehensive information, based on the 'best available evidence', the patient will look for further information: at least she will 'surf the Internet'. Perhaps, she will see another physician to get a 'second opinion'. She also asks the surgeon whether 'he has ever seen such a tumour' and 'whether he has performed the proposed operation before'. If she is brash, she may even ask whether he would also recommend the surgery if she did not have private insurance coverage. Perhaps, she will also consult a practitioner of some type of 'alternative medicine' before she eventually decides to go ahead with the operation.

---

have not done so, the reader is solicited to read the male form in the sense of a generic pronoun implying both genders equally.

[7] 'Compatible with' is common medical usage and is not to be confused with 'proves that'.

At first glance, the two stories may appear as the short and the long version of the same story, which, indeed, they almost are. The significant, if unstated, difference is that whereas the first is from the 1970s, the second is from today. Furthermore, there are two other major differences between the stories, which can be gleaned from the description: the first refers to the amount of workup (i.e. the number of tests and exams); the second refers to the interaction between the patient and the physician (i.e. the patient–physician relationship). These differences are key to helping us understand trust.

With regard to the increased amount of workup, one might argue (1) that it reflects 'progress' and the increasing sophistication of medicine. Of course, this is true, but it is only part of the explanation. Not all of these exams are truly indicated,[8] and this amount of workup is definitely not cost-effective. If you consider that in this case the pretest probability of the lesion being a benign pleomorphic adenoma is above 90 per cent, it is questionable whether, in addition, fine-needle aspiration biopsy, CT, and MRT will add new information that would significantly change the treatment recommendation.[9] Besides, one could argue (2) that the changes in the patient–physician interaction only reflect the newer, more modern self-perceptions patients have, as seen through its focus on patient autonomy, the patients' desire of taking control and participating in decision-making, and finally their increased access to information. Yet again, this is only part of the explanation. What we want to claim is that both changes are, to a considerable part, caused by the decrease of patients' trust in physicians.

1.3   A Brief Explanation of Changing Views on Trust

A scrutiny of the second history reveals that it abounds with clues (some subtle, some not so subtle) pointing to the patient's *mis*trust.[10] Whereas the patient in the first history takes the physician's trustworthiness for granted (and therefore trusts him without further ado), the patient in

---

[8] 'Indicated' is again a standard medical term, meaning there is good evidence that an exam gives *new* and *essential* information. Unfortunately, the term is often used far too liberally.

[9] We will argue in the next section that the addition of ever more tests and exams is not so much justified by their diagnostic value but by the fact that many physicians practice what is commonly called 'defensive medicine' out of fear of litigation.

[10] '*Mis*trust' is one of a range of technical terms that form part of our account of the concept of trust. We will define this and other related terms in detail in Section 6.1.

the second story appears to have serious qualms about the physician's trustworthiness. Her question 'have you ever seen such a tumour before?' implies 'can I trust your diagnosis?', and her question 'have you performed this operation before?' means 'can I trust your surgical skills?' For the patient these questions are a means of assessing the physician's *competence*. The fact that many, if not most, patients today consult the Internet after the consultation also points in the same direction: it serves to assess the physician's epistemic trustworthiness, which today's patients no longer take for granted. The question 'would you recommend surgery if I did not have private insurance coverage?' implicitly expresses doubts about the physician's integrity. From the reaction to this and similar questions, the patient tries to gauge the doctor's honesty, to find out whether he indeed has her, rather than his own, interest foremost. In other words, she tries to assess the physician's *commitment* to her. Although the patient may not perceive (let alone intend) these questions as expressions of mistrust, the physician may perceive them as questioning his professional competence and integrity (in short, of his trustworthiness) and, hence, as a sign of mistrust.

This mistrust not only explains the changes in the patient–physician relationship that have occurred over the past decades. It also explains the ever-increasing number of diagnostic tests ordered by physicians, because the physicians (fearing that a mistrusting patient is more likely to be dissatisfied, or even litigious) react to the perceived mistrust by practising what is called 'defensive medicine',[11] i.e. they order more tests than they really think necessary 'to hedge their bets', to be on the safe side if ever they should be called to account for their actions. Nickel calls this 'positive defensive medicine' (or 'assurance behaviour'), which he defines as behaviour that "involves supplying additional services of marginal or no medical value with the aim of reducing adverse outcomes, deterring patients from filing malpractice claims, or persuading the legal system that the standard of care is met".[12] He then goes on to differentiate this type of defensive medicine from what he calls 'negative defensive medicine' or 'avoidance behaviour', which refers to situations where physicians, for example, refuse to treat high-risk patients.[13]

---

[11] Berlin 2017.
[12] Nickel 2009, p. 358.
[13] In fact, defensive medicine need not always be caused by mistrust. If a patient trusts (expects) a doctor to prescribe an antibiotic for the common cold, then the doctor's 'failure' to do so can be resented as a breach of trust. Knowing the cost of such 'failure',

The comparison of our two typical case histories (one from the 1970s and one from today) underpins our claim that trust has declined over the past forty years or so. We have also learnt from the two stories that trustworthiness and, hence, trust refer to both competence and patient-oriented commitment of the physician. Yet, there is more we can learn about trust from the two stories. The simple fact that patients feel compelled to ask these questions points to two other important features of the patient–physician relationship and, hence, of trust: *uncertainty* and *risk*. The patient is aware that she can never be sure about the physician's trustworthiness and that therefore to trust always means to run a risk. By asking such questions she tries to reduce the uncertainty and, hence, the risk. Finally, the two histories show that the reasons for which patients' trust (i.e. how they justify the risk of trusting) have changed over the years. Whereas in the past most patients trusted doctors simply qua doctors, most of today's patients trust a doctor only if they have good reason to assume that the physician merits their trust.

As such, the two histories not only show that trust has declined over the past forty years or so. They also tell us that how the patient perceives both competence and the patient-oriented commitment of the physician determines the patient's trust; that uncertainty and risk are important features of 'trust'; and, finally, that the way patients justify taking the risk of trusting has changed. Although many people share our concern about the erosion of trust and its consequences,[14] not everyone agrees that the decline of trust is real rather than imagined. Since the claim that trust has declined is a factual claim, it should be possible, at least in theory, to prove or refute it empirically. In Chapter 2, we will therefore present a brief summary of the available empirical literature on trust. Admittedly, the evidence for the decline of trust may be challenged; yet this applies to most evidence in the social sciences.[15]

---

doctors may attempt to live up to patients' trust even when this is not medically appropriate. In other words, 'trust can be bad, not because moral expectations are disappointed, but rather because they are *met*'. Nickel 2009, p. 359.

[14] See, e.g. Shore 2007.

[15] At the very least, the empirical evidence taken from this literature provides a reasonable foundation for supporting our claim about the decline of trust, and it is not the purpose of this book to engage in empirical and sociological investigations of our own. Although the authors would, of course, welcome further work in this area by social scientists interested

1.4 Outline and Structure

As we mentioned at the very outset of the book, our approach is one of analytical philosophy and bioethics. This methodological approach is one that primarily critically assesses argument and seeks to provide a clear and rigorous analysis of concepts. As such, the structure of this book reflects this approach, with an emphasis on definitions and argument analysis. Accordingly, we are interested not simply in proposing a suitable definition of trust in the medical context, although this is certainly a major aim of the book. We are interested in exploring the reasons why we need to account for trust in this way. Partly, this is the product of subjecting various possible definitions of trust to a detailed analysis to see if they are 'fit for purpose'. The other aspect of this, however, is that we want to explain why we need trust, why the loss of trust is a bad thing, and how a good account of what trust is can help us to suggest ways in which we might go about restoring the evident loss of trust that has occurred in the field of medicine.

Therefore, rather than simply going through one potential definition of trust after another, the book is structured to take on different issues that surround the question of trust in medicine.

Chapter 2 begins this process by looking at what empirical evidence we have for thinking there has been a decline in trust in the context of medicine over recent years.

Chapters 3–7 address the fundamental questions of our definition of 'trust'. We start with a critical analysis of existing definitions (Chapter 3). Next, we propose a new type of definition (Chapter 4) and then use this type of definition to define 'trust' (Chapter 5). Since 'trust' is often used interchangeably with concepts such as 'confidence', 'reliance', 'belief-in', and 'hope', we will analyse how our definition of 'trust' can separate and distinguish these concepts, both from itself and from each other (Chapter 6). Finally, we will end this part by demonstrating that our definition of 'trust' can accommodate different situations (Chapter 7).

Chapters 8 and 9 consider the justification of trust. Chapter 8 will be devoted to the justification of epistemic trust and Chapter 9 to the justification of patients' trust in physicians.

in the topic, the conceptual analysis of trust that we offer can still be understood without this contextual framework.

Chapters 10 and 11 focus on aspects of the significance of trust, first from an instrumental (Chapter 10) and then from a moral standpoint (Chapter 11).

Chapter 12 seeks to explore some of the reasons for the decline of trust.

Chapter 13, finally, will round off our analysis of trust with a few thoughts on whether and how (at least some) trust can be regained by individual physicians as well as by healthcare institutions.

Empirical Evidence for the Decline of Trust

Trust, as a concept, is not simply out there to be measured or calculated like, for example, the gross national product. Nevertheless, the level of trust can be assessed using sophisticated survey methodology.[1] The attentive reader will notice that one study presented below measures 'confidence', whereas the others refer to 'trust'. However, since, as we have mentioned in Chapter 1, folk usage does not tend to make a distinction between the two terms and since opinion polls certainly work at a 'folk level', this need not concern us here. Indeed, this very book is founded on the problem of there not being a definitive use of the concept that is understood and used by all. Therefore, all we can expect from any attempt to measure levels of trust within the general population is that of a folk-level understanding of the concept.

Most empirical studies on trust measure trust and examine the influence of certain variables (such as age, sex, education, and ethnicity) on trust at a specific moment in a specific, usually small segment of the population. Such studies can tell us a great deal about the quality and the quantity of trust at a given time in a given part of society. Yet only data collected from the general population (or at least from a representative sample of the general population) over an extended period (so-called longitudinal studies) can tell us whether overall trust has declined or not. With the exception of the study presented by the American Medical Association (AMA), all longitudinal studies come from opinion poll institutions, such as Harris Poll or Gallup in the United States and Ipsos MORI in the United Kingdom.

The Harris Polls study is the most commonly cited study.[2] For their survey, conducted annually since 1966, an allegedly representative sample of 1,010

---

[1] It is beyond the scope of this book to discuss the methodology of measuring trust. Anyone interested in the intricacies of survey methodology and scale validation is referred to the excellent book by DeVellis 2003.

[2] Although there are others, for example by Blendon 2007 and by Jacobs 2005.

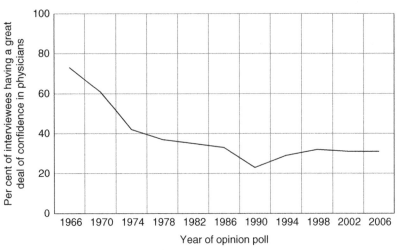

Figure 2.1   Level of trust/confidence in physicians according to Harris Polls (based on Data from Corso 2010)

adults are each asked the following question by telephone: "As far as people in charge of running (e.g. medicine) are concerned, would you say you have a great deal of confidence, only some confidence, or hardly any confidence at all in them?" Figure 2.1 shows that the confidence in physicians ('in those in charge of running medicine') has declined from about 75 per cent in the 1960s to about 30 per cent by 1986 and stayed at that level ever since.[3]

Two additional empirical studies underpin this claim[4]: one from the United States performed by the AMA,[5] the other one from the United Kingdom published by Ipsos MORI.[6] Unfortunately, neither of these studies goes as far back as the 1960s and 1970s, which is the period

---

[3] Corso 2010.

[4] We have eliminated a third survey, published by Gallup because to us it is methodologically flawed. Gallup polls are based on telephone interviews with a randomly selected national sample of 1,004 adults, 18 years and older. The interviewees are asked a single question. In principle, there is nothing wrong with measuring trust with a single question, provided the question is well formulated, offers a balanced choice of response, is asked in a clearly defined context, and unambiguously states the object of trust (Hall 2006, p. 464). However, the question *"would you rate the honesty and ethical standards of (e.g. physicians) very high, high, average, low, or very low?"* (Gallup 2003, our italics) clearly does not fulfil these conditions. Though the question sounds (deceivingly) simple, it is not clear at all: With regard to what is the doctor trusted to be 'honest'? And how many of the 1,004 people surveyed know what is meant by 'ethical standards'?

[5] Jacobs and Shapiro 1994.

[6] Ipsos MORI 2009.

when (according to Harris Polls) the most important decline of confidence took place.

The AMA study covers the period from 1982 to 1993. The interviewees were asked to state whether they agreed with the following five statements: *doctors usually explain things well to their patients, most doctors spend enough time with their patients, doctors act like they are better than other people, doctors are too interested in making money,* and *people are beginning to lose faith in doctors.* By reversely coding negatively worded statements, one can calculate an overall value for how people judge doctors. Whether the responses to these statements truly reflect people's trust is debatable, but at least the statements are understandable to everyone. Moreover, we would consider it entirely reasonable to presume that you probably do not (and should not) trust a doctor who does not explain things well, who does not spend enough time with you, and who is too interested in making money.

Ipsos MORI (often referred to simply as Ipsos) covers the period from 1984 to 2008. Ipsos MORI each year presents the following statements to about 2,000 British adults:[7] "*Generally, I trust doctors to (a) give accurate information, (b) have the most up-to-date information, (c) recommend the most effective treatment, and (d) speak up for patients when it comes to matters of health & healthcare.*" The interviewees are then asked to rate their agreement with these statements with (1) strongly agree, (2) tend to agree, (3) neither, (4) tend to disagree, and (5) strongly disagree.[8] With regard to the questions asked this is clearly the best survey. It assesses the doctors' competences (statements b, c, and d) as well as their commitment (statements a and e) (Figure 2.2).

Whereas the AMA study shows that the level of trust in the period surveyed was indeed practically identical with the level of confidence as reported by Harris Polls, there appears to be a striking difference between the confidence level as measured by Harris Polls (in the United States) and the trust level as reported by Ipsos MORI (in the United Kingdom). We have said 'appears to be' rather than 'is' because we think that the difference is spurious. Here is why. The interviewees of Harris Polls are asked one single question: "*As far as people in charge of running medicine*

---

[7] The results have been weighted by gender, age, location, and social class to reflect the known population profile of Great Britain. So, they should be representative for the entire population.

[8] Ipsos MORI 2007, p. 10.

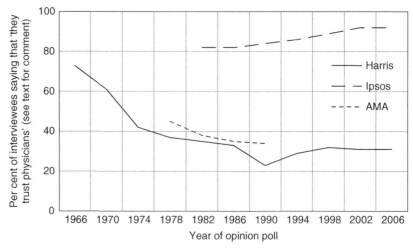

Figure 2.2   Level of trust/confidence in physicians according to Harris Polls, Ipsos MORI, and AMA (based on data from Corso 2010; Ipsos 2009; and Jacobs and Shapiro 1994)

are concerned, would you say you have a great deal of confidence, only some confidence, or hardly any confidence at all in them?" Only those answering 'a great deal' are considered to have confidence. Ipsos MORI, however, presents the interviewees with five statements regarding their trust in physicians and asks them to rate each statement with one of five options: (1) strongly agree, (2) tend to agree, (3) neither, nor, (4) tend to disagree, and (5) strongly disagree. Anyone saying that he 'strongly agrees' or that he 'tends to agree' is counted as trusting. As Figure 2.3 shows, this difference of interpreting the individual answers greatly influences the overall result.

For Harris Polls only people who have a great deal of confidence (but not those who have only some confidence) are used to calculate the 'confidence index', i.e. are said to have confidence. Ipsos MORI, however, also includes those who only 'tend to trust'. This, however, is misleading. It is a well-recognised phenomenon that people with no clear opinion tend to cluster at or around the centre options and avoid clearly taking position. Moreover, we do not think that we would count anyone who only 'tends to believe' that we are trustworthy among those whose trust we enjoy. If we exclude those who only tend to trust, the difference between the confidence level (Harris Polls) and the trust level (Ipsos MORI) virtually disappears. The claim that there is no major difference

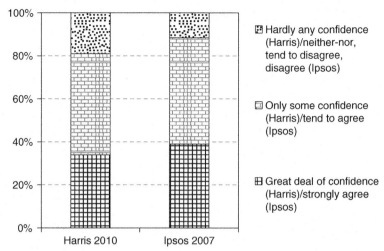

Figure 2.3   Analysis of the levels of trust/confidence reported by Harris Polls and Ipsos MORI (Corso 2010; Ipsos 2009)

between the levels of trust in the United Kingdom and in the United States is also supported by cross-national comparisons, which show similar levels in most Western societies.[9]

So, while data are fairly modest and limited to a very general folk understanding of what trust is, there is empirical evidence that trust in physicians has declined since the 1960s and that this decline is similar in the United States and in the United Kingdom (and indeed in most Western countries[10]). To conclude this brief chapter on empirical data, we would like to add a graph (Figure 2.4) that illustrates an extremely interesting phenomenon, namely that 'trust' became a topic of interest in the professional literature only once it had declined; or, in the words of Annette Baier:

> We inhabit a climate of trust as we inhabit an atmosphere and notice it as
> we notice air, only when it becomes scarce or polluted.[11]

Although we have limited our discussion to the decline of trust in the context of medicine, this decline is by no means limited to medicine. Indeed, as the data by Harris Polls show (see Figure 2.5), this decline affects many other professionals, such as the representatives of the law,

[9] Norris 2009, p. 41.
[10] By now, the decline of trust has also reached China (see, e.g. Chan 2017; Nie et al. 2017) as well as India (see Kane and Calnan 2016).
[11] Baier 1986, p. 234.

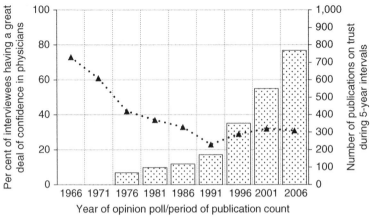

Figure 2.4   Level of trust versus number of published publications on trust

the church, and higher education, as well as the managers of major companies.

Many readers would probably like to know at this point not only *that* trust has declined but also *why* trust has declined. In Chapter 12, we will present five reasons for the decline of trust, namely the discrediting of professionalism, the difficulty of assessing physicians' trustworthiness, the crisis of modern medicine, the commodification of medicine, and changes of risk perception and risk acceptance. Readers are, of course, free to go directly to Chapter 12 to read about them in more detail. However, the reason we wait until this much later chapter in order to fully present and discuss these reasons is that at least some of our arguments as to why trust has declined may not be fully understandable without first having a good grasp of our concept of trust. We therefore believe that the reader will gain a great deal from following our arguments by proceeding through each chapter in turn.

Returning to our intended structure for this book, now that we have established that trust in physicians has declined over the past decades and shown how this decline manifests itself in the patient–physician relationship as well as in the practice of medicine, we will turn our attention to the *definition* of trust. This will form a basis for subsequent chapters, where we will use this definition to help explain the justification and significance of trust, why trust in medicine has declined, and ultimately what might be done about it. We start our account of the definition of trust with a discussion of possible ways of defining trust and a critical analysis of the most prominent definitions found in the literature

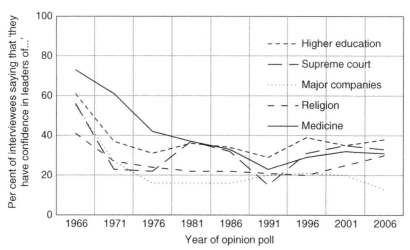

Figure 2.5   Level of trust/confidence in leaders of various social institutions in the United States (based on data from Harris Polls, Corso 2010)

(Chapter 3). Since, on our reckoning, none of the available definitions is sufficiently comprehensive to capture all that we would wish from an account of trust in medicine, we propose a new type of definition based on the pattern of characteristic features (rather than necessary conditions) of a concept (Chapter 4). Following this, we present pattern-based definitions of trust (Chapter 5) as well of some trust-related concepts, such as 'confidence', 'reliance', 'hope', and 'belief-in' (Chapter 6),[12] and (by comparing the various patterns) will explain why it is that these four concepts can be differentiated from 'trust'. We conclude our account of the definition of 'trust' by demonstrating how our definition can be adapted to various situations and therefore provide a suitable practical account of how we should understand trust in the field of medicine (Chapter 7).

---

[12] We will refer to the concept of a 'belief in something (or someone)' as 'belief in'.

PART II

The Nature of Trust

A Critical Analysis of Existing Definitions
of Trust in Medicine

Before we can judge the value of existing definitions, we have to state what conditions we believe a comprehensive definition of trust in medicine should fulfil. The importance of these conditions will become clearer as we proceed through our account of trust, but it is worth simply outlining them in the first instance. There are five conditions that we believe an account of trust in medicine should fulfil. First, the definition must be internally coherent. By this we mean that 'trust' can be understood by previously well-understood terms[1] and that the definition leads neither to inconsistencies nor to anything new that does not strictly fall under the concept being defined.[2] Second, it must be comprehensive, that is, it must encompass all *relevant* features of trust (which is not to say all features but does require that we explain what constitutes a 'relevant' feature).[3] Third, it must be applicable both to individuals (physicians and other healthcare professionals, as well as the patients themselves) and to the institutions these individuals work in. Fourth, it must be able to differentiate trust from similar concepts, such as confidence or reliance. We will call this condition 'discriminatory power'. Finally, fifth, it must be able to explain the decline of trust and the value of trust. We will call this final condition 'explanatory power'.

3.1 Types of Definition

There are, of course, many different ways of classifying definitions and many different types of definition potentially open to us.[4] However, we

---

[1] Belnap calls this the 'eliminability' criterium . . .

[2] . . . and this the 'conservativeness' criterium of a good definition (Belnap 1993, p. 117).

[3] We are aware that by insisting on coherence and comprehensiveness we may underplay the significance of the ordinary usage of these terms. For this and the previous condition, see also Wrigley (2014, p. 3).

[4] In fact, there are many ways of defining the term 'definition' itself. Yet, interesting as this would be, it is beyond the scope of this book to enter into an in-depth analysis of the term 'definition'. Anyone interested in such an analysis is referred to Swartz (2010).

will limit ourselves to a brief discussion of those few types of definition that have been used in the literature on trust in medicine or which we think would be useful.[5] To do so, we will use a very prosaic example for illustrative purposes, namely, the definition of 'beer' and some specific types of beer, such as lager, Pilsner, ale, stout, and wheat beer. To start with, however, there are a few technical terms needed to help provide a rigorous account that often underpin philosophical conceptual analysis and that need some brief explanation themselves. *Definiendum* refers to the term that is to be defined and *definiens* refers to a term (or group of terms) used to explain the meaning of the definiendum. So, for example, in the statement 'an adversary is someone who takes up a position of antagonism', the term 'adversary' is the definiendum; whereas 'someone who takes up a position of antagonism' is the definiens. A definiendum can also be said to have 'extensions' and 'intensions'.[6] *Extensions* (also sometimes called 'denotations' or 'references') designate a class of objects sharing the same attributes. They can be seen as examples of the definiendum. Ale, lager, stout, and Pilsner are, for example, extensions of the term 'beer'. *Intensions* (also sometimes called 'meanings', 'senses', or 'connotations') describe a set of attributes of the definiendum. To follow our example, 'A brew / produced by fermenting grain / and spicing with hops' is such a set of attributes of 'beer'. Both extensions and intensions can be used to define a term, albeit in different ways.

---

[5] Types of definition that (with the exception of Wittgenstein's, to which we come back later) will not play a role in the present context include the following, among others (a) Stipulative definitions, which assign a meaning to the defined term. They are typically used to show how we intend to use a term in a given context. To use an example from Moore (2009), 'Let an adversary be someone who takes up a position of antagonism' would be a stipulative definition of 'adversary'. (b) Lexical definitions seek to show how a term is commonly used. 'An adversary is someone who takes up a position of antagonism' is an example of a lexical definition. (c) Synonymous definitions define a term by giving another word with a very similar meaning that is (more) familiar to the reader and has (roughly) the same general sense (e.g. 'enemy' for 'foe'). (d) 'Theoretical definitions' are commonly used in physics, e.g. to define 'radiation' in the light of some physical theory. (e) 'Persuasive definitions' serve to influence the attitude or behaviour of others. Although they (are made to) look like lexical definitions, they are not, instead relying on a pre-desired characteristic or usage being utilised and that use being justified through rhetoric rather than appeal to general usage, in order to help establish a desired attitude or response when using the term. Not surprisingly, they are very commonly used, e.g. in political debates (Swartz 2010, chapters 5.4 and 5.7). (f) Finally, there is Wittgenstein's 'meaning as use' approach (Wittgenstein 1953, §43), to which we will come back on page 34.

[6] The terms 'extension' and 'intension' are attributable to Rudolph Carnap (Carnap 1956), but the basic distinction between meaning (sense) and denotation (reference) is that of Frege (1892).

Denotative definitions make use of the extensions of a term. They define a term by citing typical examples (e.g. Mount Everest, Matterhorn, or Ben Nevis for 'mountain'). They are very commonly used in everyday life. Just ask someone to define 'tool' without thinking first and you will almost certainly get an answer something like: 'well, hammers and pliers, and suchlike'. Although typical examples are usually easy to come by and can give a quick understanding of what a term means, they do not always provide an adequate definition of a term. 'Matterhorn' or 'Ben Nevis' no more define 'mountain' than 'hammer' or 'pliers' define 'tool'. The explanation for the rather limited defining power of denotative definitions lies in the fact that whereas (as it is commonly held among logicians) the intension determines the extension of the term, the reverse does not hold.[7] The extension does not determine the intension, since different intensions may have the same extensions. In our example, 'a beverage, produced by fermenting malt and spicing with hops' (the intension of beer) always refers to 'beer' and therefore also to lager, ale, etc. (which are some extensions of 'beer'). Lager, ale, etc., however, do not entirely define 'beer', as they will not help us to determine if something that is not lager or ale is still a beer. Whilst there might be something to be said in cases where all extensions of a definiendum are listed, this is still limited as an approach to providing a definition. For one thing, there will be many cases where it is impossible to list all the extensions of the definiendum. For another, the same extensions might be extensions of other terms, meaning that they will underdetermine what is being defined. Lager, ale, and so on are also extensions for 'types of intoxicant', 'alcoholic beverages', 'liquids consumed by humans', 'fizzy liquids', etc. So, we would be unable to precisely determine which term these are the definiens for. Most importantly, however, is the concern that simply listing extensions does not tell us anything about what the important features or attributes are of the definiendum; what is it that is common to all the extensions? Without this, it would be impossible to determine if some new object, etc., that hadn't been included in the list of extensions ought to be included. Suppose some new drink, let's call it 'schmeer', was invented. We wouldn't know if this was a new extension of beer from simply looking at the list of extensions. We would be much more interested in discovering whether schmeer was some new form of 'a beverage, produced by fermenting malt and spicing with hops' that

---

[7] Moore 2009, p. 3.

would mean it was a beer rather than some other drink. This is why another approach to provide a definition is often preferred.

Analytic definitions make use of the intensions of a definiendum. They seek to define a term by 'reducing it to simpler meanings',[8] that is, by breaking it down into its constituent elements (e.g. we might seek to define 'football' by identifying various key elements: is a game / in which two teams of eleven players / try to drive a ball / into the opponent's goal / using only their feet or head, etc.). These constituent elements are called 'conditions'. Conditions may be 'necessary' and/or '(jointly) sufficient'. To go back to our original example, 'A beverage / produced by fermenting grain / and spicing with hops' (which as we have shown is a set of attributes of 'beer') is a form of analytic definition of 'beer'. To anyone asking what 'beer' is, we could answer that beer 'is a beverage, which is produced by fermenting grain and which is spiced with hops'. Here, both 'fermenting grain' and 'spicing with hops' are necessary conditions. What is meant by 'necessary condition' is that these are elements that the definiendum could not do without, that must be there, usually formulated as 'P only if Q'.[9] In the case of our example, these necessary conditions are those things beer could not do without. Hence, anything that did not involve fermenting grain and spicing with hops could not be a beer – 'It is beer only if it is fermented of grain and spiced with hops.' This does not have to mean that other things cannot be of fermented grain and spiced with hops, just that if something is to be considered a beer, it must have both of these conditions fulfilled.[10]

However, according to the 'standard theory of definition', a 'proper' analytic definition states not only the necessary conditions but also the (jointly) sufficient conditions. This is the most demanding type of definition and is often referred to as an 'explicit definition'.[11] A sufficient condition for P tells us that if the condition is satisfied, it guarantees that P occurs. This is often formulated as 'P if Q' (or, more precisely, 'If

---

[8] Strawson 1992, pp. 17–18.

[9] 'P' and 'Q' are used in propositional logic to stand for propositions or statements. Hence 'It is beer' (P) only if it is 'a beverage produced by fermenting of grain and spicing with hops' (Q). The use of the truth functions of material implication (if . . . then . . .) from classical logic to underpin our understanding of sufficient and necessary conditions is commonplace. See, for example, Hintikka and Bachman (1991).

[10] Consider, for example, that it is a necessary condition of being human that you are a mammal. This does not mean that other things that are not human cannot also be mammals, just that you cannot be human unless you are also a mammal (and hence anything that was not a mammal could not be human).

[11] Belnap 1993, p. 117.

Q then P'). Some conditions are sufficient but not necessary. What we are interested in with an analytic definition, however, are both the necessary and jointly sufficient conditions.[12] This is commonly formalised as involving a biconditional relation 'if and only if' (sometimes abbreviated to 'iff'), whereby 'P if and only if Q' abbreviates 'P if Q' and also 'P only if Q'. A typical example is 'x is a triangle if and only if it is / a closed figure / with three straight sides / linked end-to end'. Similarly, even if neither of the two conditions alone define beer, jointly they are sufficient. You can say 'it is (only) beer if is produced by fermenting grain and spicing with hops' (because the conditions are necessary) as well as 'if it is produced by fermenting grain and spicing with hops it is (must be) beer' (because the two conditions are jointly sufficient). The advantage of analytic definitions in general is that they convey the meaning of a term as well as some of its characteristics without attributing more to the subject than is already conceptually contained in the subject.[13] The disadvantage of explicit definitions is that they are often difficult (or even impossible) to come by.

3.2   Analysis of Existing Definitions of Trust

Following this brief introduction, we can now analyse the most prominent definitions of trust in medicine found in the literature.[14] Aware that analysing 'trust' is no easy task, many authors avoid the issue by resorting to *denotative definitions*, so that they just give examples, such as 'trust means expecting caring, honesty, or responsiveness';[15] 'trust means that my interests are encapsulated in your interest';[16] or 'to trust someone is to lower one's guard, to refrain from taking precautions against an interaction partner, even when the other could act in a way that might seem to justify precautions'.[17] As stated previously, such denotative definitions

---

[12] Jointly sufficient conditions are all those conditions that, when taken all together, are sufficient.

[13] The term 'football' embraces the entire phrase 'football is a game, in which two teams of eleven players try to drive a ball into the opponent's goal using only their feet or head, etc.'.

[14] The academic literature abounds with definitions of 'trust' from diverse fields, such as economy, political science, and psychology (e.g. see Misztal 1996, pp. 12–15). However, since this book is about 'trust in medicine', we have limited our review to the context of medicine.

[15] Mechanic and Meyer 2000, p. 660.

[16] Hardin 2002, pp. 3ff.

[17] Elster 2007, p. 34.

may give us a feeling of what 'trust is about', but they do not tell us what 'trust is'; i.e. they do not define 'trust' in a way that is useful to an account of trust in medicine. For example, 'Your interest is encapsulated in mine' may refer to 'trust', but it might just as well refer to 'symbiosis'.

Therefore, of greater interest than these denotative definitions are the proposed *analytic definitions* of 'trust'. Probably the most popular of them defines 'trust' as 'the expectation that the trustee (i.e. the doctor) will act in the truster's (i.e. the patient's) interest'[18] or that 'the trustee will act as the truster's agent'.[19] Along similar lines, 'trust' is defined as a 'commitment to an on-going relationship';[20] as an 'open-ended commitment on the physician's part to continue the relationship through the unexpected, even though the form that it takes cannot be certain in the original agreement';[21] or as 'the expectation that individuals and institutions will meet their responsibilities to us'.[22] These are all, albeit very limited, analytic definitions.[23] Yet, they are all fraught with serious problems. First, defining 'trust' as having to do with 'the patient's best interests' opens the definition to radically different interpretations, depending on how one defines 'best interest', thereby obfuscating the definition by requiring the use of another concept that is itself in need of accurate definition. Second (and more importantly), all these definitions suffer from the fact that they define 'trust' solely with regard to the patient-related commitment (or agency) of the trustee.[24] However, any definition of 'trust' limiting trust to the commitment of the trustee is insufficient. Here is why. Assume that you bring your car in for its annual service. If, in the past, you have been happy with the owner of your garage, you trust him to do only what needs to be done and not to increase the bill by exchanging a few perfectly good parts as well. In other words, you trust his commitment to your interests. Yet, in addition to trusting that he does not cheat you, you also expect him to do a 'good job', i.e. you trust his competence as a car mechanic. As we will discuss later, appreciation of this aspect is important because a useful account of

---

[18]   Norris 2009, p. 32.
[19]   E.g. Goold 2001; Illingworth 2002; Iltis 2007; Mechanic 1998; Rhodes 2000.
[20]   Rowe and Calnan 2006, p. 5.
[21]   Quill 1983, p. 229.
[22]   Mechanic 1998, p. 662.
[23]   They could all be presented in the form 'it is trust if it e.g. refers to the expectation that the trustee will act as the truster's agent'.
[24]   This is equally true for Hardin's "I trust you because I think it is in your interest to take my interests in the relevant matter seriously" (Hardin 2002, p. 1).

trust in medicine must (with few, well-defined exceptions) relate to the commitment as well as the competence of the physician.

It is useful to make another distinction at this stage. The counterpart of trust on the truster's side is trustworthiness on the trustee's side. So, rather than trying to define 'trust', Russel Hardin proposes to define 'trustworthiness'. In fact, he claims that "the literature would be much clearer and less confused if all proponents of all extant theories [of trust] recognised that their theories or conceptions are about trustworthiness and only derivatively about trust".[25]

Of course, we agree that to say 'I trust you' usually (but not always, as we will show below) means 'I believe you to be trustworthy' and that, therefore, trustworthiness plays an important role in the debate about trust. And yet, we will focus on trust and not on trustworthiness. We have two reasons for this. The *first reason* is very pragmatic: everyone else (except Hardin) does so, and looking at something from the same perspective as others makes it easier to engage in comparative critical analysis. The *second reason* is more substantial. The relationship between trust and trustworthiness is not symmetric. A symmetric relationship would imply that (a) if you are trustworthy, we trust you, and (b) if we trust you, you are trustworthy. This is indeed the position of Hardin. We wish to argue that neither condition has to be fulfilled: trust is possible in the absence of trustworthiness, and trustworthiness does not a priori lead to trust. Just because someone is (or appears to be) trustworthy does not mean that we automatically trust him (or, more strongly, that we have to trust him).[26] Furthermore, while trustworthiness is a prerequisite for trust to be responsible, it is not a sine qua non condition for trust per se: sometimes we are imprudent enough to trust someone who is not trustworthy. Trustworthiness does not so much explain what trust *is* but what *justifies* our trust: we trust you *because* we believe that you are trustworthy. Your trustworthiness justifies our trust in you but does not define 'trust'. Since there is an entire chapter (Chapter 9) on how to justify one's trust, we will defer further discussion of trustworthiness until then.

Clearly, there is no lack of analytic definitions of 'trust'. Yet, it seems, all focus on one or at best a few aspects and none of them come close to meeting the condition of being genuinely comprehensive. The absence of a comprehensive analytic (or an explicit) definition of trust in medicine is surprising given that most of the definitions mentioned so far clearly

---

[25] Hardin 2006, p. 17, our insertion.
[26] Miller 2000, p. 47.

reduce trust to other, supposedly more familiar, or better understood, concepts (e.g. respect, autonomy, etc.). In fact, 'it is hard even to imagine a conception of trust that is non-reductive and still plausible'.[27]

Indeed, analytic philosophers have typically tried to clarify the concept of 'trust' through conceptual analysis, i.e. by reducing 'trust' to simple meanings and hopefully coming up with a definition that can be stated in terms of necessary and sufficient conditions.[28] And yet, there is no comprehensive or even explicit analytic definition. Jackson proposes two possible explanations for this lack:[29]

(a) There is an analysis, but we have not found it, perhaps because (to use Simpson's words) 'no one has given it a really decent shot yet'.[30] This explanation is not very plausible, given the fact that so many philosophers have addressed the issue.

(b) There is an analysis, but we have not found it, because it is beyond us. This is possible but hard to prove. Whatever the explanation is, the fact remains that we have no comprehensive definition.

This leaves a further alternative that 'trust' is not analysable, despite all the arguments in favour of it being reducible, because several different concepts masquerade under the single term 'trust', i.e. that we are under what Jackson calls a 'recognitional illusion',[31] in which case it is not possible to find a single definition that covers all concepts. This explanation is the one that Simpson favours:

> The ways that the word [trust] is used are simply too various to be regimented into one definition. Sometimes 'trust' is naturally understood as referring to a sort of affective attitude ('I will trust my husband, I will not be jealous'); at other times to a conative one ('Come what may, I will trust you to the end'); and at yet others to cognitive ones ('I know you are an honourable woman, so I trust you') ... Similarly, it is used in situations where the motivation to trustworthiness is dramatically varied: love, mutual gain, or considerations may all count as reasons not to betray someone's trust. These all support the inductive argument against the plausibility of analysing of trust. Counter-examples can be given so easily because there are so many ways the word may permissibly be used, and so it would be foolish to seek a single definition.[32]

[27] Hardin 2002, p. 57.
[28] Simpson 2012, p. 550.
[29] Jackson 2010, p. 183.
[30] Simpson 2012, p. 553.
[31] Jackson 2010, p. 183.
[32] Simpson 2012, pp. 553–4.

According to Simpson, 'trust' refers to a 'cluster concept', which means that the term is (and can permissibly be) used in many different ways. Because of this, he argues, it is easy to come up with counterexamples to any definition, making it unlikely that a single definition can be found.

Although we can see his point, we do not agree with Simpson for three reasons: first, his examples do not illustrate the different ways we use trust. Rather, they describe different aspects of trust, such as the consequences of trust ('I trust, therefore I am not jealous'), the intention to trust ('come what may, I will trust him'), the reason why we trust ('you are honourable, therefore I trust you'), and possible motivations to be trustworthy ('love, mutual gain, etc.'). We do not see why this should prove that it is impossible to define 'trust'. One of the best-known examples of an (attempted) explicit definition is 'knowledge as justified true belief'. Whilst there are counterarguments that have been offered to the adequacy of this definition,[33] the fact that we can describe the consequences of knowledge (e.g. the development of nuclear warfare), the intentions we have to acquire knowledge (e.g. 'knowledge is power'), or the reasons why we know certainly do not count among them. Second, although counterexamples are strong arguments against the validity of any *given* definition, they do not rule out the possibility that there exists *a* valid definition. Take, for example, the definition 'a king is a hereditary, male ruler of an independent state'. It is easy to find examples of kings that do not fit this definition, such as the king of chess or the lion as king of the animal world. These counterexamples show that the proposed definition is, in certain senses, wrong. Yet, they do not prove that there cannot be a valid conceptual definition of 'king'. Finally, third, just because people use 'trust' in different ways does not prove (and Simpson does not supply proof) that these uses are indeed *permissible* (as he claims).

The fact that people use a term in different ways does not prove that these uses are a priori permissible. To illustrate this, we briefly leave 'trust' and move to something more mundane. In their ignorance, many people call any sort of bug that crawls around on more than two pairs of legs a 'spider'. Of course, anyone with just some basic knowledge of zoology can come up with counterexamples, e.g. examples of bugs that crawl on more than four legs and are not spiders. This does not prove that we cannot define 'spider'. All it proves is that these people are using 'spider' far too indiscriminately. Similarly, we argue that people use 'trust'

---

[33] Such as those proposed by Gettier (Gettier 1963).

too indiscriminately. To coin a phrase, not everything that 'has trust on the label has trust inside'; hence, not every use of 'trust' is permissible.[34] As we have said earlier, 'we trust that the weather will be good tomorrow', 'we trust that our car will keep running another year', 'we trust the brakes of our bike', 'we trust in the faithfulness of our partner', and we (or at least some people) trust in homeopathy. We claim that it is not permissible to use the term 'trust' in all these statements.[35] Of course, even if we weed out the non-permissible uses of 'trust' (such as using it instead of 'confidence', 'reliance', etc.), trust may still refer to a cluster of different concepts (and Simpson may still, in this sense, be right in his analysis). At least, however, we will have removed a number of arguments against the possibility of a comprehensive analytic definition of 'trust'.

3.3   Summary and Conclusions

In this chapter, we have stated the criteria a comprehensive account of trust must meet. We have briefly discussed the types of definition used in the context of trust in physicians, namely denotative and analytic definitions, and we have critically looked at the existing definitions of 'trust', only to find them all wanting. In the next chapter, we will present a type of analytic definition which, as we hope to show in the later chapters of this book, when applied to 'trust' will fulfil the five conditions a comprehensive account of 'trust' must meet.

---

[34] Our use of 'permissible' is meant to be understood in terms of 'in accordance with an accurate account'. This may, of course, be questioned by advocates of very liberal forms of 'meaning as use' approaches to definition, but it is not intended to suggest such approaches cannot provide meaningful definitions. This instead implies that, were people given greater insight into classification, they would not use the term in this context (this also raises interesting questions about the possibility of community-wide error that we shall not go into here). Suffice it to say at this point that there are good grounds as to why certain (even widespread) usages of terms can be considered to be erroneous and, as such, not 'permissible'.

[35] We will present our arguments why we believe that we can and should discriminate between 'trust' and these other concepts in Chapter 6.

Proposing a New Type of Definition

The Pattern-Based Definition

In this chapter, we present what we believe is a development of an analytic definition that is apt for use in defining trust in medicine, one which does not state necessary conditions but which is based on what we recognise as the pattern of characteristic features common to various applications of the concept to be defined. There are two reasons prompting our utilising such an approach. First, defining a term and diagnosing a disorder have a lot in common, and many diagnoses are made by recognising the pattern of symptoms and signs which are characteristic for a disorder. Second, we believe that we all use this approach to some extent, even though we may not be aware that we are de facto defining something.

4.1 Clinical Diagnosis by Recognising the Pattern of the Symptoms and Signs of a Disease

Defining a term and diagnosing a disorder have a lot in common. Some diagnoses are similar to analytic definitions. Just as a beverage is a beer (only) if it is produced by fermenting grain and spicing with hops, a patient is diagnosed as having Menière's disease (only) if he suffers from recurrent episodes of vertigo, (fluctuating) hearing loss on one side, tinnitus, and a fullness sensation in the affected ear.[1] In both instances, all criteria are necessary (and even jointly sufficient). In clinical practice, however, this type of diagnosis is probably the exception rather than the

---

[1] The precise criteria in the medical literature for the diagnosis of Menière's disease are: (1) two or more spontaneous episodes of vertigo, each lasting 20 minutes to 12 hours; (2) audiometrically documented low- to medium-frequency sensorineural hearing loss in the affected ear on at least 1 occasion before, during, or after one of the episodes of vertigo; (3) fluctuating aural symptoms (hearing, tinnitus, or fullness) in the affected ear; and (4) not better accounted for by another vestibular diagnosis (Seemungal et al. 2015, p. 624).

In fact, this list of criteria has a stipulative character, because it reflects the consensus of a panel of experts (Lopez-Escamez et al. 2015).

rule.[2] Much more typically, clinical diagnoses are made by looking for the diagnosis that fits (or, at least, best fits) the pattern of symptoms and signs presented by the patient. Here is another example, again referring to a disease characterised by vertigo attacks. Often, patients consult a neuro-otologist[3] for dizzy spells that occur when the patient lies down or turns in bed. On detailed questioning, the physician will learn that the dizziness starts a few seconds after changing position (what is called a 'latency'), increases up to a maximum, and dwindles after up to 30 seconds. Often the dizziness returns when the patient sits up or turns to the other side. Very discerning patients may even notice that the direction of the spinning sensation changes and that on repeated position changes the spells peter out. This is the typical (full) pattern of the symptoms of a vestibular disorder called 'benign paroxysmal positional vertigo' (BPPV).[4] However, very few patients present this full pattern of symptoms (it may well be that many are probably too scared to notice the finer details). Obviously, the dizzy spells and the positional triggering are essential (or necessary) conditions. However, they are not, by themselves, sufficient to make the diagnosis. Other disorders, such as carotid artery stenosis or cervical spine disorders, also cause position-dependent vertigo. Therefore, to make the diagnosis, some of the other features must be present, and the more features are present, the likelier becomes the diagnosis of a BPPV.

So far, we have only discussed symptoms or features which are important if they are present. However, often the absence of certain symptoms is almost equally important in making a diagnosis. Pleomorphic adenomas (to come back to the example presented in the Introduction) are typically slow-growing, firm, well-defined, and mobile swellings in front of the ear. Firmness, slow growth rate, etc. are, accordingly, parts of the typical pattern of the symptoms and signs of a pleomorphic adenoma. However, none of these features is limited to pleomorphic adenomas and few pleomorphic adenomas will show all features to the same degree, although all will show some of them. Yet, even if all these features are present, the diagnosis becomes highly unlikely if the tumour is fixed to

---

[2] Although we acknowledge that this is only a viewpoint based on the clinical practice and teaching experience of one of the authors (M.W.).

[3] Neuro-otology is a sub-specialty of otorhinolaryngology, dealing primarily (although not exclusively) with disorders of hearing and equilibrium.

[4] This type of vertigo is called 'benign', because it is self-limiting; 'paroxysmal', because it is characterised by recurrent attacks, and 'positional' (or more correctly 'positioning'), because it is triggered by position changes.

the underlying tissue, shows signs of skin infiltration, or if it causes facial weakness or pain. So, the *absence* of tumour fixation, skin infiltration, pain, and facial weakness are as important parts of the typical pattern of a pleomorphic adenoma as the mentioned positive signs. This means that, because our patient with the pleomorphic adenoma of the parotid presented with a typical pattern, the clinical diagnosis was justified. Had the lesion been, for example, tender or fixed to the underlying tissue, it would not have fitted the pattern, and the clinical diagnosis would have had to be revised.

It is often the greater ability to recognise patterns that makes 'old hands' the better diagnosticians. This is a claim that needs some clarification and support, but it is one that is ultimately useful to grasp to help understanding of the pattern-based approach to definition. To avoid any misunderstanding, we are not talking about an ability to 'intuitively' recognise patterns. Of course, such abilities do exist. For example, Jackson describes the example of a group of people who, after being shown several examples of ellipses and non-ellipses, were able to recognise ellipses intuitively, that is, without knowing what (in mathematical terms) an ellipsis is.[5] What the good diagnostician does, however, is to compare the signs and symptoms presented by a patient with the patterns of signs and symptoms of various disorders and pick out the 'best fit'. This is an analytic process and not an intuitive one. Also, where the clinician uses the pattern of symptoms and signs to make the diagnosis of a BPPV, the textbook author will use the same pattern to define the BPPV.

4.2 Recognising the Pattern that All Examples of a Concept Share

Irrespective of whether a comprehensive or explicit analytic definition of 'trust' is theoretically feasible (although we have not found it) or not (perhaps because 'trust' is not a single concept), the fact remains that we can *recognise* trust just as we can recognise (to use Jackson's example) a 'liberal society':

> Each of us uses 'is a liberal society' to capture a pattern in nature, and we know a good deal about which societies satisfy the pattern, and which don't, and why. However, we will never find anything of the form 'x is a liberal society if and only if'. It is enough that we can recognise a liberal society if we have enough data about it.[6]

[5] Jackson 2010, p. 181
[6] Jackson 2010, p. 183.

Or, stated more generally:

> We pick up terms like 'knowledge', 'free society', 'pain' and so on by being exposed to examples and somehow latching onto the relevant commonality. We recognise the relevant pattern and thereby acquire mastery of the terms.[7]

The key term here is 'pattern'. A pattern is what all examples of a concept share, at least (and this is important) 'to some extent'. Patterns are something we can recognise, even in cases in which there is no comprehensive analytic definition. 'Liberal society' is such a "pattern in nature", and so (we argue) is 'trust'.[8] Although Jackson does not refer to it, we think that there is a certain similarity (or even indebtedness) to Wittgenstein's concept of 'family resemblance' in this sort of approach to defining a concept, something that is unlikely to have escaped the notice of readers familiar with Wittgenstein's work.[9] Given such a connection, it is worth briefly outlining what this is. This is something best done through example. Here is an example of 'family resemblance'. We all know what animals are. Take, for example, fish, dolphins, and rabbits. Whereas fish and dolphins live in the water, rabbits do not. Whereas dolphins and rabbits are mammals, fish are not. And whereas some fish and dolphins are carnivores, other fish and rabbits are vegetarians. Obviously, there is no single feature that is common to all of them and that is unique to them, and yet, we recognise them as animals. To use Wittgenstein's words, 'what we see is a complicated network of

---

[7] Jackson 2010, p. 179.

[8] Such an approach is not without difficulties, however. Since we have no gold standard to tell us which examples are, indeed, examples of the concept under scrutiny, there is a risk of circularity. Circularity is a notorious problem in attempting to provide definitions, as any circular definition would require us to already understand the *definiendum* because that term, at some point, appears as part of its own *definiens*. Unfortunately, it often appears that definitions turn out to be circular at some point in tracing their definiens back. This has led to different philosophical concerns over the challenge to conceptual analysis as a practice, such as Moore's paradox of analysis (simply put, that if a definition is accurate we therefore must know it is so and hence it cannot be informative, and if it is informative there is no way of judging that it is accurate) or Quine's rejection of the possibility of (non-trivial) definitions for particular expressions. In response to such concerns, various attempts have been made to claim there is no circularity in their definition or to consider ways in which circularity is non-vicious; see the discussions in, for example, Burgess 2008; Keefe 2002; Quine 1951. By appealing to a form of pattern recognition and family resemblance, we are accepting a form of Wittgensteinian approach to addressing such concerns.

[9] Or '*Familienähnlichkeit*', as Wittgenstein calls it in the original German text. Wittgenstein himself uses the example of 'games' to illustrate what he means by 'family resemblance'.

similarities overlapping and criss-crossing' (i.e. a 'family resemblance').[10] By following the analogy made to medical diagnosis, we are drawing upon this sort of pattern recognition, akin to family resemblance, to provide us with a means of defining trust.

In the next chapter, we will present a definition of trust that is based on what we believe to be the typical pattern of characteristic features (the relevant commonality) of trust. At its heart, this is a form of conceptual analysis:[11]

> The kind of conceptual analysis I am discussing ... is about capturing patterns ascribed by certain descriptive terms in a language using other terms in a language in ways that illuminate the structure of ascribed patterns.[12]

One may argue that the individual features that make up a pattern are similar to the individual conditions of an analytic definition. This comparison may be suitably apt. There are, however, several major differences between a definition based on necessary conditions and the pattern-based approach, which we are pursuing. Therefore, before we go any further, it is worth making these differences clear.

As an example of a necessary conditions-based definition, we can again utilise the example of beer. As we previously outlined, two necessary conditions define 'beer': 'fermenting grain' and 'spicing with hops'. These two conditions can be used to formulate an affirmative, unequivocal definition ('if it is produced by fermenting grain and spicing with hops it *is* beer'). The same is not true for pattern-based definitions: 'living in water' and 'reproduction by spawning' are features of 'fish'. However, 'if it lives in water and spawns it is a fish' is false, because frogs fulfil these conditions as well. You cannot formulate a positive, unequivocal definition based on the features of a pattern. You can, however, formulate a negative definition ('if it does not live in water and does not spawn, it is

---

[10] Wittgenstein 1953, §§66–67. Apart from the concept of 'family resemblance', Wittgenstein also proposes that "the meaning of a word is its use in the language", often shortened to 'meaning as use' (Wittgenstein 1953, §43). Apart from the fact that both deal with concepts with vague boundaries, we think they should not be conflated: 'Family resemblance' is an account of analytic definition, whereas 'meaning as use' is not. We hope to show in Section 6.2 that the way the word 'trust' is used in ('folk') language confuses rather than clarifies the meaning of 'trust'.

[11] Jackson himself writes "We analytical philosophers might describe it [i.e. this approach] as 'conceptual analysis using the method of intuitions about possible cases' but that should not disguise that it is folk wisdom and not some arcane bit of technology special to our profession" (Jackson 2010, p. 174, our insertion).

[12] Jackson 2010, p. 186.

not a fish') as well as a conjectural definition ('if it lives in water and spawns, we may assume it is a fish'). Obviously, a negative formulation is not very helpful, although it does do some work by determining what won't fall under the definiendum. Similarly, 'firmness', 'well-defined contour', 'slow growth', 'painlessness', 'movability', 'absence of skin infiltration', or 'facial weakness' are all features of pleomorphic adenomas. However, even if we integrate all these features, we cannot formulate an affirmative definition, because not even a tumour which presents all these features is, with absolute certainty, a pleomorphic adenoma. It may still be, for example, an acinic cell carcinoma. Yet there is an element of probability that comes with such an approach, and the more features are present, the more likely the diagnosis becomes.

Adding an additional condition to a necessary conditions-based definition will make the definition more specific. However, it will no longer define the original term. Here is the beer example again: '*top*-fermenting grain and spicing with hops' will define beers such as ales or stout, but it will no longer define beers in general (because not all beers are top-fermented). The same is not true for pattern-based definitions: just as adding more features will make a presumptive diagnosis more likely, adding additional features will make a definition more stringent (albeit narrower) and bring it closer to an affirmative definition. In fact, the more features we add, the more certain such a definition captures the essence of a concept. Let us illustrate this with another (non-beer) example, that of 'peach'. Here are the characteristic features of a peach. It has an almost spherical shape. Its skin is velvety. It is moderately hard. If we take a bite, the fruit pulp has a smooth, almost squidgy texture. It has a fairly typical taste (mostly sweet, but with a hint of sourness), etc. None of these features unequivocally identifies or defines a peach: not all are spherical (wild peaches are more doughnut-shaped). Some are hard. Some have almost no taste at all, etc. In fact, not even the full set of characteristics defines a peach unequivocally. However, the more features are present, the more likely the fruit in front of us is a peach. With a grain of salt, one can say that definitions based on necessary conditions are about certainty, whereas pattern-based definitions are about probability.

There is yet another important difference between the two types of definitions. In a necessary conditions-based definition, the individual conditions (definientes) are individually necessary to define the definiendum, and since all conditions are necessary, there is no hierarchy among them. In a pattern-based definition, not all features have to be present, and the features do not necessarily have the same value. Some may be essential,[13] whereas others have a supporting character. Accordingly, the pattern-based approach may still admit necessary criteria into the definition, although this might not be the case for all definienda. To illustrate what we mean, consider again the example of the pleomorphic adenoma of the parotid. A pleomorphic adenoma of the parotid gland is *in most cases* a firm, well-defined, slowly growing preauricular swelling; it is *usually* non-tender and mobile, but it *never* infiltrates the skin. In the next chapter, we will show that the same approach holds for 'trust'.

There is an obvious snag with this approach. Where do we draw the line? What does still count as trust, and what does not? Again, we think this is a problem which both Jackson's and our own approach have in common with Wittgenstein's concept of 'family resemblance':

> What still counts as a game and what no longer does? Can you give the boundary? No. You can draw one; for none has so far been drawn. (But that never troubled you before when you used the word 'game').[14]

In other words, there is no clear-cut boundary, but we can 'draw one'. We can even make the decision of where and why we are drawing such a boundary non-arbitrary, based on its usefulness within the context in which we are seeking the definition. The way we do this is by comparing the patterns of different concepts. Later, we will show that by comparing the pattern of 'trust' with the patterns of 'confidence', 'reliance', 'hope', and 'belief in', we can 'draw the boundary' of what still counts as trust (in a broad sense). Moreover, we will show that by 'moving this boundary' we can obtain both very narrow and wider definitions of 'trust' and thus adapt it to different situations and needs.

4.3 Summary and Conclusions

So far, we have argued that even if we have no comprehensive analytic definition of a term 'X', we can often recognise and understand 'X', and that one way of doing this is by recognising the pattern of characteristic features (or 'family resemblance') common to different examples of 'X'. Whereas in a definition based on necessary conditions all conditions must be met, in a pattern-based definition not all features (or even none

---

[13] In the example of BPPV described above, only the vertiginous attacks and the triggering by position changes must be present, but they must be accompanied by at least some of the other features.

[14] Wittgenstein 1953, §68.

of them) are essential. It may still be 'X' if not all features of the pattern of 'X' are present, but the better a case fits the pattern, the more likely it is 'X'. We will proceed in the next chapter to present a definition of trust in medicine based on what we believe to be the pattern of characteristic features of 'trust'.

5

A Pattern-Based Definition of Trust

We start this chapter with a brief outline of the individual characteristic features of the pattern of trust as far as it regards medicine.[1] Once we have completed this outline, we will flesh out each feature separately and try to respond to possible objections in order to give a solid foundation to our definition of trust from which we can make subsequent refinements in later chapters.

5.1 Preliminary Outline

To explore what 'trust' means, we will begin by analysing the use of the concept in context by considering its use in the sentence 'a patient trusts his doctor'. In principle, we will argue, this sentence refers to an expectation the patient has regarding the contingent behaviour of his doctor. Or, more explicitly, an *expectation* the patient has regarding the doctor's *competence* as well as his *commitment* to the patient's interest. Since trust is an expectation regarding a contingent behaviour, it implies a situation of *uncertainty* and hence *a certain risk* that the patient's trust may be breached, in which case that patient will feel *betrayed* (or let down). The patient who says that he trusts his doctor obviously accepts this risk. However, this is only reasonable (a) if the patient can decide whether he wants to trust or not (i.e. if he has a *free choice*) and (b) if the patient has good reason to believe that the doctor is trustworthy (i.e. if his *trust is justified*). From all this it follows that trust refers to a *relationship* or, more specifically, to a relationship between autonomous agents.

The italicised terms we have just presented in this brief initial outline denote the key features of the pattern of trust, which is to say: (1)

---

[1] To avoid any misunderstanding, we do not claim that these features hold for trust in any situation or relationship. Our claim refers solely to trust in medicine.

expectation, regarding (2) the competence and commitment of the physician, (3) uncertainty and risk, (4) free choice, (5) a feeling of betrayal following a breach of trust, (6) justification of trust, and (7) trust as relationship.

In the following short sections, we will present a brief summary of what these features mean and imply. Some of the statements and claims may be obvious, which is hardly surprising given the widespread use of the concept of trust by many people. Others may be less obvious or even contentious, which reflects something of the particular status of trust in this context. Following this outline, we devote the rest of the chapter to fleshing out each feature and then try to vindicate them against possible objections, which is where much of the discussion, explanation, and justification for these features will be offered.

5.1.1   Trust Expresses an Expectation

The first thing that will doubtless not have escaped the reader's attention is that this statement concerning the first feature of trust is very vague and in need of specifying. Nevertheless, it is central to the account of trust that we want to give, as it forms the foundation from which many of the subsequent features are derived. There are a number of key elements which need individuating and unpacking from this feature of expectation, as follows:

(a) If the patient says that she trusts her physician, then it implies that she expects him to do certain things and/or to be something (e.g. be honest).

(b) As an expectation, trust is, by definition, future-oriented.[2]

---

[2] That is, expectations are themselves beliefs that are always orientated towards the future, albeit in some cases to the very near (almost immediate) future. In cases where this concerns an event in the past, one can instead hold an assumption but not an expectation because of this future orientation. For any event that happened to occur in the past that one might think one has an expectation about, the unpacking of that purported expectation will turn out to be a combination of an assumption about the past event together with a future-orientated expectation along the lines of 'I expect that it will prove to be the case that my assumptions about past event x will be met by the revealing of evidence to that effect in the future'. Hence, the expectation is still a future-oriented belief about what evidence will reveal, rather than about the past event itself (about which, one only has assumptions). See Lazarus R 1991, p. 150 and Sztompka 1999, pp. 19ff. However, as we discuss in the next section, we reject the idea that trust can apply to features of an agent in the past precisely because they are things that one can know.

(c) The expectation in trust must regard something, which we perceive as positive, that is, something we wish.

(d) It does not make sense to say that one trusts someone if the trustee is not (at least implicitly) aware of what is expected of him.[3]

(e) The expectation can never be general (you cannot trust 'wholesale') but must be specified with regard to what you expect of the trustee. These specifications are generally referred to as 'trust domains'.

(f) The expectation must encompass both the competence and the commitment of the trustee. In other words, the expectation refers to characteristics of the trustee; it is agent-related.

(g) The expectation must be realistic, that is, it must refer to something that the trustee is capable of doing. This must not be confused with whether the trustee has the competence to do so or not.

(h) Finally, saying 'I trust A to do x' generally (although not necessarily always) means 'I believe A to be trustworthy with regard to x.' Consequently, trustworthiness, like trust, must encompass both competence and commitment.

5.1.2 Trust Always Implies Uncertainty of Outcome and Risk for the Truster

This aspect implies the following:

(a) Whereas an expectation in general may refer both to something that we know will happen[4] (e.g. we expect the sun to rise at five o'clock tomorrow morning) and to something of which we are not sure that it will happen, trust always refers to something that is uncertain. More formally, 'I expect you to do x' can only mean 'I trust you to do x' if 'I expect' cannot be replaced with 'I know'.

(b) Since trust always implies uncertainty, the truster runs the risk that his trust will be breached, which in the case of trust in physicians may mean being poorly advised or badly treated.

(c) Since, following (b), to trust implies to run a risk, the patient will want to make sure that his trust is justified.

(d) If it does not matter (or if we do not care) whether our expectation is met, then we do not trust; we simply wait and see.

---

[3] Although we are aware that there may be cases that are trust-like, in which it may be that the trustee has no awareness of this. We shall discuss such cases later.

[4] Within certain epistemic limitations, as knowledge that is neither analytic nor a priori may always be subject to probabilities or errors.

5.1.3   Trust Is a Free Choice

This implies the following:

(a) Trust is never accidental. Although you occasionally hear people say 'I just happen to trust him', this does not mean that they trust fortuitously. A phrase like 'I simply trust him' or 'I just happen to trust him' only means that the speaker trusts without too much (or no) deliberation.

(b) Trust does not follow automatically from the fact that you believe someone to be trustworthy. However, this is an asymmetric aspect of the relationship between trust and trustworthiness because trust does have to be grounded in the trustworthiness of the trustee, even if trustworthiness does not guarantee trust.

(c) Trust is always intentional. Moreover, the decision to trust is not only intentional; it is also your free choice to decide whether you want to trust someone or not.

(d) If you decide to trust someone, this implies that you consciously accept the risk inherent in trust.

(e) You may be forced by circumstances to *rely* upon someone or to *cooperate* with someone, but you cannot be forced to trust someone.

5.1.4   A Breach of Trust Causes a Feeling of Betrayal

In general, if something that you expect to happen does not happen, you feel disappointed. However, if you trust someone and they breach your trust, you feel betrayed rather than just disappointed.

From what we have seen so far, it is clear that on this account there is also another feature, discussed in the following section.

5.1.5   Trust Presupposes a Relationship between Two Moral Agents

We have just two points to make about this feature at this stage:

(a) Since trust refers to what one person expects another person to do, trust must be relational. Trust always implies a relationship between one who trusts (the truster) and one who is trusted (the trustee). This relationship may vary from a hearsay relationship (e.g. you trust the physicians at the local hospital, whom you do not know personally) to an intimate or long-standing relationship.

(b) Both truster and trustee must be autonomous and competent because only autonomous and competent persons can make free decisions and show commitment in the way required for trust. We realise that this is something that may seem rather a stringent feature of trust, given the variety of patients in the medical setting who might not be considered autonomous or competent agents, such as children in the paediatric setting or patients with certain types of mental illness in the psychiatric setting, but with whom one might still expect a level of trust to be created in their relationships with the doctor caring for them. The reason why we maintain this feature of trust given these types of trust-like relationships is an issue that we will discuss separately and in greater depth in Chapter 7.

To sum up, this is an account of trust as an expectation of the truster on the trustee's contingent behaviour towards the truster under conditions of uncertainty and risk – a risk that the truster freely choses to accept provided that he has reason to believe that his belief in the trustee's trustworthiness is justified. In other words, trust is not only a reasonable expectation but also a justified expectation.[5] On this account, a breach of trust causes a feeling of betrayal rather than just a disappointment. Finally, trust refers to a relationship between competent autonomous agents. This is the 'full pattern' of 'trust' that will serve us in providing an analytic definition akin to a comprehensive definition based on necessary conditions, albeit with some differences. It will suffice at the present time simply to repeat that this is a pattern-based definition, for which not all features must be present. We are also aware that some people may object to such a seemingly narrow definition of trust. We will return to this concern again in Chapter 7.

Having given the basic outline of the pattern-based definition of trust, we can now turn to analyse each of the individual features that form this pattern in more detail (with the exception of the justification of trust, which is so important and complex that we will devote two separate chapters to discussing it[6]). Moreover, for each feature we will aim to (a) show why we believe it to be important, (b) try to refute possible objections to its inclusion, (c) specify the feature further, where necessary, and (d) indicate whether we consider a feature essential.

---

[5] We will explain the difference between a merely rational belief or expectation and a justified belief or expectation in detail in Section 6.2.

[6] See Chapters 8 and 9.

5.2   Trust as a (Specific) Expectation

To some, it may come as a surprise that we define trust as an expectation rather than as a belief. Intuitively, the claim that 'trust' refers to a belief may sound right. And yet, we claim that it is wrong or, given that expectations might arguably require that one hold a form of belief, insufficiently precise for our purposes. Here is why. Assume that you trusted your doctor to tell the truth. If it turns out that he lied to you, you will (quite rightly) say that he breached your trust, i.e. you blame him for the breach. If trust were simply a belief, however, you could only blame yourself for having held a false belief.[7] Hence, only if trust refers to an expectation rather than a belief *simpliciter* can you blame your doctor.[8] Moreover, we might add that the term 'belief' underplays the significance of trust. To believe something need not involve actively reflecting on it,[9] whereas trust always follows from an assessment of the trustee's trustworthiness.

This emphasis on expectation as an aspect of trust is not something new but, rather, has often formed a central feature of attempts to analyse the concept. In this we entirely agree with Hardin, that "in virtually all conceptions of trust, there is an element of expectation".[10]

We can refine this feature of expectation further. The statement 'we trust you' implies that we expect you to behave in a certain manner, to do or to be something. Whereas a belief may refer to an outcome, trust refers to the person acting in a certain way and not to the outcome. On our account, trust is *agent-related* and not outcome-related. It is important to keep this in mind. 'We trust you to help us paint our house' therefore means that we expect you to help us, and not necessarily that we expect the house to be painted in the end. More precisely, trust is based on the expectation "that the person, who has a degree of freedom to disappoint our expectations, will meet an obligation under all circumstances over which they have control".[11]

As an expectation, trust is *future-oriented* or forward-looking. Quite aptly, Sztompka calls trust "a bet about future contingent actions of others".[12] Statements like 'I trust the show last night was good' express

---

[7] Luhmann calls this 'internal attribution' . . .
[8] . . . and this 'external attribution' (Luhmann 2000, pp. 97–8).
[9] Schwitzgebel 2011.
[10] Hardin 2006, p. 29.
[11] Misztal 1996, p. 24.
[12] Sztompka 1999, p. 25.

the speaker's belief that the show was good but does not actually express their trust, primarily because it refers to something in the past, i.e. to something the speaker can know.

Moreover, the expectation in trust always refers to something that has a *positive value* for the truster.[13] The statement 'we trust you will be late as usual' only makes sense if it is to our advantage if you come late (i.e. if it is what we hope for). Otherwise, it is simply a (sarcastic) statement about our unfavourable beliefs regarding your punctuality.

Another relevant feature of expectations is that an expectation may be vague, but it cannot be general. You cannot expect *'tout court'*. Likewise, trust cannot be general or absolute;[14] you cannot 'simply trust'. Both the object of trust (the trustee) and the content of your trust (i.e. what you expect of the trustee) must be specified.[15] If we trust someone, we expect him or her to do (or to be) something particular. We may also say that we always trust someone with regard to something particular. As we noted in our outline of the features of trust in Section 5.1.1(e), these 'regards' are usually referred to as 'trust domains'.[16]

The following quotation directs us to two key expectations (or trust domains):

> [T]rust definitions generally combine expectations about the ability or competence of the other with expectations about her value orientation, that is her ethics, integrity, and motives.[17]

In other words, the expectation of the truster regarding her physician always refers to both the 'competence' (knowledge, skills) and the *'commitment'* (or agency) of the trusted physician.[18] Since 'competence' and 'commitment' together define 'trustworthiness', one could also say that trust is an expectation regarding the trustworthiness of the trustee. There are two exceptions to this rule, to which we will return momentarily. As we have seen earlier, many authors define 'trust' solely with reference to

---

[13] This does not imply that the value is morally positive. In the example of a wife trusting her lover to kill her husband, the expectation may be positive (i.e. wished for) for the wife but is clearly morally reprehensible.

[14] Iltis 2007, p. 45.

[15] Hardin therefore talks of trust as a three-part relation (Hardin 2002, p. 9).

[16] Some authors also use the term 'trust dimensions'. We prefer not to use the term 'dimension' because it has too many connotations.

[17] Gilson 2006, p. 360.

[18] McKnight and Chervany (2001, p. 31) add another domain (they call them 'trust referents'), namely predictability. While we agree that predictability is important, we would subsume it under the domain 'commitment'. If someone is not predictable, he is not committed.

commitment. We believe that this is insufficient. In addition to being committed, you also want your doctor to be competent. The patient does not only want a fine, empathic doctor but also a competent and skilled one. Conversely, nor does she want a top-notch, highly skilled surgeon who clandestinely lets his junior assistant do the surgery or lies about the chances for success of the operation.

We now come back to the two exceptions to the rule that trust always refers to both the competence and the commitment of the trustee.[19] First, if we trust someone to have a certain attitude (such as open-mindedness) or to be something (say, to possess a character trait such as to be honest or faithful), competence plays no role. We must be careful, however, because 'to be' has to refer to something which we are intrinsically (such as possessing an aspect of character like being honest), and not to something which we are because we are doing something ('I trust you to be knowledgeable' really means 'I trust you to know a lot') or which itself expresses a competence (such as to be skilled). Second, if we trust someone to abstain from doing something, competence again plays no role. If I trust you not to lie to me, you do not need any particular competence. All you need is a commitment to veracity. In these two (and, as far as we are able to ascertain, only in these two) cases, trust refers to commitment alone.

Placing such emphasis on competence and commitment as features of trust naturally leaves us open to the requirement to expand on these two aspects. Surprisingly, to construe trust and trustworthiness with reference to competence and commitment sounds so intuitively right that remarkably few people have taken a closer look at analysing what 'competence' and 'commitment' actually mean in the real world of medicine. Yet competence and commitment of the physician together define his trustworthiness. Since the concept of trustworthiness plays such a key role in the debate as to how patients justify their trust in physicians, we will meet the challenge of providing some additional explanation by defining 'competence' and 'commitment' in the later chapter on the justification of trust in physicians.[20]

Where we first outlined the key elements of trust as expressing an expectation in Section 5.1.1, we emphasised the importance of the trustee also being *aware* of what is expected of him. The statement 'I trust my son to water the garden during my absence' does not make sense if he does

---

[19] Kohn 2008, p. 59.
[20] See Sections 9.2.1 and 9.2.2.

not know that I expect him to do so. What this sentence means without such an awareness is 'I assume (or I hope) my son will water the garden'. However, the awareness may be (and in many cases, is) implicit. You do not have to tell your doctor that you expect him to help you. The fact that you consult him implies your expectation.

There is an important limitation of what we can expect of the trustee, something that also has been noted elsewhere: "Trust demands . . . that the party being trusted . . . is capable of the actions required."[21]

In other words, *trust presumes capability*[22] on the part of the trustee. This is an important distinction to make because capability must not be confused with competence. Capability simply means that the trustee is (in principle) in a position to do what he is trusted to do, irrespective of whether he has the competence to do so or not. Alternatively, one might say that the *expectation must be realistic*. This condition is similar to the Kantian position that "duty commands nothing but what we can do",[23] often more broadly cited as "ought implies can". Accordingly, it does not make sense to trust your neighbour to look after your garden during your absence if he is on vacation at the same time. Or, to take an example from medicine: if you are not willing to tell your physician honestly what ails you, he will not be capable of helping you, because (not knowing what bothers you) he is not in a position to do what you trust him to do despite his competence as a physician. Of course, it is often difficult for the truster to know what lies within the trustee's capability. In fact, many patients overestimate the capabilities of a physician. In most cases, this will not be a problem. The 'misunderstanding' will be resolved during the discussion. It does become a problem, however, when patients have highly unrealistic or even irrational (or outcome-related rather than agent-related) expectations regarding the physician's capabilities. In Hertzberg's words, "trust can only concern that which one can rightfully demand of another".[24] If a patient with an incurable cancer trusts her doctor to cure her, she expects him to achieve something which is not within his capabilities (irrespective of his competence), and which she cannot demand of him.

To have specific expectations is, therefore, an essential feature of trust, although in everyday life they are often not consciously spelt out. In many

---

[21] Kohn 2008, p. 59.
[22] Tuomela and Hofmann (2003, p. 165) call this the 'ability condition' of trust.
[23] Kant 1793, p. 94 in referenced edition.
[24] Hertzberg 1988, p. 319.

situations, we have 'default' expectations. If you ask a stranger for directions to the railway station, you expect him to indicate the correct way and to tell you honestly if he does not know himself. Similarly, your expectations are mostly implicit rather than formulated when you consult a doctor. Such implicit or default expectations might be considered simply part of the social norm aspect of the practice of trust and trusting within society, whereby rigorous adherence to strict reliance on highly specific definitions as to what constitutes trust is unlikely to form part of our everyday practice or usage.

5.3   Trust Presupposes Uncertainty and Risk

In considering this next feature of trust, we look to argue that trust is a concept which only makes sense (a) under conditions of uncertainty and (b) if there is a risk for the truster.

5.3.1   Trust Implies Uncertainty

The basis for the uncertainty feature of trust is that, if we are certain how the other person(s) in a given relationship will act, we do not have to trust – it is simply not a relevant position to be in. Trust only comes into play if we cannot be sure of how the other will act:

> The need to trust presumes a state of incomplete knowledge. A state of complete certainty regarding a partner's future actions implies that risk is eliminated and trust is redundant.[25]

In other words, you do not have to trust someone to do something if you know that he will do it. Likewise, you do not have to trust someone to do something he would do (or abstain from doing) anyway. For example, one might think it unnecessary to trust your friend who is a strict Muslim not to drink your whisky on the grounds that their religious practice precludes drinking alcohol and that they are sincere adherents of that belief. Admittedly, this example shows that there is a certain leeway because even a Muslim may drink alcohol. It would be a sin, but then that it is a sin implies the individual has free will and the opportunity to do otherwise. In many cases, the uncertainty may be minimal, but at least it exists. It may therefore be that on a strict application of this feature, trust extends

---

[25] Johnson and Grayson 2005, p. 501.

to almost all aspects of human behaviour because of the minimal levels of uncertainty that may surround any decision to act.

While we agree that we do not have to trust if we have certain knowledge as to what the other will do, we do not concur with the rather broader criterion proposed by Hardin, who contends that we do not have to trust if we know that the other shares our interests.[26] We think that whether we still need to trust or not depends on the extent to which the other shares our interest. Even if both parties have an interest in cooperating, you can rarely be sure that the interest is equal on both sides and that the person will act in accord with one's own interests. As long as there remains some uncertainty, there is room for trust.

Finally, there is the question whether we 'truly' trust if the trustee has an obligation[27] to do what we trust him to do. We would argue that the answer is 'yes' if we are talking about a moral obligation because, just as with the earlier point about religious belief and free will, we can never really know whether the person will behave morally, and this creates the circumstances of uncertainty that are prerequisite for trust. If, however, we are talking about a legal (or contractual) obligation, there is no need for trust, because the other is bound to do what we expect him to do by the law or by the contract. Of course, it is not that the individual could not break the law or contract, just as they might choose to behave against their religious or moral codes, rather that the law or the contract is replacing the *need* for trust by offering certain commitments and safeguards concerning the actions of individuals. Religious and moral codes, on the other hand, do not offer quite the same safeguards. That being said, there may be cases where even the more demanding legal or contractual safeguards are not seen as sufficient to reject the requirement to trust. For example, the view that one doesn't need to trust because any deviation from the law or contract will provide sufficient recompense for any such breach (by punishing the offender and awarding damages) may not be an adequate resolution, either because the system itself is inadequate to ensure resolution or where an individual stands to lose something irreplaceable, or experience severe harm or even death. In such cases, the uncertainty generated over the efficacy of the alternative system to trust – the legal system – might still warrant grounds to have to trust as well. We will return to these concerns later in Section 10.3.

---

[26] Hardin 2006, p. 17.
[27] We will come back to this problem on page 65.

So, how should we deal with this uncertainty? Uncertainty is so relevant to trust that trust can even be seen as a strategy of "coping with uncertainty over time".[28] Admittedly, trust is not the only strategy we can adopt in the face of uncertainty. Alternatively, we can (a) abstain from interacting, (b) resort to some form of contract, or (c) gamble.

Concerning (a), *abstaining from action* may be all right (and prudent) if done occasionally. Used as a general strategy, however, it will paralyse us. And if we abstain from action because we are habitually unable to trust, the lack of trust will eventually lead us to withdraw from society.[29]

Concerning (b), *contracts* and trust may complement each other. Yet, contrary to what many people think, contracts may increase reliability,[30] but do not per se increase trust. In fact, they will more likely decrease trust. At best, contracts will replace trust (in fact, this is what they are often intended to do). Yet, as we will discuss later, contracts are poor substitutes for trust.[31]

This leaves (c), the option of *gambling*. Both trusting and gambling carry the risk of losing and offer the chance of gaining. In both cases, loss and gain are defined by the quantity (of what we can lose or gain) and by the probability (that we will lose or gain). Entrusting the latchkey of your house to your neighbour while you are on vacation is a good example of trusting. Buying a lottery ticket is the prototype of gambling. If you entrust your latchkey to your neighbour, your possible gain is small (your key is kept safe), whereas your possible loss is potentially big (if, for example, he uses your house to stage a riotous party). However, the probability that you 'win' is high (your key is safely held), whereas the risk that you 'lose' is small (a mature neighbour is unlikely to throw a riotous party). Conversely, if you buy a lottery ticket, your gain may be enormous, whereas your loss is at worst the price of the ticket. Also, contrary to the situation of trust, the probability of winning is minimal and the probability of losing is very high. In other words, with trust, the potential loss (if your trust is betrayed) is great relative to the gain (if your trust is honoured), but the probability (or risk) of a betrayal is small (unless you have misplaced your trust, i.e. made an unwise choice). If you gamble, the possible gain is big relative to the possible loss, but the probability of winning is very small.[32] Of course, not everyone might characterise the

---

[28] Dunn 2000, p. 73.
[29] Luhmann 2000, p. 104.
[30] We will discuss the difference between 'rely' (or 'reliance') and 'trust' in Chapter 6.
[31] See Section 10.3 for a detailed discussion of these claims.
[32] Deutsch 1960, pp. 124–5.

distinction between trust and gambling in this way. Counterexamples presenting clear types of gambling with low gain but high probability, such as betting on a dead-cert favourite with very low odds, are likely to be uppermost in people's minds (and *mutatis mutandis* for counter-example cases of trust). This would be to miss the point, however. These appeals to probability are not what define trust or define gambling per se. They are markers of commonplace features that distinguish the two in situations of uncertainty.[33]

To place the strategy towards uncertainty in context, many people likely believe that gambling has no place in medicine, yet to believe this would be an error. Many patients, in fact, take a gamble. Classic examples often involve patients with chronic pain or with an incurable disease. Having been frustrated by the failure of orthodox medicine, many will eventually consult a practitioner of some type of alternative medicine (or even a 'miracle healer'). It is wrong to assume that they trust the healer, but since they have a lot to gain (even if the chances are minimal) and virtually nothing to lose (if the 'miracle cure' does not work, they are usually no worse off than before), they will take the gamble. Of course, not all patients who seek help from an alternative practitioner gamble. Many of these patients cannot cope with the uncertainty inherent in medicine and prefer the professed security of alternative medicine. These patients do not gamble and may actually trust the alternative practitioner. Finally, there are those patients who consult both, an orthodox physician and an alternative practitioner. Often, they are at least sceptical of orthodox medicine and follow the old adage 'better safe than sorry'.[34] They do not gamble, although it may often be difficult to determine whom these patients trust.[35]

5.3.2   Trust Implies Risk

Acting under conditions of uncertainty implies running a risk. Since the uncertainty of trusting pertains to the behaviour of the other, this risk is a 'moral risk' or a 'moral hazard'.[36] If we do not care how 'the other' will

---

[33] We remind the reader that our approach to providing a definition for the concept of trust in medicine is pattern-based rather than an attempt to only present necessary criteria.

[34] This may remind one of a form of Pascal's Wager.

[35] As M.W. anecdotally notes from his experience of years of professional medical practice, many of these patients are difficult to manage for practitioners in terms of building relationships of trust as they have a tendency to attribute successes to alternative medicine and failures to orthodox medicine.

[36] Smith 2005, p. 300.

act, we do not run a risk. Therefore, we do not have to trust him. Here is an example. If we invite you to a party, but do not care whether you come or not, we do not trust you to come. We simply wait and see. In the words of Luhmann, "trust is only required if a bad outcome would make you regret your action",[37] i.e. if there is a risk. A statement like 'we trust you will win the competition tomorrow' does not express trust as long as there is no risk to us.[38] Such a statement simply expresses our opinion and 'trust' can effectively be replaced by some other, more precise term, such as 'believe', 'hope', etc. Similarly, if the worst possible outcome is no worse or even better than the present situation (i.e. if things can only get better), there is no need for trust because there is no risk; one would choose this action anyway.[39] The incurable cancer patient does not have to trust a healer because he will be no worse off if the hoped-for 'miracle cure' does not work.

In many people's minds, uncertainty and risk are synonymous. However, although they do have a lot in common, risk is always about a potential loss (you would not say 'you risk winning in a lottery'), whereas uncertainty may refer to wins and losses. Negative uncertainties are often referred to as 'dangers', positive ones as 'chances'. Moreover, whereas risks can be assessed and/or quantified, uncertainty 'just is', that is, uncertainties are inherent; they are 'simply there'.[40] There is no doubt that risk presupposes uncertainty. If a student knows that he will fail an exam because he has not prepared himself at all, it does not make sense to talk of a 'risk of failing'. So, without uncertainty, there is no risk, but (and this is important) uncertainty does not necessarily imply risk. With any surgical procedure there are inherent uncertainties (e.g. will the surgeon be able to remove the parotid tumour without injuring the facial nerve?). Yet this uncertainty only becomes a risk when the patient decides to undergo the operation.

As we will come back to the concept of risk repeatedly, it is worth spending some time at this point to provide a clear definition of it. We shall start with the definition itself and then go on to explain the features of that definition:

---

[37] Luhmann 2000, p. 98.
[38] We will lose nothing if you do not win unless we have made a heavy bet on your win. And even then, we can only trust you to play as well as you can, and not to win (remember that trust is agent-related and not outcome-related).
[39] Brown 2008, p. 356.
[40] Luhmann 2000, p. 100.

The risk (of a scenario) is a function of the probability (of an adverse event happening) and the consequences (of the adverse event).[41]

As an example, let us use the scenario of skiing down a slope. Here, the adverse event happening could be falling or colliding with someone else, and the consequences could range from a few bruises to more significant injuries.[42] If we know (or can calculate or estimate) the probability of the adverse event happening and its consequences, we can calculate or estimate the risk. Moreover, we can make a risk/benefit analysis before we decide to act. To avoid any misunderstanding, by 'adverse effect' we are referring to something which we know may happen, either because it has happened in similar situations or because it is bound to happen eventually. 'Adverse effect', however, does not refer to anything unknown of which people are afraid that it might happen (but have no good reason to do so). As we will discuss later,[43] changes in risk perception and risk acceptance play a major role in the decline of trust.

Trusting implies two risks. The first risk is that our trust is breached. This risk is inescapable. The second risk is that an inherent risk (e.g. of a surgical procedure) materialises (i.e. becomes reality). An example of this second risk would be that the patient wakes up after a parotidectomy with a facial palsy. So, part of the overall risk is secondary to trusting (the risk of a breach of trust), and part of it is prior to trusting (the physician's competence is independent of whether he is trusted or not).[44]

Somehow, we feel that the two risks are tied together, and yet they do not necessarily come together. Here is the same example again. Let us assume that the surgery has gone well. There was no complication. But the patient finds out that the surgeon has lied about his qualification regarding the operation (in fact, he has never done it before). So, the first risk has materialised (because the patient's trust was breached), but, fortunately, the second risk has not materialised. Unfortunately, it may also be the other way around; the complication materialises despite the fact that the physician was competent and did everything correctly so that the patient's trust was justified. Contrary to the first situation, which many patients might simply accept with just a shrug due to the beneficial outcome, a waning number of patients are willing to accept that complications can happen (i.e. that risks can materialise) even if nobody is at

---

[41] In fact, insurance companies calculate their premium by multiplying the possible damage of an accident with the probability of the accident happening (Helg 2018, p. 57).

[42] Huang 2013, p. 393.

[43] See Section 12.5.

[44] Sztompka 1999, pp. 31–2.

fault. We will return to this point later as an aspect of yet another reason for the decline of trust.[45]

The fact that to trust means to run a risk does not imply that trust is an incalculable risk. On the contrary, we tend only to trust if we are reasonably confident that the trustee deserves our trust. We assess the trustworthiness of the trustee and we weigh the possible gains and losses, taking into account the respective probabilities of losses and gains. Obviously, there is interplay between these various factors. The higher the potential gain is (especially in comparison with the potential loss), the lower the evidence for, or the probability of, the trustee's trustworthiness that is required for trust to be responsible (and vice versa).[46]

Uncertainty and risk are essential features of trust, although most of the time we are not aware of them. This is fortunate because, if we were aware of the risk all the time, we would probably lose 'trust in trust'.

5.4   Trust as Free Choice

With our account of trust, we posit that one can freely choose whether (and to what extent) one wants to trust someone. This presupposes that trust is an act (or, more cautiously formulated, that trust may also be an act). To be able to defend our position we will have to refute claims that trust is purely cognitive (i.e. a mental state), such as that offered by Hardin:

> All three extant standard conceptions of trust are therefore cognitive, . . .
> *If trust is cognitive, then we do not choose to trust.*[47]

---

[45] See Section 12.5.

[46] We are taking 'responsible' to mean 'having good reason to believe x is trustworthy', that is, justified in a reasonable belief in the trustee's trustworthiness. We will say more about justified expectations in Section 6.2, in particular on page 77.

By referring to responsibility here, the reader will note that we are moving away from providing a form of purely 'rationalist' account of trust, whereby a decision to trust is considered 'rational' if there is a certain probability ratio inherent in the risk calculation. As noted, trust is a sufficiently broad concept to allow for strategic judgements involving weighing of evidence but an important element of a substantive account of trust is that it does not involve such purely rationalist strategies and instead involves considering other, often normative, justifications (McGeer 2008, pp. 240–1). Whilst McGeer's interest is in how one might maintain trust based on an account of hope, the point is well made. Rather than engaging in a discussion of what would constitute 'rational' and 'rationality', we prefer to couch our justification for trust in terms of making responsible choices. Although one can be both rational and responsible, there may be times where these come apart. We shall develop this normative aspect of the justification for trust as we progress.

[47] Hardin 2006, p. 17, his emphasis.

Or claims that it is solely non-cognitive (i.e. an affective attitude), such as that offered by Jones:

> I defend an account of trust according to which *trust is an attitude* of optimism that the goodwill and competence of another will extend to cover the domain of our interaction with her.[48]

If, as Hardin claims, trust were solely cognitive or if, as Jones claims, trust were purely an attitude of optimism, we would agree that we could not choose to trust. However, we disagree with both claims.[49] We have two motivations to defend our position of 'trust as choice': first, the position that we cannot choose whether to trust or not is not plausible to us. Second, conceiving trust as choice has significant implications. Or, inversely and more to the point, trust loses important qualities if we cannot choose whether we want to trust or not.

Here is a little thought experiment to illustrate why we think that it is not plausible to claim that we cannot choose whether we want to trust someone. Suppose that you are to undergo dental implantations. Since you believe that your dentist is honest and will not overcharge you, you trust him and do not ask for a cost estimate before he embarks on what you know will be an expensive treatment. But then (for whatever reason) you suddenly realise that your belief might be false and that the dentist might betray your trust. It dawns on you that you run a considerable financial risk and, since you are, in general, rather risk-averse, you decide that it is safer not to trust him after all (better to be safe than sorry), despite the fact that you still believe him to be honest. The thought is that if you can decide (or choose) to *mis*trust (i.e. not to trust), you must logically also be able to decide (or choose) to trust.

Moreover, it is *not trivial* whether we conceive trust as something we can choose or not for two very good reasons. First, (a) to trust means to take a risk, and if you do this at your own choice, you want to make sure you have good reasons. So, to be responsible, trust has to be well grounded. Second, (b) if, on the other hand, trust is purely cognitive, any decline of trust must be due to a decline of trustworthiness (on which trust is based) and thus be external to the truster. In this case, we would have to explain why trustworthiness has declined rather than why trust has declined. Both points need further elaboration. We will address the issue of how we justify trust in Chapters 8 and 9, and also answer the

---

[48] Jones 1996, p. 4, our emphasis.
[49] To forestall any misunderstanding: we do not deny that cognition and attitudes are important aspects of trust. All we claim is that they are not sufficient.

question as to whether trustworthiness rather than trust has decreased in Chapter 12.

5.4.1   Trust as Attitude versus Trust as Choice

In the literature, 'trust' is often seen either as a cognitive mental state or as an attitude, as we can see from the following passage from Becker:

> To fix ideas, let us call our trust *'cognitive'* if it is fundamentally a matter of our beliefs or expectations about others' trustworthiness; it is *'non-cognitive'* if it is fundamentally a matter of our having trustful attitudes, affects, emotions, or motivational structures.[50]

However, although this seems intuitively intelligible, it is in some ways confusing: first, because the characterisation of trust as "trust is having trustful attitudes" is circular and, second, because the term 'attitude' is itself ambiguous and needs to be defined. This second aspect may seem to be straightforward, but, as Bem points out, "our attitudes are our likes and dislikes".[51] This may sound a bit simple, and it is, but it illustrates once again that when it comes to defining commonly used concepts, very often "we recognise the relevant pattern and thereby acquire mastery of the terms".[52]

That being said, it is beyond the scope of this book to go into the immense scholarly literature on what attitudes are or how they can be defined. There are a few points, however, which we want to make. One of the most frequently cited definitions of 'attitude' is from Gordon Allport,[53] according to whom an attitude is

> [a] mental and neural state of readiness, organised through experience exerting a directive or dynamic influence upon the individual's response to all objects and situations.[54]

So, in this definition, an attitude has a cognitive component ('it is a mental state') and a behavioural component ('exerting an influence'). Moreover, it is acquired ('organised through experience'). This definition was later expanded by authors such as Rokeach and Smith to include an affective component.[55] It has also been noted that attitudes (like trust or

---

[50] Becker 1996, p. 44, our emphasis.
[51] Bem, 1970, cited in Schwarz and Bohner 2001, p. 436.
[52] Jackson 2010, p. 179.
[53] The statement refers to the social science literature.
[54] Alport, 1935, cited in Lind 1984, p. 5.
[55] Rokeach and Smith 1968.

trustworthiness) are not general but must have an object;[56] that is, they must refer to someone or something. Whereas 'most young people have a negative attitude' does not make sense, 'most young people have a negative attitude towards older people' would make sense (irrespective of whether it is true or not).

This means that we can reasonably define attitudes in the following way: attitudes are acquired; they have a cognitive component and/or[57] an affective as well as a behavioural component; and they must refer to an object. The fact that *attitudes are acquired* and may be modified (mostly through learning processes) distinguishes them from personality traits (which remain more stable throughout life). The *cognitive component* refers to such mental states as knowledge and beliefs, to what we know or believe about others. The *affective component* refers to our stance or disposition towards others. It may, but does not necessarily have to, follow from the cognitive component. Finally, the *behavioural (or conative) component* refers to how we behave towards specified others.

This discussion of attitudes has implications for our account of trust. So, rather than saying that trust is *cognitive* if it is fundamentally a matter of our beliefs and *non-cognitive* if it is fundamentally a matter of our affective attitudes, it would be less confusing if we talked of trust as a matter of the cognitive or of the affective component of our attitude, that is, of our cognitive or our affective attitudes.

Accordingly, we shall first turn to discuss trust as a matter of *cognitive attitudes*. One of Hardin's major arguments against 'trust as choice' is that "just as you cannot look at the evidence and then decide to know, you cannot [assess the other's trustworthiness and then] choose to trust".[58]

Of course, we agree that we cannot look at the evidence and then decide whether we want to know or not. However, there is a major difference between 'knowledge' and 'trust'. If we are told that the average distance from the earth to the moon is 384,400 km, we know this (in the vernacular sense of the word). We cannot choose whether we want to know it or not. Once we have been told, we know it. So, 'to know' is purely cognitive. We may forget the exact figure, but as soon as you mention it, we will say that of course we know this. Similarly, once we have assessed your trustworthiness, we believe that you are trustworthy. So far, this is no different from 'to know'. In this sense, trust is cognitive.

---

[56] Koballa 1988, p. 117.

[57] We say 'and/or' because an attitude does not necessarily concern all components (see below).

[58] Hardin 2002, p. 58, our insertion.

But whereas 'to know' refers to the content of what we know (the distance from earth to moon), 'to trust' also refers to how we interact with others based on our beliefs. In other words, whereas 'to know' is only self-referential, 'to trust' is also relational. For example, the claim 'We believe that you are honest' expresses our belief but has nothing to do with our relationship, whereas 'We trust you to be honest' expresses our belief and, in addition, informs about our relationship. We cannot choose whether to believe that you are trustworthy (if according to our assessment you are trustworthy), but we can choose to trust you or not.

Of course, Hardin admits that, somehow, we have to apply our belief of trustworthiness if it is to have any practical use. So, he proposes that we should distinguish between 'trust' and 'acting on trust' by claiming: "That trusting someone and acting on that trust are different is trivially evident."[59]

We agree with this statement, but not with the conclusion he subsequently draws, namely that 'to trust' cannot itself be an act. This requires some further explanation of both Hardin's position and our own. To underpin his point, Hardin argues that we may trust you (which for him means that we believe that you are trustworthy) but not act on this trust. Here is an example. You may trust your doctor to always tell you the truth but, in fact, never ask him to do so because, being healthy, you see no reason to do so. So, for Hardin, you trusted but did not act on your trust. Along similar lines, Simpson claims that "defining trust as an action, which one places or not, fails to describe situations where trust is latent".[60] To use the same example: assume that you told your physician to always tell you the truth (even if it was bad news) and you trust him to do so. Luckily, until now, he never had to give you any bad news. Therefore, so Simpson would argue, you were never exposed to risk; your trust was only latent. So, you did not trust.

To our thinking, both arguments are flawed. To trust (in a relational sense) is something we do, irrespective of whether our trust is ever put to test or not. When you decided to trust your doctor, you could not know whether you would ever have to rely on his integrity or not. So, you did put yourself at risk. In both examples, you trusted, but your trust was not put to test. In Hardin's case this was because you had no reason to act on your trust; in Simpson's case because the situation did not arise.

---

[59] Hardin 2002, p. 58.
[60] Simpson 2012, p. 553.

It is also worth noting that, linguistically, Hardin claims that 'to trust', like 'to know', is a stative verb.[61] To the contrary, whereas we agree that 'to know' is indeed purely stative, we take 'to trust' as both stative (with regard to our belief in your trustworthiness) and non-stative (inasmuch as it refers to our relationship with you).[62] To limit the concept of trust just to the belief component is insufficient and neglects an important aspect of 'trust'.

Rather than always saying 'we *act* on trust', we think that at a 'street level'[63] we may safely use 'to trust' when we refer to the relational aspect of trust. Whether we say that we trust you to behave in a certain manner or that we act on our belief that you are trustworthy does not make a difference. Either way, and this is the important point, we can choose whether we want to act, i.e. to trust you or not.

To conclude this discussion on cognitive trust we want to add a final argument for 'trust as choice'. We think that there is a major difference between knowing the distance from earth to moon and believing in your trustworthiness: the former is an empirical fact, whereas the latter is a judgement; even more to the point, it is our personal judgement. Everyone who measures the distance to the moon will come up with the same result (assuming they all use a reliable measuring method). Trustworthiness, however, is not definite; it has degrees, and it is situational. It is the patient's choice whether she considers the available information adequate to believe in the physician's trustworthiness. So, even if (as Hardin argues) trust inevitably follows from the assessment of trustworthiness, this assessment is subjective and hence subject to choice.

We can now turn our attention to the affective (or, as Becker calls them, non-cognitive) attitudes. Karen Jones, one of the major proponents of 'trust as an affective attitude',[64] writes:

> I defend an account of trust according to which *trust is an attitude of optimism* that the goodwill and competence of another will extend to cover the domain of our interaction with her.[65]

---

[61] Contrary to this, McKnight and Chervany argue that 'trust' is an action verb, the truster being the subject, the trustee being the direct object (McKnight and Chervany 2001, p. 40).

[62] Stative verbs may be non-stative if they refer to an action in progress, e.g. 'I am thinking about . . .' (www.annies-annex.com/dynamic_verbs.htm).

[63] This is a term which Hardin himself uses in the context of epistemology.

[64] This is also the title of one of her papers.

[65] Jones 1996, p. 4, our emphasis.

This definition, however, relies on too strong a connection between trust and optimism whilst leaving understated what optimism actually is. Looking more closely at what optimism amounts to, the definition offered by Jones starts to look less convincing. There are numerous ways of defining optimism, and these can involve some reference to optimism being an attitude.[66] However, almost every available account of optimism also treats it as a 'mode' of viewing the future with an emotional or motivational component, so that it is more of a general stance towards life.[67] This is perhaps best summed up by Garrard and Wrigley, where they say that "optimism is the belief that everything will turn out for the best. It focuses on some better future in a way which is detached from the individual; it is a stance which is ultimately that of the spectator."[68]

If we are optimistic, our optimism usually pervades most of our actions.[69] Attitudes, however, tend to be more specific. Someone's political attitude may be left or right wing, but this has nothing to do with whether he is an optimist or a pessimist. Admittedly, people with a more optimistic outlook on the world[70] are likely to trust more easily. However, our point is that simply to equate trust with optimism as Jones does is not plausible. This claim will require some additional elucidation.

We prefer to start from Eagly and Chaiken's definition of (affective) attitudes as "a psychological tendency that is expressed by *evaluating* a particular entity *with some degree of favour or disfavour*".[71] Using this definition, what is called 'identification-based trust'[72] becomes the 'psychological tendency' to positively judge the trustworthiness of people with whom we share, for example, values, gender, or ethnicity 'with a degree of favour'. We think it is fair to say that a 'benign (or malign) affective attitude' often influences our choice to trust. However, we would not go as far in this as Govier, who claims that "[t]rust *is in essence* an attitude of positive expectation about other people".[73]

---

[66] Bennett 2011.

[67] Bennett 2011; Peterson 2000.

[68] Garrard and Wrigley 2009, p. 42.

[69] We admit that 'optimism' may also be specific (e.g. 'we are optimistic that on this occasion it will not rain again').

[70] McKnight and Chervany use the term 'faith in humanity', by which they mean the general belief that others are trustworthy (McKnight and Chervany 2001, p. 39).

[71] Eagly and Chaiken 2007, p. 582, our emphasis.

[72] Goold 2002b, p. 79.

[73] Govier 1998, p. 6, our emphasis.

Just as we disagree with Hardin that 'trust is solely a rational assessment' (i.e. purely cognitive), we disagree with Govier that 'trust is purely affective'. Rather, our position is that for trust to be responsible our decision to trust must be grounded in some belief;[74] that is, it *must have* a cognitive component,[75] but as well as that, in addition, it *may be* (and often is) supported by a positive affective attitude.

Having said all this, we want to clarify that we are not claiming that trust is always a deliberate, conscious choice. In this, we agree with Holten, who says that "I think that in some circumstances we can decide to trust. I do not say that every case of trust is a case of a decision to trust."[76] In most cases, it is quite plausible that our choice is unconscious. In fact, most of the time we are not even aware that we are trusting.[77] There are far too many situations in which we simply have to trust in order to function efficiently. Since this limitation is nowhere as evident as it is in the continuous necessity to trust other people's testimonies, we will discuss this in further detail in Chapter 8 (justification of epistemic trust). What is important is not so much that we choose to trust in every case but that we have the option to choose if we want to.

So, we have argued that trust is a cognitive mental state, in so far as it refers to our beliefs (i.e. the assessment of someone's trust-worthiness), and that it is an act, in as much as it refers to how I interact with the trustee. Whereas we cannot choose to believe (this is the cognitive part), we can choose to act on what we believe (this is the relational part). Moreover, we have argued that the decision to trust may be supported by (but cannot be solely based on) an affective attitude. The arguments presented so far thereby underpin our claim that we can choose whether we trust or not. We will now go a step further and argue that we cannot only choose but choose freely, i.e. that trust is a *free* choice. It will come as no surprise that 'free choice', being a key concept itself in our account of trust, needs to be defined and, hence, is what we shall turn to next.

---

[74] We will show why in Chapter 9.

[75] In a more recent paper, Karen Jones has changed her position to a position very close to what we have just outlined: "Perhaps sometimes there is an affective component to trust, and sometimes not, but trust always works by shaping the agent's interpretation of reasons ... Call these 'trusting interpretations'" (Jones 2013, p. 16).

[76] Holton 1994, p. 69.

[77] Lagerspetz and Hertzberg 2013, p. 32.

5.4.2   Trust as Free Choice

To avoid any misunderstanding, we are here using the term 'free' in a descriptive rather than in a normative sense. Here is an example of what we mean by this: If 'coercion' is used descriptively, it refers to any form of external influence irrespective of whether this influence is morally wrong or not. If it is used normatively, it refers only to those cases where the influence is morally wrong. Similarly, if 'free' is used descriptively, it refers to any act performed in the absence of controlling influences; if it is used normatively, it assigns some moral value to the act. In this latter case, to say that 'trust is a free choice' would imply that trust is a moral notion.[78] Although as part of our overall account of trust we agree with this, it is not in this (normative) way that we are using the term 'free'. Despite the potential for such ambiguity between the two uses of the term, we nevertheless decided to use the term 'free' rather than 'voluntary'. We are well aware that the two terms are not synonymous (although they overlap to some extent). However, since much of the literature is on 'voluntariness', we will occasionally use the term 'voluntary' in lieu of 'free' where we think this provides greater precision in the point we are making.

In the previous section, we explained that we can choose whether we want to trust or not. Yet, the fact that we choose something does not necessarily imply that our choice is free. The mugger's demand of 'your money or your life' obviously leaves us a choice (albeit one that is not what we would usually consider 'free').[79] We could even argue that we hand over our wallet intentionally (after all, we do not accidently drop it). Yet, it would be stretching the truth to claim that we hand over our wallet freely. Obviously, 'intention' alone does not make a choice free. So, how can we define 'free choice'? Nelson et al. offer the following definition of 'voluntary' action:

> We propose that the concept of voluntary action be understood in terms of two necessary and jointly sufficient conditions: intentional action and the absence of controlling influences.[80]

If this is correct, 'voluntary' (which is here being used in place of our preferred use of 'free') implies both intention and absence of controlling

---

[78] Wilkinson 2013, pp. 85–7.
[79] See Wilkinson 2013, Chapter 6 on coercion, for an excellent discussion as to whether there is an element of a 'free' choice in such situations.
[80] Nelson et al. 2011, p. 6.

influences. As we have just seen (in the example of the wallet), intention alone is not sufficient to define 'free'. As regards the necessity of the second condition (absence of controlling influences), we think that it is undisputed, although, as we will see, it is often difficult to decide what exactly counts as a controlling influence. So, the question that remains to be answered is whether we need the first condition (i.e. intention) at all or whether doing something without controlling influences is implicitly intentional, in which case 'absence of controlling influence' would be sufficient to define a 'free choice'. Obviously, Nelson thinks it is not. To the contrary, we hold that whatever we do in the absence of controlling influences, we do intentionally. Here is why. If no controlling influence induces us to do 'x', we have two options: we can abstain from doing 'x', or we can do 'x'. No matter what we choose (to do 'x' or not to do 'x'), our acting and our non-acting is intentional. Therefore, we argue that 'absence of controlling influence' is not only the *key feature of 'free choice'*; it is also a sufficient condition.[81] We admit, though, that a controlling influence may at times be difficult to detect,[82] (a) because not all influences are per se controlling and (b) because there are external as well as internal influences (which may be more difficult to detect).[83]

Having defined 'free choice', we will now turn our attention to its practical application. In the medical context, the concept of 'free choice' is often referred to as 'voluntary choice' and discussed within the framework of 'informed consent'. Consent is considered ethically valid (i.e. establishes the permissions it is designed to generate) if the patient is given the necessary information, has the competence to understand this information, and acts voluntarily.[84] Even if trusting someone and consenting with what someone proposes are not necessarily the same, much of what is said about voluntariness in the context of informed consent is useful in the context of trust. It is therefore worth taking a closer look at voluntariness briefly.

---

[81] We are here excluding cases where there is an absence of controlling influences but no choice to be made (or no one to make that choice). This is because we are taking 'free choice' to mean 'types of decision that an intentional agent would make', which means that there is an intentional component to the definition but it is a trivial part of it. Given such a context, 'absence of controlling influence' is a sufficient condition for free choice, so interpreted.

[82] One might add 'and to define': e.g. the question whether dipsomania is a vice or a disease largely depends on how we define (and hence, what we regard as) 'controlling influence'.

[83] Nelson et al. 2011, p. 8.

[84] Wilkinson 2013, p. 76.

According to the Nuremberg Code of 1949 "voluntariness is the free power of choice without undue influence or coercion".[85] This sounds intuitively right, and yet it is not very helpful, because it replaces one unknown with another. Instead of having to define 'voluntariness', we now have to define what we consider as 'undue influence' or 'coercion'. Whereas coercion may be relatively obvious, it is rather difficult to decide what counts as 'undue influence'. Since we are not making decisions in the void, we think it is reasonable to assume that all our decisions are made under *some* influence (even if at times we may not be aware of it). This influence may be external (i.e. coming from outside) or internal (i.e. relating to our own beliefs or feelings).[86] Irrespective of whether influences are external or internal, they may be fully controlling (in which case our decision is not free), partly controlling (in which case the voluntariness is questionable), or not controlling. So, voluntariness is not black or white; it admits of degrees. One may therefore say that "voluntariness is the degree of control that an agent has over his behaviour".[87]

Moreover, influences may be objective/objectifiable (such as if a doctor makes it clear to the patient that unless she follows his recommendations, he will refuse to see her again) or subjective (e.g. if the patient fears that the doctor will abandon her if she does not follow his advice). Whereas the first case is one of coercion, the second case is more difficult to judge. *Being free* and *feeling free* from controlling influences are not the same.[88] In the first case, the patient is not free; in the second case, she may be free but does not feel free. The opposite situation (i.e. a patient who feels free although in reality he is not free) is also possible, probably more common, and certainly more problematic.

In other words, there is not just free and not free; there are all shades in between. So, where should we set the cut-off point? The same applies to influences: they are not just harmless or coercing; they may be anything in between. Nor are influences either entirely objective or purely subjective; many of them have a touch of both. Moreover, are objective or subjective influences worse? And which of them trumps the other? Rather than trying to answer these questions (which we believe would be bordering on the futile), we will discuss three potential limitations of the 'freedom of choice': (1) How much persuasion is permissible? (2) Do

---

[85] Cited in Miller et al. 2009, p. 25.
[86] Nelson et al. 2011, p. 8.
[87] Wall 2001, p. 130.
[88] Berghmans 2011, p. 23.

obligations a priori render choices unfree? And (3) what if there are no alternatives?

(1) The art of persuasion (i.e. the physician's ability to persuade the patient to follow his advice) is part of what makes up the physician's competence (which, as we have previously argued, is part of a physician's trustworthiness). If he does not try to persuade the patient, she may think that he is not sure (or convinced) himself. However, it is often difficult to decide when exactly persuasion becomes coercion. Whether an argument is perceived by the patient as persuasive or as coercive often depends on what the patient prefers to hear. If the patient with the pleomorphic adenoma goes to see her physician with the idea of 'having this lump removed', she will freely agree to the proposed surgery. If, however, she does not feel inclined to undergo an operation, she may think that the doctor is trying to bully her into consenting to surgery. To paraphrase Appelbaum et al. 'applying pressure may be reprehensible, but, if it is not causally related to the decision, it does not render the decision involuntary'.[89] To come back to our example: if the patient's decision to undergo surgery is *not* due to the physician applying some 'pressure' but to her preconceived idea 'to have this lump removed', the decision may be considered her free choice.

(2) Trust does not exist in a void. It happens in a relationship (see below), and in relationships, people have *obligations*. The question is, does a patient trust freely if she has (or thinks she has) an obligation towards her physician? The first impulse would probably be to say no. But if any obligation automatically renders an act 'unfree', then all actions, which we perform because we feel that we have a moral obligation, likewise become unfree. This cannot be right as it sets a standard far too high for free choice and would run counter to a central tenet of moral philosophy that it is precisely that we have free choice when it comes to acting on our moral obligations that lends them their value. In this, we are not alone and agree with Wertheimer that a (real or imagined) obligation per se does not render a decision unfree.[90]

(3) Perhaps even more difficult to answer are the following questions: Is the patient's trust his free choice if he has no (acceptable) alternative? And, does it matter whether the patient effectively has

---

[89] Appelbaum et al. 2009, p. 34.
[90] Wertheimer 2012, p. 238.

no alternative or just thinks he has no alternative? From a legal standpoint, Appelbaum et al. argue that "constraints – such as poverty, [or] the lack of alternative treatment options … . – may have a profound influence on … choice, but with the possible exception of some extraordinary cases, they do not make the choice involuntary".[91]

Of course, legal arguments are not necessarily congruent with ethical arguments. Yet, even from an ethical standpoint, we believe that this analysis is right. An oft-used example in discussions of informed consent is to imagine a case where there is a patient with a life-threatening disease who has to undergo emergency treatment. The question is, is this patient's consent to the treatment free, and, consequently, is the consent he gave to undergo the treatment valid? There are three possible answers to these questions:[92] (a) the consent is not free. This means that the consent is not valid. We think that this is clearly unacceptable because it would render one of the most important parts of medicine a priori unethical. (b) The consent is not free, but the consent is still valid. Again, this is not satisfactory, because it would undermine the entire concept of informed consent, which would be too high a price to pay. (c) It is free despite the lack of choice, and hence the consent is valid. Even if no one is probably completely happy with this answer, we think it is the best possible solution. The main reason for accepting this solution is, as Wilkinson points out, "that it will be difficult, if not impossible, to specify non-arbitrarily what counts as a sufficient good number of sufficiently good alternatives".[93]

If consent is free in the absence of an alternative, we take it that, on the same grounds, trust must likewise be free in the absence of an alternative. Moreover, we do not think it matters whether the absence of an alternative is real or surmised. Nor does it matter whether there is no alternative or simply no time to evaluate potential alternatives (as in emergency cases).

In summary, trust is essentially a free choice. Even if in the great majority of situations trust is not a deliberate choice, having the option to choose is an important (albeit not essential) feature of trust. Moreover, neither obligations on the part of the truster nor lack of alternatives renders our choice to trust a priori unfree. Having the option of choosing

[91] Appelbaum et al. 2009, p. 33, our insertion.
[92] Wertheimer 2012, p. 236.
[93] Wilkinson 2013, p. 80.

whether one wants to trust someone or not is an important, albeit not an essential, feature of 'trust'.

5.5   The Feeling of Betrayal after a Breach of Trust

We have previously argued that to trust means to accept the risk of a breach of trust. This is, in one sense, nothing special to trust itself. We all run risks all the time. What differentiates the risk in trust from other risks is our reaction if the risk materialises. If something we simply rely upon fails, we are usually just disappointed (or, depending on the situation, angry). A breach of trust, however, engenders something more substantial and complex in terms of a feeling of betrayal or deception. To illustrate this, here are two examples:

Example 1:   Every morning at ten you go to the post office to pick up your mail. So far, it has always been ready by that time – but today it is not.

Example 2:   Your friend has promised to help you set up your new computer. Having known him for years, you expected him to show up – but he did not come.

Both times your expectation was not fulfilled. Yet, upon reflection, it is most likely that your reaction was different in each case. When your mail was not on time, you were somewhat annoyed (perhaps even slightly angry if it was something important or if you had other pressing things to do), but when your friend did not show up it was most likely a different sort of reaction: you felt let down or even betrayed. So, what is the difference between the two cases? The answer is that you trusted your friend but relied upon the mail service. It was your friend's breach of your trust that engendered a feeling on your part of being let down in a way that constituted a form of betrayal, whereas the unreliability of the postal system only leaves you disappointed or annoyed. It is this feeling of betrayal[94] that distinguishes trust from other types of expectations.[95]

Admittedly, the answer that we feel let down in the case of trust but not in the case of reliance somewhat begs the question. It does not explain *why* we feel betrayed in one case but not in the other. Our answer to this question is that the feeling of betrayal (which is often referred to as

---

[94]   The fact that the feeling of betrayal admits of degrees does not change this because even a minimal feeling of betrayal differentiates trust from other expectations.
[95]   Baier 1986, p. 235.

a 'reactive attitude') is constrained to 'disappointments of moral expectations'.[96] You feel betrayed if your friend does not keep his promise (keeping a promise is a moral obligation), but not if the mail is not on time (delivering the mail on time is not a moral obligation). In other words, we claim that the fact that you typically react to a breach of trust with a feeling of betrayal shows that 'trust' belongs to the realm of morality.

We are well aware that this is a difficult and potentially contentious claim, which demands considerable elaboration. For the moment, we let the claim stand as it is. We will, however, present a detailed discussion of the moral value of trust in Chapter 11. As a final comment on this issue, it is worth emphasising that, although it is not an essential feature, the feeling of betrayal engendered by a breach of trust is, nevertheless, conceptually an important feature of 'trust'. To what extent people feel betrayed if their trust is breached, however, will depend on their attitude and on the circumstances.

5.6   Trust as Relationship

From what we have said so far, we think it follows that trust is always relational and can only prevail between competent autonomous agents.[97] The *relationship character between truster and trustee* is usually clear in the case of a patient and his physician. Yet, we also trust doctors (or other professionals) *qua* role representatives.[98] We trust hospitals or other medical institutions, and we can even trust healthcare payers (at least theoretically) such as medical insurance companies. In all these instances, the relationship is neither immediately evident nor is it personal. Yet, we still hold that in all these cases there is a relationship between the truster and the trustee.

To explain why we believe this to be so, let us use another example. You may hear people say that they trust the BBC weather forecast. Most of these people have no personal relationship with the forecaster (or the meteorologist responsible for the forecast). Their statement about their trust in the BBC forecast means that they believe in the competence and the commitment of the meteorologists. So far, there seems to be no difference between trust in your doctor and trust in the meteorologists.

---

[96] For a more detailed discussion of this, see Section 11.1.
[97] We will discuss this claim and qualify this statement further down as well as in Chapter 7.
[98] Schermer 2002, p. 171.

And yet, we claim that there is a difference here, despite the use of the same term, in that you *trust* your doctor but *rely on* the competence of the meteorologist.[99] The picture is even more complicated because you not only trust your own doctor but you also trust the doctors at your local hospital to be medically competent and to be committed to their patients. After all, this is what they profess to do. Of course, you may say that the meteorologists are competent and committed as well, which is certainly true. So, where is the difference? The difference lies in the relationship aspect of trust. The commitment of the hospital doctors is to their patients, i.e. to you personally, if ever you happen to become a patient at their hospital. So, there is (even if only potentially) a relationship between you and the hospital. This is also true in the case of, e.g. an insurance company, and even in the case of a health authority. In all these instances you trust their representatives to be competent and (what is more important) committed to make decisions that are in your (or at least your fellow humans') interest. In the case of an insurance company, this may mean, for example, that you trust its personnel to put your personal interests above the company's financial gain by not contesting reasonable insurance claims. In sum, trust in institutions is possible via trust in representatives.[100] In contrast, the meteorologists may be committed to do a competent job, but they are not committed to you (or any of us). It is not their job to make a prognosis that is in your (or actually in anyone's) interest.[101] In the words of Lagerspetz and Hertzberg, "trust means we are prepared to enter in some kind of cooperation",[102] and whereas there is 'some kind of cooperation' between you and your doctor, hospital, or insurance company, there is clearly no cooperation between you and the meteorologist.

From the fact that trust is relational it follows that we can only trust in persons (interpersonal trust) and (indirectly, through representatives) in institutions (institutional trust) but not in technology. Nor can we trust 'in medicine', where 'medicine' refers to a body of knowledge or to

---

[99] We will detail the (important) differentiation between trust and reliance in Section 6.2.3.

[100] Sztompka 1999, pp. 19–20.

[101] There may be some concern over the example of the BBC weather service because both the BBC and the Met Office who provide the weather data are public services in the United Kingdom. This may mean a certain set of expectations, governance, reliance, etc. is attributable to the weather forecast because of its public status. However, the point remains that it is not a meteorologist's role to make weather predictions that are in anyone's interest, only that they are committed to high standards of competency in providing this service.

[102] Lagerspetz and Hertzberg 2013, p. 34.

a mode of decision-making and of judging medical interventions.[103] Moreover, the fact that trust is about a relationship does not imply that the beneficiary of the trust is always the truster himself.[104] For example, if we trust you to help your sister, then the relationship is between you and us, but the beneficiary would be your sister.

Both truster and trustee must be autonomous and competent (not in an absolute sense but with regard to what trust is about in the specific case),[105] because only autonomous and competent persons can make free decisions and show commitment. Moreover, since only an individual can make an autonomous choice, the truster must always be an *individual*. If a group of individuals (or 'the public') claims to trust 'A', this may mean either that each individual has decided to trust 'A' based on his or her own assessment of the trustee's trustworthiness or that the members of the group individually trust the assessment of 'A's trustworthiness by one member of the group'.[106] Contrary to this, it is possible to trust a group of moral agents or even institutions (e.g. a healthcare organisation) on the assumption that the members of the group are jointly committed and jointly have the necessary competence. Again, this feature is conceptionally important, although in many cases of trust it may not be present (e.g. cases involving small children or individuals with certain mental disabilities).

5.7   Summary and Conclusions

So, to sum up, we have applied the approach of basing a definition on the pattern of characteristic features of a term to that of 'trust'. Then, by analysing the sentence 'a patient trusts his doctor', we have stepwise identified the following characteristic features of 'trust':

(1) Trust refers to an expectation regarding the trustworthiness, i.e. the competence and commitment, of the trustee.
(2) Trust presupposes a situation of uncertainty and risk.
(3) Trust is responsible if this expectation is justified.
(4) This expectation must be realistic (i.e. the trustee must be in a position to do what he is expected to do).

---

[103] As we will discuss in the next chapter, we can believe in medicine and we can rely on technology, but we cannot trust in either of them.
[104] Holton 1994, p. 65.
[105] This may reduce the scope of 'trust of' and 'trust in' children but does not rule it out. We will discuss this in more detail in Chapter 7.
[106] Sztompka refers to this as second-order trust (Sztompka 1999, pp. 46–7).

(5) Trust is a free choice and implies the (at least unconscious) acceptance of the trust's inherent risk.

(6) A breach of trust causes a feeling of betrayal on the part of the truster.

(7) Trust refers to the relationship between agents who are competent and autonomous with regard to the topic of trust.

Of the seven features, 1, 2, and 3 are essential. If one of them is absent, it is simply not a case of trust. Together, they form the basis of our definition of 'trust': 'trust refers to a justified expectation regarding the trustworthiness of the trustee under conditions of uncertainty and risk'. However, as we will go on to explain in the next chapter, they are not sufficient to define 'trust'.

So far, this definition satisfies the first three of the five conditions for a satisfactory definition, which we set up in the introduction to Chapter 3:[107] First, it fulfils the eliminability and conservativeness criteria of a good definition.[108] This means that 'trust' can be understood by previously understood terms (expectation, competence, commitment, risk, etc.), and that replacing these previously understood terms with 'trust' leads neither to inconsistencies nor to anything new. Second, it is comprehensive, i.e. it encompasses all relevant features of trust. Even if there were additional features, which we have not identified, it is unlikely that they would improve the power of the definition to identify cases of trust.[109] It may seem that a definition of 'trust' that is based on the full pattern described above will be very narrow and, arguably of limited use in everyday practice. However, this need not concern us here, as we will go on to show in later chapters how the method of pattern-based defining can be used to come up with wider definitions of trust and definitions that are better adapted to various situations or needs. Finally, third, it is applicable both to individuals (physicians and other healthcare professionals, as well as patients themselves) and (through representatives) to institutions, in which these people work.

Having defined 'trust', we will now turn our attention to a series of related concepts, namely to trust's opposites ('mistrust' and 'distrust'), and to those terms which (at least in folk usage) are often used interchangeably with 'trust', namely 'confidence', 'reliance', 'hope', and 'belief-in'.

---

[107] See page 21.

[108] Belnap 1993, p. 117.

[109] Such a claim has parallel examples in all sorts of areas. For example, in an in-depth study undertaken with the aim of developing a computer-based prognostic model in aero-digestive tract carcinomas, out of more than twenty parameters three or four key parameters were sufficient to make an accurate prognosis. Adding additional parameters to these key parameters did not significantly improve the prognostic accuracy of the statistical model (Wolfensberger 1992).

6

Differentiating Trust from Related Concepts

If trust in medicine has declined, this raises the question whether trust has simply disappeared or whether it has been replaced by a rise in something else, most notably by its opposite. And furthermore, if it has been replaced by its opposite, what do we call this opposite? In the first section of this chapter, we will defend the position that trust has not one opposite but two: *m*istrust and *d*istrust. Further, we claim that these two concepts can, and should, be clearly differentiated in order to avoid additional misunderstandings as to the nature of trust. In our Introduction, as the reader may recall, we claimed that many people use 'trust' in situations in which it would be more appropriate to use 'confidence', 'reliance', 'hope', and 'belief-in'. However, this presupposes that we can differentiate trust from 'confidence' and other such similar concepts. Therefore, in the second section of this chapter, we will explain how we can do this by applying the concept of pattern-based defining to these five terms and comparing the various patterns. With this we will have completed the initial stages of offering an account of trust by distinguishing it from these various and often conflated concepts in a way that other accounts of trust have not overtly or systematically achieved. This will allow us the opportunity in subsequent chapters to expand on some of the advantages of our pattern-based account of trust.

6.1 Mistrust and Distrust

Most terms have one opposite. This opposite may express either a meaning contrary to that of the term (such as love versus hate or hot versus cold) or simply the absence of the meaning of the term (such as knowledge versus ignorance, where ignorance is simply the absence of knowledge). Trust has both types of opposites: 'mistrust' and 'distrust'. In this short section, we will show that the two terms (although they are often used interchangeably) can (and should) be clearly distinguished. To introduce the subject, here is a short example: if you answer 'no' to an opinion pollster's question as to whether you are familiar with a certain brand X, he knows what he wants to know from your response, namely that you have not heard of brand X. However, if you answer 'no' to a standard poll question such as "would you tell me whether you trust doctors to tell the truth?",[1] the interviewer may think that he knows what he wanted to find out. Yet, the fact is that he does not yet know. Here is why: if you say that you are not familiar with brand X, there remains no ambiguity. Either you know it or you do not know it. If, however, you say that you do not trust (i.e. expect) doctors to tell the truth, this still leaves room for two different interpretations:

(a) You may generally expect doctors not to tell the truth.

This may mean either that you expect them to tell outright lies or that you expect them to withhold the (whole) truth.

(b) You do not generally expect them not to tell the truth, but neither do you expect them to tell the truth.

We call this second interpretation the suspension of trust.[2]

Trust, mistrust, and distrust differ with regard to the truster's expectations. Trust is about positive expectations. Of the two other terms ('distrust' and 'mistrust'), one expresses a negative expectation (as we saw in the example as to whether you expect doctors not to tell the truth), whereas the other simply refers to the suspension of trust.[3] Consequently, 'I don't trust you' may either mean 'I believe that you are not trustworthy' or 'I do not know whether you are trustworthy'. In the vernacular, the two meanings are often not differentiated. Also, semantically, the two prefixes 'dis' and 'mis' are very similar, although we think that overall 'dis' has a more negative connotation than 'mis'. However, because of the commonplace conflation of meanings in the vernacular, both are often given negative connotations. In our more precise usage of the two prefixes, 'mis' should not be read as having such negative connotations. There is clear precedence for such a technical

---

[1] Ipsos MORI 2007, p. 7.

[2] There is yet a third potential option, namely to withhold trust even though one believes that the other is trustworthy. Since, in our definition of trust, trust is a choice, this is of course true. Yet, we do not believe that this type of 'not-trust' plays an important role in the patient–physician relationship.

[3] Hall et al. call this "a sense of agnosticism but not active distrust" (Hall et al. 2001, p. 618).

use. With few exceptions,[4] 'distrust' is used to refer to the negative expectation, 'mistrust' to the suspension of trust.[5] We will follow these examples by using the following definitions. *'Trust'* refers to a positive expectation (as it typically does). *'Distrust'* refers to a negative expectation (you believe that the trustee[6] is not trustworthy). Finally, *'mistrust'* refers to the suspension of both trust and distrust; i.e. you do not expect the trustee to be untrustworthy, but neither do you expect him to be trustworthy.[7] In a way, mistrust is a negation of both trust and distrust.

In practice, there is often a certain overlap of the two terms. The statement 'I don't know whether I can trust him' (indicating a suspension of trust) also implies the likelihood of at least a grain of the 'expectation that he will not be quite trustworthy'. Nevertheless, we believe that we should make a clear distinction between the two terms. One significant reason for maintaining such a distinction is that, overall, to distrust someone is a far more severe moral criticism than to mistrust someone.[8] Here is why: if someone tells you that he *dis*trusts you, this implies that he believes you to be dishonest, unreliable, etc. All these terms are far from complementary, suggesting numerous failings of one's moral character. If, on the other hand, someone tells you that he *mis*trusts you, this (on our definition) simply implies that he does not know you well enough or that he is not yet sure whether you are trustworthy. The moral distinction is not the only one, however. Distrust also has far more negative consequences than mistrust. Outright distrust is detrimental to social interactions, whereas a certain amount of mistrust may at times be indicated and even prudent. We can see it as a "form of wariness that generates caution and verification ('trust but verify')".[9]

This view is probably correct as long as mistrust does not become habitual, because every time we mistrust we miss an opportunity to trust and, hence, to benefit from the advantages that trust offers.[10] Take, for example, the increasing number of parents who forego the protection that vaccination would offer to their children because they mistrust their GP's (or, depending on the healthcare system prevalent in the country,

---

[4] For example, Omodei 2000, p. 279.
[5] See also Rose et al. 2004; Shea et al. 2008; Sztompka 1999.
[6] Strictly speaking, he will not be a 'trustee'. We still use the term for convenience sake.
[7] One might argue that 'mistrust', meaning the suspension of trust, is not truly an opposite of trust. Yet, even if one agrees with this, mistrust is perceived as negative, and in this sense it is the contrary of trust, which is a positive expectation.
[8] Hawley 2012, p. 9.
[9] Hall et al. 2001, pp. 618–19.
[10] See Section 10.1.

the paediatrician's) recommendation. Moreover, wholesale distrust is pragmatically incoherent.[11] In the end, you will always have to trust someone. Paradoxically, or perhaps ironically, people who say that they no longer trust doctors often do so because of what they have learned from the media, as was seen in the case of various vaccination 'scares', yet this information comes from journalists – exactly the profession whom many of the same people claim to trust even less than doctors.

It is worth noting some other key distinctions between trust and distrust. Whereas trust is a way to handle uncertainty and risk,[12] distrust is not. It simply avoids the issue. If you distrust someone, you will have to use other means to cope with uncertainty. If you trust someone, you are willing to render yourself vulnerable,[13] to transfer power to the trustee. If you distrust, you will not do either. Finally, just as there is only conditional trust, there is only conditional distrust. Like trust, distrust must always be specified. This is best exemplified by the fact that you can trust and distrust the same person at the same time,[14] but with regard to different issues.[15]

There is yet another important point about this distinction: whereas it is often rather difficult to build trust, mistrust and distrust come easily. This is not surprising, because to trust (contrary to mistrust and distrust) needs courage (to run the risk of trusting). Also, the transition from trust to distrust is much easier and happens much faster than the opposite. Moreover, it is probably easier to pass from mistrust to distrust than from mistrust to trust.[16] If we remember that "the surest way to make someone untrustworthy is to distrust him and show your distrust",[17] it quickly becomes obvious that distrust is self-reinforcing.[18] With this in mind, and to sum up briefly, we have a view of trust as a positive expectation on one side, distrust as a negative expectation on the other side, and mistrust as the suspension of both somewhere in between.

---

[11] O'Neill 2002a, p. 121.

[12] See page 148.

[13] We are aware that this term is poorly defined (Wrigley 2014), but here we are simply using it in its vernacular sense.

[14] See, e.g. McKnight and Chervany 2001, p. 42, or Hawley 2015, p. 799.

[15] If you know that your doctor is a good surgeon but an inveterate womaniser, you may trust his medical judgement but would never trust him to take your daughter camping.

[16] Sztompka 1999, p. 27.

[17] Henry L. Stimson, United States Secretary of War from 1911 to 1913 and again from 1940 to 1945.

[18] Miller 2007, p. 59.

6.2   Confidence, Reliance, Hope, and Belief-In

Of course, one may ask why we want to differentiate as precisely as we do between trust and some other terms that are so clearly used interchangeably by many people. Previously, we argued that 'not everything that has trust on the label has trust inside', i.e. that not all uses of the term 'trust' are permissible, and that in many situations the use of 'confidence', 'hope', 'reliance', or 'belief-in' would be more appropriate than the use of 'trust'. Here, we will expand on this argument and defend the position that a differentiation between 'trust' and 'confidence', 'reliability', 'hope', and 'belief-in' is not only possible but also advisable, both from a conceptual standpoint and for practical reasons, because the indiscriminate intermingling of these terms leads to confusion and misunderstanding, particularly when applied to the focus of trust in medicine. We can illustrate what we mean by this through a simple example which shows that the equation of 'trust' with 'belief-in' leads to false conclusions being drawn from the use of trust discourse. Take the often-heard statement 'I don't trust in medicine any more'. This is usually interpreted to mean that patients have lost trust in physicians when, in fact, it only means that patients no longer *believe in* the paradigms of modern medicine.[19] It is confusions like this that we will seek to elucidate and remedy through our account of trust. We will start by outlining why these concepts are neither synonymous with trust nor with each other and then take a closer look at the role that these four often-conflated concepts play in the patient–physician relationship, focusing on each one separately in turn.

As we have seen, within our everyday discourse we say that we trust (among other things) 'that the weather will be good tomorrow' and 'that our car will keep running another year'; we trust 'the brakes of our bike', we trust 'in the faithfulness of our partners'; and we may even 'trust in homeopathy'. In our account of trust, most of these everyday uses of 'trust' are misapplications of the concept. We *may say that we trust* but we *cannot effectively trust* the weather, our car, and the brakes of our bike, because trust is always about a personal relationship and these are attitudes towards objects or natural events, not persons.[20] Furthermore, just as we cannot trust in medicine per se, we cannot trust in homeopathy, as trust would only make sense with regard to relationships to the *practitioners* of medicine or homeopathy. Only in the case of our

---

[19]   We will come back to this example in Section 12.3.
[20]   See Section 5.6.

partner's faithfulness can we talk of trust in the strict sense. In the other cases it would, instead, be correct to express our beliefs by saying that we *hope* (or, depending on the situation that we *are confident*) that the weather will be good or that our car will keep running another year; that we *rely* on the brakes of our bike; and that we *believe* in homeopathy.[21]

Trust, according to our pattern-based account, is an expectation of the truster regarding the trustee's behaviour under conditions of uncertainty and risk. Of the four concepts, only 'confidence', 'reliance', and 'hope' refer to an expectation of the speaker and, so far, fit the pattern of trust, whereas a 'belief-in' is not an expectation but simply an affirmation of the speaker's belief.[22] Clearly then, 'belief-in' does not fit the pattern and, therefore, it can be differentiated from 'trust' relatively easily on these grounds.

To differentiate 'trust' from the remaining concepts of 'confidence', 'reliance', and 'hope', we need to take our analysis further. To do this, let us look at the level at which the expectation is situated. To explain what we mean by this, we can compare 'expectation' with 'belief'. Beliefs can be irrational, rational, or justified.[23] Similarly, expectations can be irrational, rational, or justified.[24] Let us start from the bottom of this

---

[21] In fact, trust is used in lieu of even more terms. Faith is one of them. Since faith belongs almost exclusively to the discourse of religion, we will not include it in the discussion. Another use of trust is illustrated by the sentence 'I trust you will come to the party tonight'. Of course, this may mean that the speaker trusts you to come. Yet, more likely, it simply means that the speaker 'assumes you will come'.

[22] That is, the cognitive attitude of belief that the speaker has. See Section 5.4 (in particular page 58).

[23] Of course, these are not the only possibilities, but they are the only ones in which we are interested in the present context. The analysis of belief has, unlike trust, been subject to considerable discussion, particularly concerning its characterisation as a propositional attitude, by some of the world's leading philosophers. While this makes the literature too extensive to even begin to enumerate here, it is worth noting (and to some extent in support of our selecting these three key aspects of belief relevant to our comparative analysis here) a recent interest in irrational beliefs. See, for example, Borlotti 2010.

[24] We have not given a detailed account as to exactly what we mean by the terms 'rational', 'irrational', and 'justified', although we have alluded to their interpretation in various places. These are all meant to be understood as epistemological terms, although we recognise that they are still all terms used in multiple different ways, and open to very different interpretations.

We take '*rational*' as a model of human thought based on certain types of reasoning – logical inference, analysis, and probability. 'Irrational' means to think in other ways, such as guessing, or rejecting logical inference, or based on very low-to-zero probabilities. For some attempts at providing a detailed account of rationality, see: Audi 2001, or Nozick 1993.

We take '*justified*' to mean something akin to 'having good reason to believe true (or at least probable)' or 'having good reason to hold that belief'. Of course, this begs the

hierarchy. Take the belief that the moon is inhabited and populated by pink piglets. Given everything we know and all the evidence we have about the moon and about piglets, this belief is irrational because the probability of piglets on the moon is fractionally small to zero. Moreover, by the same set of standards, so is the expectation that one day we will find piglets on the moon.[25] The important point here is that irrational expectations have nothing to do with trust and yet they are often confused with trust.

Contrary to the belief that there are pink piglets on the moon, the belief that somewhere in the wide universe there is another form of life is perfectly rational given that there is a possibility that this will turn out to be true,[26] and, likewise, so is the expectation of scientists that, given enough time and resources, they will eventually find signs of life elsewhere in the universe. Contrary to irrational expectations, *rational expectations* can manifest themselves as holding true in the world. Indeed, if they refer to something positive, they are often called 'hope'.[27] This is why it can be said that many scientists hope to find signs of life in the universe – they have a rational expectation of doing so and see this as a positive outcome. It is worth noting, as we will discuss in the section on 'hope' below, that it is important not to confuse irrational wishes (which often take the form of 'false hope') with hope.

Let us move one more step up the hierarchy of beliefs and consider a different example. Most kids love dolphins and (like many kids) they initially believe that dolphins are fish. Even if they eventually learn that dolphins are mammals, we think that their belief is perfectly justified

question as to what a 'good' reason is in this context. This is one of the major questions in epistemology and we do not intend to address it here. Instead, we think it sufficient to characterise it as taking a stance as to what conditions we want for our knowledge base through evidence derived from such things as empirical observation/perception, memory, testimony, or rational inference. Of course, this still allows scope for a belief to be justified but turn out to be false. See Audi 1993.

[25] At least as long as 'pink piglets' refers to what we call pink piglets in the vernacular, the chances (or the probability) that we will ever find pink piglets on the moon are exceedingly small (or even zero).

[26] We are of the view that, given the immense size of the universe, it is (for purely statistical reasons) probable that life has evolved more than once. We recognise that there exist sceptics as to the possibility of this, although many of these are based on non-rational (e.g. faith-based) reasons. There may also be some disagreement as to the statistical probabilities associated with this. However, we should distinguish between the possibility that we will ever encounter other life and the possibility that other life exists – both reasonable positions to hold given the immense size of the Universe.

[27] We can rationally wish for something negative. But this would not be 'hope' because of the innate positive future-orientation of hope. See Garrard and Wrigley 2009.

because it is based on a reasonable inference from the knowledge and evidence available to children; after all, dolphins look and behave like fish in many ways (although, admittedly, not in all ways). This means that children's belief that dolphin are fish is justified because they have reason to believe it is true. Following this, just inasmuch as there are beliefs that are both rational and justified (even though they may not be true), there are also expectations that are both rational and justified (even though they do not necessarily have to become fulfilled). As we have argued in the preceding paragraph, hope is a rational expectation when it is possible (at least to some degree) that it may become true.[28] Yet, hope is not a justified expectation because we have no reason to believe that our hope will become true, other than the tiny possibility that buying the lottery ticket brings with it. Justification requires some stronger basis than simply relying on luck to manifest a fractionally small possibility – we require some reason to believe it is true.[29] So, 'hope' does not belong to the category of rational *and justified* expectations, and hence is different from 'trust'.[30]

Contrary to 'hope', both 'confidence' and 'reliance' do belong to the category of justified expectations because (as they are based on past performance) we have reason to believe that they are true. Yet, even though confidence and reliance, like trust, are justified expectations, this does not mean that they are synonymous with trust. Another essential feature of trust is uncertainty and risk. Of course, this is also true of confidence and reliance. However, there is a major difference between how trust, on the one hand, and confidence and reliance, on the other hand, handle uncertainty and, above all, risk. The difference is this: if we trust, we always know (at least 'subconsciously') that we are running

---

[28] This may apply even to the rather unrealistic hope of winning the jackpot in a lottery, although some prefer to view rational hope as also being probable, rather than simply to some degree likely, and defer unlikely hopes to the category of wishes. See Meirav 2009.

[29] See footnote 24 on page 77 concerning what we take justification to be.

[30] Following on from our previous note defining the terms 'rational', 'irrational', and 'justified', it is worth noting that the rational component in discussions concerning hope has often taken the form of the belief being based on an assessment of the probability that the desired outcome will turn out to be true. What is crucial is that the belief component of hope (if taken as a belief-desire pairing) excludes certainty as much as it excludes impossibility. Although this goes some way to restricting the sorts of thing one can legitimately hope for, further distinctions on this front have also been added by some authors to distinguish 'substantial' from 'superficial' hopes based on the probability of the desired outcome obtaining. Hence, superficial hopes simply involve some non-zero level of probability, whereas substantial hopes require a good chance of obtaining. See Day 1969; Kadlac 2015; Meirav 2009; Pettit 2004.

a risk. The same is not true for reliance and confidence. Reliance refers to a (perceived) certainty based on past performance.[31] In fact, reliability means something close to a 'faultless track record'. Once a machine fails, for example, it is no longer considered reliable. Of course, we know that boarding an airplane implies a risk, but we do not consciously consider it a real danger. Similarly, confidence implies stability. In the case of confidence and reliance, risk (although inherent) is not perceived as such.[32] So, confidence and reliance can be differentiated from trust by the way they perceive uncertainty and handle risk.

Alongside this way of perceiving uncertainty and handling risk there is yet another important difference between trust and confidence: trust is always agent-related. You can only trust your doctor to act in a certain way but not to achieve a specific result.[33] On the other hand, you may well be confident that he will act in a certain way *or* that he will achieve a specific result (e.g. because he has repeatedly done so in the past). So, confidence may be agent- and outcome-related. Finally, it is worth noting that a person or a technology may be reliable. Yet, there is no such thing, however, as a 'reliable outcome'. Therefore, reliability cannot be outcome-related.

Now that we have outlined how (and why) the four trust-related concepts differ from trust as well as from each other, we want to briefly look further at each of the four concepts and of the role that they play in the patient–physician relationship to help contextualise their links with trust.

6.2.1   Hope

To begin with, it is worth outlining some of the key distinctions between trust and hope. Firstly, whereas trust is active, hope is passive – once you have formed your hope you are just in a position of 'wait and see'.[34] Furthermore, whereas you commit yourself if you trust, hope is non-committal, in that it does not require you to do anything further for or with anyone. In other words, trust belongs to the discourse of agency; hope belongs to the discourse of fate. It is also important not to confuse (true/genuine) hope with false hope because false hope belongs to the category of irrational expectations. To have a false hope means hoping for

[31]   O'Neill 2002b, p. 15.
[32]   Brown 2008, p. 351.
[33]   See page 44.
[34]   Sztompka 1999, p. 24.

something that 'in the real world' will not come true, or at least is extremely unlikely to become true. It is, instead, better characterised as 'wishful thinking', where wishing allows one to engage with impossible outcomes. Contrary to this, (true/genuine) hope is rational. It is standardly considered a combination of a belief and a desire, which we can rationally expect to be fulfilled. This distinction between false hope and true hope touches upon an ethically important issue in medicine. Patients with incurable cancers (or other terminal diseases) often say that they do not (or refuse to) give up hope, and their relatives often ask the doctor 'not to destroy this hope', that is, not to plunge the patient into despair (which in fact is the opposite of hope, but which is also often considered to be the absence of hope) by revealing the full extent of their diagnosis and poor prognosis. This places doctors and other healthcare professionals involved in the care of such patients in a position often referred to as "the paradox of hope".[35] Although not a genuine paradox, it arises from a seeming conflict between truth-telling and beneficence. We do not agree that there genuinely is such a tension in such cases if by 'hope' they mean 'hope for a cure', because this hope (at least in this situation) is irrational. Contrary to what people believe, supporting false hopes should not be treated as a benevolent act but rather one that is deceitful.[36] It does not respect the patient's autonomy. And besides, it violates the doctor's integrity. Of course, there are occasionally patients who can keep up this (false) hope to the very end.[37] Whether this is positive, we do not want to discuss here. In most cases, however, the patient will eventually come to realise that there is no cure, and that his hope was false. He will then potentially resent that his doctor, in collusion with his family, has not been honest. We subscribe to the theory that in these situations the physician's task is to help the patient not to fix all his thoughts on the inevitable (death), not to hope for the unachievable, but instead to locate hope in other areas with a genuine possibility of being fulfilled, so that they may hope that the remaining time is meaningful, that it is still "containing the possibility of new experience, rather than the closed experience of life as having nothing more to offer".[38] This approach is summed up by the following: "Fostering ... hope provides the welfare benefits of helping patients to cope with a terminal

---

[35] See Cohen 2013; Garrard and Wrigley 2009; Merrick 2016; Tanis and DiNapoli 2008.
[36] Some might argue that it may be benevolent despite being deceitful. We agree. But then we are back to good old 'benevolent paternalism', an attitude that we do not endorse.
[37] In the experience of M.W., they are the rare exception and not the rule.
[38] Garrard and Wrigley 2009, p. 41.

condition, while also respecting their autonomy by providing a full and accurate explanation of the prognosis."[39]

In linking hope back to its association with trust, hope often stands at the beginning of a trust relationship. On the way to your first appointment with a physician, you can hope that he is competent and emphatic, in which case your hope is agent-related. Or you may even hope that he will be able to cure you, in which case your hope is outcome-related. Goold refers to this situation as 'presumptive trust'.[40] We can understand what he means by this by a small reflection upon our commonly held experiences: because we usually trust doctors, we presume that we can (or will) trust this doctor as well, although we have not yet met him and, therefore, are not yet in a position to trust him. Nevertheless, we think that it would be better not to talk of 'trust' in this situation in order not to confuse the issue and instead prefer to consider Goold's 'presumptive trust' as a form of hope that stands at the beginning of a trust relationship.

6.2.2   To Believe in Someone or Something

It is often easy to confuse 'trust' with 'believe in', but to conflate the two would be to miss something quite substantial about what 'believing in' requires. To 'believe in' someone or something (as opposed to 'believe that', which concerns an attitude towards propositions rather than persons) may have two different meanings, only one of which is relevant to our discussion of trust.[41] (a) It may simultaneously note and reject a claim to existence of something or someone. A statement like 'John believes in Santa Claus', implying 'he is very naive', exemplifies this meaning. This is more of a speech-act than a genuine cognitive attitude, and, for obvious reasons associated with such speech-acts, first-person statements rarely refer to this meaning. (b) More commonly, 'believe in' has an acknowledging meaning. Contrary to the first meaning, this meaning affirms or even requires the existence and functioning of the entity one believes in. 'I believe in God' acknowledges His existence. Yet, in addition to simply meaning 'I believe that God exists' it also adds a statement about my belief in His 'power' or 'work', etc. On a more down-to-earth example, 'I believe in homeopathy' means that I approve of homeopathy, that I believe it works, etc. We will come back to

[39] Garrard and Wrigley 2009, p. 42.
[40] Goold 2002, p. 79.
[41] Honderich 2005, p. 86.

interesting examples such as this in Section 12.3, as part of our discussion as to how physicians are losing the authority they used to have when people's belief in scientific medicine was much more widespread, on the grounds that, now, ever-more people have become disenchanted with (i.e. no longer believe in) science and scientific medicine. For now, it is worth simply noting that when people say that they no longer *trust* in medicine they actually mean that they no longer *believe in* medicine, that they no longer believe it works, or that they no longer approve of its paradigms.

6.2.3   Reliance and Reliability

Like 'trust' and 'trustworthiness', 'reliance' and 'reliability' are twins. You (usually, but not always) trust only people whom you believe to be trustworthy and you (usually, but not necessarily) rely only on someone you believe to be reliable. Yet, here the relationship ends. Even if reliability leads to confidence, and confidence is a basis for trust, trust and trustworthiness cannot simply be reduced to reliance and reliability.[42] There are good reasons for this. Trust presupposes uncertainty and risk whereas reliance refers to certainty based on past performance; risk, although it may be inherent, is future-orientated in a way that is not conceived as part of the reliability judgement. For example, one relies on the brakes of one's bike if (and because) they have never failed in the past. One does not conceive of their failure in the future. Of course, one might object at this point and say that past reliability combined with an awareness that brakes wear over time might mean a good reliability judgement would involve an assessment of the likelihood of future risk. This would be to miss the point about reliability judgements, however. There is nothing to stop people thinking through future risks, but this is not a reliability judgement but rather a different form of judgement that is being shaped – reliability is, by definition, orientated towards the past.

As we have seen, a breach of trust generally produces a feeling of betrayal, while misplaced reliance merely produces a feeling of disappointment.[43] But, and this is important, trust often survives

---

[42] Jones 2012, p. 62.

[43] Hieronymi 2008, p. 215. This need not always be true, because occasionally there may be a certain overlap in ordinary usage of the terms. For a detailed discussion of the role that the feeling of betrayal plays in conceiving 'trust' as a moral notion, see Section 11.1. Moreover, the reader is referred to Section 11.2, in which we defend the position that we have a moral obligation to honour trust with the help of the obligation-ascription thesis.

a breach, reliance usually does not: you may still trust someone who has breached your trust, but if a system fails, you will no longer rely on it (at least not until you have sufficient evidence that the fault has been fixed).

Whereas (according to our account) we can only trust in agents, we can rely on a variety of different things: on agents, on technology, and on things happening. With regard to agents and technology, reliance has something of a double meaning in that it may implicate that we believe the person or technology to be reliable or it may signal that we are dependent on that person or technology. Let us consider this from the perspective of a small story based on one of the author's (M.W.'s) experience in medical practice. The day before carrying out surgery, he usually had a long talk with the patient (explaining the goal of the procedure, the procedure itself, and the risks involved). From his perspective, the purpose of these discussions was to build up trust. At the end of this talk, many patients said to him that 'they put themselves into his hands'. In some cases, this may have meant that they trusted him, whereas in other cases it merely implied that they relied upon him. Since most patients have had no prior experience with him, this could only mean that they felt they had to depend on him because there was no past basis upon which they could properly make a reliability judgement.

This still leaves the third possible area of reliance where we rely on something to happen. In this context, reliance may have yet another meaning, neatly described by Holton: "I need not believe that it will happen. But I do need to plan on it happening: I need to work around the supposition that it will."[44] Take the following scenario: "relying on her cough to clear up by the weekend, she plans to go skiing". This has a very different meaning to how reliance was used in the case of people or technology: of course, she does not consider her cough reliable in that sense; nor can she be said to depend on the cough. What she does is that she plans to go skiing in Holton's sense of reliance, that is, 'under the condition' that her cough clears by then.

'Reliance' is an important concept in medicine. Not only because we (may have to) rely on persons, but because we rely on technology and on tests or exams, and so forth. At first glance, this may be surprising, because hardly anything in medical practice ever reaches the level of certainty.[45] Yet the requirement for certainty as a feature of reliance and

[44] Holton 1994, p. 65.
[45] Schwab 2008, p. 308.

reliability is less puzzling if we remember that we are talking of *perceived* certainty, where risk is simply not conceived. This illusion of certainty and the denial of risk can help explain the massive frustration of patients if an allegedly reliable procedure fails or a risk materialises.

6.2.4 Confidence (versus Trust and Reliance)

If we keep the etymology of the two words 'trust' and 'confidence' in mind, it may not be so surprising that they are very often used inter-changeably. 'Trust' comes from the Old Norse *traust*, whereas 'confi-dence' comes from the Latin *confidentia*. Interestingly, both roots have survived in English, whereas only *traust* has found its way into the Germanic languages and only *confidentia* survives in the Romance lan-guages. Nevertheless, we think that the fact that some languages only have one term is no argument to use the two terms synonymously, as, for example, Calnan and Sanford do.[46] The Inuit (allegedly) have approxi-mately one hundred words for (different types of) snow,[47] yet the fact that we have only one word certainly does not signify that the one hundred Inuit words are all synonyms.

Here, we wish to make it quite clear that the two terms 'trust' and 'confidence' are not synonyms and their use in everyday sentences, such as 'I trust you to help me' and 'I am confident that you will help me', are not equivalent.[48] In Section 5.4.1, we argued that trust is a cognitive mental state insofar as it refers to our beliefs (regarding the trustee's trustworthiness), and it is an act in as much as it refers to how we interact with someone. Contrary to this, confidence is purely cognitive. To trust, as we have already established, implies a commitment; it belongs to the discourse of agency. Confidence, on the other hand, is passive and non-committal; it belongs to the discourse of fate.[49] So far, this distinction is similar to that between trust and hope. However, we can go further in distinguishing trust and confidence. Trust implies choice; confidence is more like a "habitual expectation".[50] This is because trust judgements are made in the face of uncertainty about the motivations of others, whereas

---

[46] Calnan and Sanford 2004, p. 94.
[47] See: http://ontology.buffalo.edu/smith/varia/snow.html.
[48] Even in German (in which *Vertrauen* indeed means both trust and confidence), one can make the difference by using *Zuversicht* for 'confidence', if one really wants to differ-entiate between trust and confidence.
[49] Sztompka 1999, p. 25.
[50] Misztal 1996, p. 16.

confidence in others, by contrast, "implies a situation of relative stability and security where judgements about others are based on what is predictable, involving little risk for the person making the judgement".[51]

To make this point even clearer, in Misztal's words, "the main difference between trust and confidence is connected with the degree of certainty that we attach to our expectations".[52]

Trust implies *consciously* taking a risk. Confidence, however, implies that negative consequences (risks) are not conceived,[53] either because there are no risks (certainty of outcome[54]), because a person (or a system) has proved to be reliable, or because we are not aware of risks. Moreover, a breach of trust leaves a feeling of betrayal. Not so confidence: if you find that your confidence was not justified you only feel disappointed.[55] Yet, like reliability (but contrary to trust), confidence is usually lost with failure.[56]

Of the two (trust and confidence), confidence comes easier; it is "the normal case".[57] Yet confidence 'carries less weight' in that, whereas lack of confidence only leads to alienation, lack of trust leads to withdrawal from society.[58] Familiarity typically leads to confidence rather than trust.[59] Like trust, confidence always refers to something specific. You are never confident 'tout court'. Yet, importantly, whereas trust is always and only agent-related (so, for example, you cannot trust that your team will win the tournament),[60] confidence may be agent-related or outcome-related (so that you may be *confident* that your team will win the tournament).

Although confidence plays a key role in the patient–physician relationship, it does not of itself lead to (or increase) trust. This is perhaps the key motivational reason for making sure we distinguish 'trust' from 'confidence', even though there is a strong connection and association between the two concepts. You may be quite confident that someone is reliable and yet decide not to trust them. Consequently, to believe that

---

[51] Gilson 2006, p. 36.

[52] Misztal 1996, p. 16.

[53] Brown 2008, p. 351.

[54] "When expectations are strongly positive, we may begin to speak of confidence" (Hardin 2006, p. 29).

[55] See Section 5.5.

[56] Pieters 2006, p. 290.

[57] Luhmann 2000, p. 97.

[58] Luhmann 2000, pp. 103–4.

[59] For a further discussion of this, see page 185.

[60] See page 44.

measures which aim at improving confidence will *automatically* encourage trust is wrong.[61] On the other hand, it is rather unlikely that we would trust someone if we were not confident that they would meet our expectations. Consequently, a decline of confidence will almost certainly lead to some decline of trust. As we will argue in Section 11.3, patients' loss of confidence (as well as belief) in scientific medicine is one of the reasons why trust has declined.

6.3 Summary and Conclusions

In most of the literature, 'trust' is treated as a binary concept: either you trust or you do not trust. Here, we hope to have established both that this is wrong and the reasons for this. Whereas many familiar concepts can be treated as binary, for example, the opposite of knowledge is ignorance, which is simply the absence of knowledge; this does not hold true of trust. The opposite of trust (which is a positive expectation) is not simply the absence of this positive expectation; rather, it is also the presence of a negative expectation. We have, accordingly, defined the absence of trust (i.e. the absence of a positive expectation) as 'mistrust' and the presence of a negative expectation as 'distrust'. Although this adds a certain complexity to the account of trust, to disregard this distinction has serious consequences that can be seen even in some of the most basic applications of the concept: opinion polls traditionally ask people whether they trust doctors or not. This is fine as long as people answer 'yes'; but if people answer 'no', it remains unclear whether they have simply suspended their trust (i.e. that they mistrust) or whether they actually harbour negative expectations vis-à-vis their physicians (i.e. that they distrust).

'Belief-in', 'hope', 'reliance', and 'confidence' are (not only in the vernacular) often used interchangeably with 'trust'. Contrary to this, we have argued that all four concepts are distinguishable from each other as well as from trust. We have attempted to systematically account for these distinctions. 'Belief-in' is an affirmation of one's belief, but without expectation, while 'trust', 'hope', 'reliance', and 'confidence' are all expectations. More than that they are rational expectations. However, of these, only 'trust', 'confidence', and 'reliance' are also justified expectations. (True/genuine) 'hope' (i.e. contrary to false hope) is a rational expectation because it may in principle become true. However, 'hope' is not

---

[61] Smith 2005, p. 312.

a justified expectation, because we have no reason to believe that what is hoped for will effectively become true. 'Confidence' and 'reliance', on the other hand, differ from 'trust' with regard to how they handle uncertainty and risk. Moreover, they can refer to technology, whereas 'trust' can only refer to people. Finally, contrary to 'trust' and 'reliance', 'confidence' may also be outcome-related.

With this, we have made the case that our definition of 'trust' has the discriminatory power to differentiate trust from trust-related concepts and thus fulfils the fourth condition of a satisfactory definition of trust that we have outlined.[62]

To conclude our definition of 'trust', we will, in the next chapter, explain and illustrate how our pattern-based definition can be adapted to different needs and situations.

---

[62] See page 21.

Adapting the Definition of Trust to Different Situations

In the preceding two chapters, we presented the full patterns of the characteristic features, which we take to define the concepts of 'trust', 'confidence', 'reliance', 'belief-in', and 'hope'. Moreover, we have shown that by comparing the full patterns of each, it is possible to differentiate how 'confidence', 'reliance', 'hope', and 'belief-in' differ from 'trust', as well as from each other – something no other definition of 'trust' we know has provided. Admittedly, a definition of 'trust' based on the full set of characteristic features is very narrow, whereby 'trust' refers to a justified expectation regarding the behaviour of the trustee (and hence is agent-related) under conditions of uncertainty and risk, that it implies the conscious choice of accepting the trust-inherent risk, that a breach of trust engenders a feeling of betrayal (rather than just a disappointment), and that it refers to a relationship between competent autonomous agents.[1]

Such a narrow definition may be interesting to a philosopher who is analysing the concept of trust or who is interested in a 'thick'[2] definition of 'trust' with the associated detail its use and attribution may have. To others, we recognise it may be far less useful. In this chapter, we attempt to demonstrate how our definition can be adapted to different (or very specific) situations.

7.1 Maximally Comprehensive versus Lowest Common Denominator

What we have described so far represents the maximally comprehensive definition of 'trust'. However, and as we have said

---

[1] See Section 5.7.
[2] 'Thick' evaluative concepts are those which are typically richer in detail and content than general or 'thin' evaluative terms, such as 'good/bad' or 'right/wrong'. Such thick concepts offer a greater sense of detail, description, character, etc. when they are attributed. See Kirchin 2013 for an excellent contemporary overview.

earlier,[3] a pattern-based definition does not have to be based on the full pattern. By reducing the number of features we use to define 'trust', we can adapt the definition to different situations or needs. This may sound arbitrary, but it is not. To explain why, let us briefly return to Wittgenstein:

> Consider for example the proceedings that we call 'games'. Don't say: "There must be something common, or they would not be called 'games' "– but look and see whether there is anything common to all. – If you look at them you will not see something that is common to all. . . . The result of this examination is 'what [you] see is a complicated network of similarities overlapping and criss-crossing' (i.e. a 'family resemblance') . . . What still counts as a game, and what no longer does? Can you give the boundary? No. [But] you can draw one.[4]

The possibility of 'drawing a line' is what makes the concept of pattern-based definitions so attractive. To illustrate how pattern-based definitions (contrary to necessary conditions-based definitions) can be adapted to different situations and needs, let us use an abstract example (see Table 7.1). Assume that we have four terms, M, N, O, and P, and a set of six defining features, a, b, c, d, e, and f:

If a, b, . . . f each correspond to *necessary* conditions, then M, N, O, and P all differ from each other, because none of them fulfils the same set of conditions. The same is true if a, b, . . . f correspond to features of a pattern, as long as we define the term using its full pattern, i.e. as long as we use a very narrow definition of the term under scrutiny. However, whereas in a necessary conditions-based definition *all* conditions must be

Table 7.1 *Defining features (a . . . f) of the terms (M . . . P)*

M	N	O	P
a	a	a	a
b	b		
c			
d		d	d
	e	e	
			f

---

[3] See page 37.
[4] Wittgenstein 1953, §§66–68, our insertions.

met, the method of pattern-based defining permits us to include only a selection of the features. If, in the above example, we draw the line below b, then M and N can no longer be differentiated. If we draw it below a, then none of the terms can be differentiated. Whereas the narrow definitions based on the full patterns are maximally comprehensive, the definitions based on the first two features could be said to represent the 'lowest common denominator' of M and N and the definitions based on the first feature only could be said to represent the common denominator of all four terms.

Let us see how this works in application by returning now to trust. Table 7.2 compares the patterns of trust with the patterns of the four related concepts.[5]

As we can see, the minimal definition of trust must comprise the first four features because they are essential features. Accordingly, we can say that 'it is *not* trust if it does not refer to a justified expectation, regarding the behaviour of the trustee, under conditions of uncertainty and risk'. We cannot say, however, that 'it *is* trust, if it refers to a justified expectation, regarding the behaviour of the trustee, under conditions of uncertainty and risk', because these four features are not sufficient to differentiate between the concepts of 'trust' and 'confidence'. A definition based on these four features differentiates 'trust' and 'confidence' on the one hand from 'reliance', 'belief-in', and 'hope' on the other. So, drawing the line below these four features would exclude the concepts of 'reliance', 'belief-in', and 'hope'.

It would exclude 'reliance' because it is based on past performance and does not presuppose uncertainty; it would exclude 'belief-in' because it does not refer to an expectation; and it would exclude 'hope' because it is not a justifiable expectation. However, it is evident that this minimal definition does not differentiate 'trust' from 'confidence'. This may be of no concern to the pollster, who wants to measure the 'level of trust' in the population and who does not care whether the interviewees have 'trust' or 'confidence' in mind when he asks them whether they 'trust physicians'. Likewise, it may not overly concern a social scientist, who analyses the influence that different variables (such as socio-economic status, education, age, gender, etc.) have on the level of trust. Many people,

---

[5] Of course, it can be argued that some of the features of the various patterns are (or at least border on the) stipulative. We can understand this concern. We cannot refute it. All we can say is that we derived all features of our definitions from a detailed analysis of the literature rather than simply by stipulation and hope that we have given sufficient grounds for accepting these features in our earlier discussion of the concepts.

Table 7.2 *Features of the patterns of trust, confidence, reliance, belief-in, and hope*

Concept / Feature	Trust	Confidence	Reliance	Belief-in	Hope
1 Refers to expectation	✓!	✓	✓	No	✓
2 Regarding trustee's behaviour (i.e. is agent-related)	✓!	(✓)	(✓)	No	(✓)
3 Presumes conditions of uncertainty and risk	✓!	✓	No	No	✓
4 Must be / is justified	✓!	✓	✓	(✓)	No
5 Expectation must be realistic	✓	✓	✓	No	✓
6 Must be rational	✓	✓	✓	(✓)	✓
7 Free choice	✓	No	✓	✓	✓
8 Risk is consciously accepted	✓	No	No	No	No
9 Breach engenders feeling of betrayal	✓	No	No	No	No
10 Refers to relationship between moral agents	✓	(✓)	(✓)	(✓)	(✓)
11 Can refer to technology	No	✓	✓	✓	✓
12 Can be outcome-related	No	✓	✓	✓	✓

✓ = applies   (✓) = may apply   No = does not apply
✓! = essential (or necessary) features of trust (see page 71)

however, will still want a definition which differentiates 'trust' from 'confidence' for all sorts of reasons. In this case, we must add at least one more feature, such as 'trust as free choice', 'conscious acceptance of risk', or 'feeling of betrayal following a breach of trust'. On the other hand, someone working with small children or mentally handicapped patients may not want a definition which stipulates that 'trust' necessarily refers to a relationship between competent and autonomous agents, and the patient, who is to undergo emergency surgery, will say that he 'trusts the physician', even though he has no choice other than to trust.[6]

Consequently, the difference between the two concepts (in this case, 'trust' and 'confidence') may occasionally be blurred. This is the essence of the 'family resemblance' or 'commonality' approach. We would even go as far as to claim that this is not just the essence; it is the beauty of this

---

[6] For a detailed discussion of the 'no choice' (or 'no alternative') situation, see page 65.

type of approach. Contrary to a definition based on necessary conditions, the pattern-based approach leaves a certain leeway in deciding what still counts as trust and yet remains adequate for everyday purposes or can be honed into a very narrow definition for more technical requirements.

7.2 Summary and Conclusions

A maximally comprehensive definition of 'trust', i.e. one that includes the full pattern, will be very narrow and arguably of limited use in everyday practice. However, through the pattern-based approach we are at liberty to use a less selective definition that covers only a number of the five terms depending on the situation. In fact, we have a spectrum of definitions of 'trust', ranging from the basic definition based on the lowest common denominator of 'trust', 'confidence', and 'reliance' to the maximally comprehensive (i.e. very narrow) definition of 'trust'.

To sum up, pattern-based definitions may not offer unequivocal definitions as necessary conditions-based definitions do. In compensation, they are much more flexible and can be adapted to different situations and different needs.

With this, we conclude the part of this book we have devoted to defining the concept of trust itself. Nevertheless, it does not conclude the broader task of accounting for trust – and its decline – in medicine. Since trust implies risk, it must be justified if it is to be responsible. Although we have identified this need for justification as a characteristic feature of 'trust', we have so far not addressed the question whether trust can indeed be justified at all, and if so under what conditions trust is justified. Nor have we answered the question how patients in reality justify their trust in physicians. We will try to answer these questions in the following two chapters.

PART III

Justification of Trust

8

Justification of Epistemic Trust

Since to trust implies to run a risk, you want to make sure your trust is justified before you decide to trust someone. In other words, for trust to be responsible, it must be justified. In the presentation of our definition of 'trust', we have argued that 'justification' is *not simply a* feature of the pattern of 'trust'; it is an *essential* feature. To see why this is, a brief look back at Table 7.2 shows that, if your expectation regarding the behaviour of the trustee is not justified, 'trust' becomes indistinguishable from mere 'hope'. Yet so far, we have not addressed the issue *whether* trust can be justified,[1] nor, if so, under what conditions. We also have not answered the question of how patients justify their trust in physicians. Of course, it is this last question that interests us most. However, before we try to answer this question (which we do in the next chapter), we want to look at a much more mundane example of trust: trust in what we are told by others. All day long, we are literally bombarded with information. We read the paper, we listen to the radio, and we listen to other people. We may not believe all of what we read or hear, but at least some of it we do believe. In other words, we trust that some of what we are told is true, or (more correctly) we trust other people to tell us the truth. This trust in testimony is commonly referred to as 'epistemic trust'. With two exceptions,[2] trust bears upon the trustee's competence, and, as competence implies knowledge, trust must therefore entail epistemic trust.

We will devote this chapter exclusively to the question of whether and how we can justify epistemic trust for two reasons. First, epistemic trust is an integral, non-eliminable, part of trust in physicians (such that, if you

---

[1] As we will show below, John Locke, e.g. argues that trust is not justified.

[2] As we have shown on page 46 only when we trust someone to have a certain attitude (such as open-mindedness) or to abstain from doing something, competence, and hence epistemic trust, plays no role.

do not trust in what your doctor tells you, you are unlikely to trust him at all). Second, it offers us the opportunity to discuss the question of whether trust is *at all* justifiable (and, if so, under what conditions) in a well-defined context, rather than in the somewhat 'messy' context of the patient–physician relationship.

Let us briefly expand on this to add some context to the motivations for this chapter. Whereas epistemologists[3] debate whether 'knowledge' acquired through testimony qualifies as true knowledge (i.e. whether epistemic trust is justified),[4] to the proverbial 'man of the street' this question may appear almost absurd, since most of what we 'know' is based on testimony from others. In most aspects of life, we depend on the knowledge of others. And yet, "almost all [epistemologists] seem united in the supposition that *knowledge rests on evidence, not trust.* Thus, for most epistemologists, it is not only that trust plays no role in knowing; trusting and knowing are deeply antithetical."[5]

And indeed, since trust implies risk (in this case the risk that the information is false), one would be inclined (on rational reflection) to reject information based on trust and prefer to rely solely on evidence. In other words, epistemic trust would appear irresponsible or hard to justify. We can see two problems with this position. First, there is no way around the fact that our daily life would be impossible without acquiring knowledge through testimony, i.e. without epistemic trust, because our "intellect is too small and life is too short"[6] to get direct evidence of (or on) everything we need to know and to check every bit of information which we receive and process almost continuously. Second, if we reject epistemic trust, the entire construct of trust collapses: how can we trust someone if we do not trust his testimony?[7] This leaves us in the uncomfortable situation that we have to rely on something that we cannot justify.

In this chapter, we defend a position that steers a course between the extremes of complete rejection and an almost unquestioning acceptance of epistemic trust, namely that *it is responsible to grant derivative*

---

[3] See, e.g. Faulkner 2003, p. 36, Fricker 2006, p. 596, and Mcmyler 2007, pp. 517 and 537.

[4] Formally speaking, the question is whether 'we know that p' if we know that 'someone else knows that p'.

[5] Hardwig 1991, p. 693, both emphasis and insertion are ours.

[6] Hardwig 1985, p. 335.

[7] It may be argued that the concept of trust need not collapse because we can base our trust on published data, league tables, etc. rather than on the trustee's testimony. We do not think, however, that this saves the concept of trust, because published data are just another form of testimony.

authority, i.e. to accept testimony, if and only if we have sufficient reason to do so. To determine what counts as 'sufficient reasons', we will propose two strategies: 'epistemic vigilance' and assessing the 'epistemic trust-worthiness' of the trustee.

We will start our arguments by defining what we mean by 'testimony'. Contrary to what we have done so far, this will not be an analytic definition but a 'stipulative definition'. We will then show why epistemic trust is unavoidable (on the grounds that 'most of the time most of us are laypeople on most subjects') and why it is often more prudential (and hence more responsible) to accept testimony than to insist on gaining knowledge from direct evidence. Finally, we will reject both the reductionist position[8] (which holds that epistemic trust is never justified) and the permissive 'acceptance principle'[9] (according to which epistemic trust is justified unless we have stronger reasons not to do so), and argue in favour of the position that it is responsible "to accept testimony to p, if and only one has sufficient reason to believe that p".[10]

8.1 Defining Testimony

From the moment we wake up to the moment we go to bed we are flooded with information. If all this information counts as testimony, the concept of 'epistemic trust' becomes absurd. For our discussion of 'epistemic trust', we need a more specific definition of 'testimony'. Let us start with what is probably the simplest definition:

> Testimony consists in imparting information without supplying evidence or argument to back one's claims.[11]

'Imparting information' means that testimony always needs two people, one who imparts the information and one who receives it.[12] We might also say that testimony refers to what someone asserts that he claims to know vis-à-vis an audience.[13] Given this, we can apply such a definition

---

[8] Exemplified by Locke (Locke 1690, Book I, chapter 3, #24).

[9] ... which would amount to granting 'fundamental authority' and is exemplified by Burge (Burge 1993, p. 469).

[10] ... which amounts to granting 'derivative authority'. Faulkner claims that this is in fact Locke's position. It is beyond the scope of (and irrelevant to) our argument, whether this claim is warranted (Faulkner 2003, p. 37).

[11] Elgin 2002, p. 291.

[12] Fricker 2006, p. 597.

[13] An early articulation of the point that testimony is a form of assertion can be found in Searle J 1969.

to understand that if the physician tells the patient 'what you have is a benign pleomorphic adenoma', he wants her to believe him and to share this knowledge with her. He wants her to go away 'with the knowledge' that she does not have to worry. But what he does not do is supply her with arguments to underpin his information that are comprehensible to her. It is also worth noting that, although most testimonies are verbal communications, they do not necessarily have to be so: "Testimony, that is communication of knowledge, through the hearer's trust in what the speaker presents as being so, can occur also when a shared language is not used literally."[14]

In other words, testimony does not have to be verbal. An assertion may be made with a facial expression or with body language. Again, to place this in context, physicians quite often try to reinforce good news by being particularly voluble. Or, conversely, they may precede the conveyance of bad news with a moment of 'speaking silence'.

Testimonial knowledge is always (at least) second-hand.[15] That is, behind any item of testimonial knowledge must (ultimately) be an equivalent item of first-hand knowledge, i.e. knowledge which is based on some form of direct, non-testimonial evidence.[16] Take the following example: if a physician makes an ultrasound exam of the preauricular tumour and then tells the patient that the tumour is well defined and measures 27 mm in diameter, he is the author (or 'producer') of the information. In this case, the patient's knowledge is truly second-hand (the physician's knowledge being first-hand knowledge, based on direct evidence). If, however, the physician tells the patient that pleomorphic adenomas are benign lesions, he himself is only the 'transferor' of information which was produced by someone else. So, the patient's knowledge might well be described as, literally speaking, third-hand knowledge. In

---

[14] Fricker 2006, p. 593.

[15] Fricker 2006, p. 603.

[16] We recognise that there is an ongoing philosophical debate between anti-reductionists, who argue that testimony can be a basis source of knowledge, and reductionists, who argue that the justifications for accepting testimonial knowledge must ultimately reduce to a justification provided by some other means. By 'direct' knowledge, we are primarily concerned with empirical knowledge derived through forms of perceptual observation (e.g. experiment, trial, and error, etc.), as this is of primary concern for the medical context that we are discussing. However, it is also possible to consider pure reason as a direct source of knowledge (e.g. by making deductive and, perhaps, inductive inferences. Mathematical knowledge may be a good example of this). See Lackey J and Sosa E. (eds.) 2006 for an excellent collection of papers on this issue. In particular on the point of reductionism, see the paper by Goldberg S 2006.

fact, it is not even 'third-hand' but more likely 'umpteenth' hand.[17] The knowledge that pleomorphic adenomas are benign rests on a statistical analysis of the course of the disease of hundreds of patients with pleomorphic adenomas. Moreover, the histological diagnosis 'pleomorphic adenoma' in these patients was made by many different pathologists who all relied upon criteria as to which tumours are pleomorphic adenomas set up by others, etc. In short, there is an almost infinite regression surrounding the foundations and justifications of our knowledge.[18] Sztompka quite aptly speaks of a 'pyramid of trust'.[19] However, irrespective of whether the testimony refers to information that the informant has produced himself or to information that he is only conveying, the question of under what conditions epistemic trust is responsible remains the same.

Although what we have said so far tells us something about the quality of the information, it does not tell us which communicated information counts as testimony. Here we want to argue that only information which (once we have received it) we treat as our own (albeit second-hand) knowledge counts as testimony.[20] To illustrate what we mean by this, here are four examples that are variations on our original example of a patient presenting with a likely pleomorphic adenoma tumour:

(1) Two days after the physician has taken the fine-needle aspiration biopsy the patient calls him to ask whether he already has a result. The doctor tells her that he has not had time to look at his mail because he was away at a conference, but that he will call her as soon as he has had a chance to look at his mail.

(2) After the physician has listened to the patient's history, has asked a few additional questions, and has palpated the tumour, he tells her that on his reckoning this is most likely a pleomorphic adenoma.

(3) At a consultation, a GP tells the patient that he should stop smoking because smoking is unhealthy.

(4) A patient consults his doctor because for two days he has felt an itching, slightly painful nodule on his back. The physician looks at the lesion and tells the patient that, to him, this looks like a tick. The

---

[17] Convention, however, means that we simply treat anything that is not first-hand knowledge as second-hand knowledge to avoid any complications over iterations of transfers of knowledge.

[18] We will come back to this on page 117.

[19] Sztompka 1999, p. 47.

[20] We owe this and the following distinction (at least in part) to Mcmyler 2007, pp. 516–20.

patient finds this hard to believe because, as he says, he has not been 'crawling through bushes' lately. The doctor then proceeds to remove the 'offender', puts it under a microscope, and lets the patient see for himself that it is indeed a tick by comparing it with a picture of a tick.

The four examples illustrate four different types of information. The information in the first example, namely that the physician did not have time to read his mail because he was away at a conference, may be true or not and the patient may believe it or not, but, at any rate, the patient is not actually interested in knowing whether the physician was at a conference. Since it is not relevant to her, it does not matter whether she trusts the physician on this or not. So, this type of information does not count as testimony, albeit that some information has been transferred between two agents.[21] A vast amount of the information that we receive continuously belongs to this type. Similarly, information that only serves the purpose of confirming what we already know does not count as testimony (although in a legal context it is often used for exactly this).

The physician's information in the second example that 'on his reckoning this is most likely a pleomorphic adenoma' (which implies that it is a benign tumour) is different from the information transferred in the first example. In this case, this information is what the patient wants to know. This information is relevant for her. She now knows (and thereby is reassured) that her tumour is most likely a benign pleomorphic adenoma. If someone asks her why she knows this, she will cite the physician's authority. She will say that she trusts her physician. To us, any information that is relevant to us and that we accept because of the authority of the informant is 'testimony'. In this case, the patient bases her knowledge on the authority of a single individual (i.e. her physician). However, this does not always have to be so. I know, for example, that Rome was founded in 753 B.C. This knowledge is not based on just one individual's assertion but is "justified by appeal to authority, but the authority appealed to is communal".[22]

In the third example, the GP does not pass on his *personal* knowledge that smoking is bad for that patient's health. Rather, what is conveyed is *general* knowledge. The GP simply conveys a well-recognised argument, namely that the patient should stop smoking because smoking is unhealthy. There is a major difference between this situation and the

---

[21] We will expand on this in the section on 'street-level' epistemology below.
[22] Mcmyler 2007, p. 519.

situation in the preceding example. In the preceding example, the patient trusts her physician's testimony that her tumour is, in all likelihood, a pleomorphic adenoma. The responsibility for the truth of this information rests with the physician. If his testimony turns out to be false, the patient may rightly feel betrayed, albeit perhaps depending upon the reasons why this testimony turned out to be false. In the third example, however, the physician supplies the patient with an argument that the patient can comprehend himself. Whether the patient heeds this advice is his responsibility and not the physician's. So, conveying an argument transfers the responsibility to the patient,[23] but it does not count as testimony.

Finally, in the fourth example, the physician does not merely claim that the patient has a tick but provides proof of it. In this case, the patient will know by direct evidence that it is a tick. He will not have to base his knowledge on the physician's authority. Hence, this is not testimony but rather a presentation of direct evidence.

So, to sum up, neither information that is irrelevant to the receiver, nor the supply of arguments, nor the provision of direct evidence counts as testimony. Only information that is relevant to the receiver *and* that she trusts (based on the informant's authority) counts as testimony.

Having established what we take testimony to be, we are now in a position to apply this to trust and will argue (a) that epistemic trust is (at least very often) inevitable, (b) that beliefs based on testimony are often more responsible than (and hence preferable to) beliefs based on direct, not-testimonial evidence (for reasons of prudence or of probability), and (c) that (under these conditions) epistemic trust can be justified. By this, however, we do not mean that we have to trust every testimony; nor do we imply that epistemic trust is always responsible; nor that there are certain conditions under which direct evidence is not in some ways epistemically more powerful than testimony.

8.2 Epistemic Trust Is Inevitable

The amount of knowledge that we possess today is exceedingly vast and its justification a complex subject. To simplify the discussion, let us go back in evolution to a time when the amount of knowledge was still far more limited and when our earlier ancestors (the australopithecines) had not yet developed language. Having no language does not mean having

---

[23] Hinchman 2005, pp. 563–4.

no means of communication. According to Dunbar's 'grooming as gossip' theory, grooming (which most people simply take for 'delousing') was used to foster social interaction (as it is today, though under different names) and alarm cries were used to warn others of predators.[24] Much as language does today, grooming and alarm cries raised expectations in the recipient which could come true or not. We know that animals use false alarm cries, for example, to lure competitors away from prey that they want to have all to themselves. So, it is reasonable to assume that our predecessors did the same. If true alarm cries were not heeded, the consequences could very well have been fatal. Yet, acting on faked alarm cries could have equally dire consequences as not heeding true alarm signals. So, at least in a very broad sense, even these hominids had to trust each other with regard to intention upon hearing an alarm cry. However, since alarm cries always pointed to something that was happening 'then and there', the recipient of the signal could check whether the signal was warranted or not; that is, he could rely on direct evidence; there was no need for epistemic trust.

Once language had emerged (anthropologists disagree about why and when that happened[25]) the situation changed; things became vastly more complex. For the first time in history it became possible to convey information about facts and events that were distant in time and/or location[26] from the 'interlocutors'.[27] From then on one could convey information that the recipient could not verify 'on the spot'. And although the amount of information was assumedly small (at least compared to today), it was still impossible for an individual hominid to verify (i.e. to have direct evidence of) everything she was 'told'. She had to decide whether to trust the testimony of others. So, there is a reasonable case to be made that epistemic trust probably developed alongside language.

We do not know at what moment during evolution our hominid ancestors began to gossip (i.e. to pass on otherwise irrelevant information), but it is fair to assume that in the early stages of language development much of the information transmitted concerned such relevant

[24] Dunbar 1996, pp. 1ff.
[25] Anyone interested in this fascinating subject is referred to Donald Johanson's and Edgar Blake's (1996) superbly illustrated book *From Lucy to Language*, Simon and Schuster.
[26] The technical term for this feature of language is 'displacement'. Whether displacement is possible without language and hence in animals is discussed controversially in the literature (see, e.g. Cuccio and Carapezza 2015).
[27] Bickerton 2009, p. 47.

things as food sources or identifying dangers. Consequently, a distrusting hominid probably had little chance to prosper because he would starve or run into the next predator. Even if not every testimony was true, overall trusting was the better strategy. Not every testimony had to be accepted of course, but refusing every testimony was not compatible with survival in the group (and of the group). So, overall, epistemic trust was the inevitable choice.

Let us now return to the present. If our ancestors had not accepted testimony, knowledge would have forever remained minimal, and without epistemic trust, the acquisition of testimonial knowledge would have been impossible. Yet we know that during the intervening hundreds of thousands of years not only the world's population but also collective knowledge has literally exploded, which strongly implies that hundreds of generations have trusted the testimony of others. Without epistemic trust, whatever knowledge one individual had acquired during his lifetime would have been lost at his or her death. In short, epistemic trust is a fact; moreover, it is a tremendous 'success story'.

As a consequence of this knowledge explosion, "most of the time and on most subjects all people are laymen".[28] In other words, most of the time and on most subjects we all have to rely on testimony, i.e. we have to exercise epistemic trust. Much of today's knowledge is empirical knowledge developed by teams in which each member has to trust the other members. Although occasionally empirical knowledge can be verified by replicating an experiment, very often this is practically not feasible. Creating knowledge has become a global enterprise in which we are all participating both as producers and as recipients of knowledge.[29] So, what was true for our hominid ancestors is even more so for us: our time and intellect are too limited to gain first-hand (direct, non-testimonial) knowledge of everything we need to know to survive and to prosper. We are

---

[28] Baurmann 2010, p. 186, our translation of "Die meiste Zeit und in den meisten Bereichen sind alle Leute Laien". This status of lay knowledge is also an issue that has been addressed in recent discussion of the nature of expertise. See, e.g. Collins and Evans 2007; Collins and Evans 2010; Priaulx et al. 2016.

[29] We think it happens to all of us that we 'know' something and think we have seen it ourselves, when, in fact, we have only heard or read about it. Shapin (1994), cited in Misztal 1996, p. 13, has called this "the great civility of granting the conditions in which others can colonise our minds and expecting the conditions which allow us to colonise theirs".

bound to trust others to supply us with (correct) information.[30] In short, epistemic trust is inevitable.[31]

There is one more reason why epistemic trust is important in the context of this book. As we have seen, knowledge is produced by a myriad of people (they are the 'experts who know that p'). But unless this knowledge is used not only by the experts themselves but also by others (those who only 'know that p because an expert knows that p') it remains useless. One of the greatest (and certainly most beneficial) discoveries of all times is the discovery of penicillin by Alexander Fleming in 1929. However, Fleming had discovered penicillin quite fortuitously and had abandoned research on penicillin when clinical tests were inconclusive and when he could not convince chemists to produce penicillin on a larger scale. Just imagine what would have happened if Howard Florey and Ernst Boris Chain (who took up where Fleming had left off and in the early 1940s started to produce penicillin) had not believed in what Fleming had published in 1929.[32] Many of us would probably not be here. We may say that epistemic trust bridges the gap between the producers and the recipients of information.[33] Indeed, all our scientific networking is based on epistemic trust. In short, and yet again, it is clear that epistemic trust is inevitable.

8.3   Epistemic Trust Is Often Responsible

The fact that epistemic trust is necessary does not per se make it responsible.[34] In this section, we want to advance the claim that epistemic trust is often preferable to direct evidence and, hence, is responsible both for prudential reasons and for reasons of probability.[35] To illustrate this, let us briefly return to our hominid ancestors and start with the *prudential reasons* for trusting testimony. If 'Lucy' saw a ferocious predator, she knew she was in trouble and had better run.[36] In short, 'she knew that p' (where 'p' may stand for predator). However, if a tribesman told her that

---

[30] Hardwig 1985, p. 335.

[31] For a discussion of the problem of 'inevitable trust' (i.e. trust if we have no alternative), see page 65.

[32] The fact that the three jointly received the Nobel Prize for the discovery of penicillin in 1945 nicely emphasises the relevance of epistemic trust.

[33] Baurmann 2010, p. 190.

[34] For a definition of what we mean by 'responsible', see footnote 46 on page 54.

[35] This in fact amounts to the (pragmatic) claim that the responsibility of trusting testimony is more important that the truth-value of the testimony.

[36] Lucy is probably the most famous Australopithecine, who lived some 3 million years ago.

he had seen a ferocious predator 'roaming beyond the next mound', she probably sensed that she was in trouble but, of course, she did not truly know it. She did not herself 'know that p' (in fact, her direct evidence at that point told her 'that not p', since she could not see a predator); she only 'knew that p', because her tribesman 'knew that p'. In simpler words, she only knew there was a predator lurking about if she trusted her fellow's testimony. Given the situation, there can be no doubt that the prudential decision was to trust the tribesman's testimony rather than to rely on direct evidence. Needless to say, the same argument very often applies today as well (even if, fortunately, under different circumstances).

Another argument in favour of epistemic trust is *probability*. Assume that you have just looked at your watch and seen that it was twenty minutes past eleven o'clock. Accordingly, you consider that you have direct evidence that it is twenty minutes past eleven. Yet, this very moment you hear the speaker on the radio announce that it is now exactly twelve o'clock. The probability that the radio speaker is right and your watch is wrong is certainly higher than the opposite. So, at least under certain conditions, trusting the epistemic testimony rather than your direct evidence is entirely responsible.[37]

8.4   Epistemic Trust Is Justified

So far, we have argued that epistemic trust is inevitable and (at least very often) preferable to direct evidence. However, we have not yet shown that (and if so, why) epistemic trust is justified. In order to do so, assume that we ask you what time it is and, after looking at your watch, you tell us that it is exactly twelve o'clock. To the 'man in the street', this is a trivial situation. To the philosopher it is not. To him, the question arises whether, and if so, under what conditions we are justified to trust your information. Or, put differently, whether, and if so, under what conditions epistemic trust is justified. Two classic answers to this question have been given by John Locke (in 1690) and by Thomas Reid (in 1764). Here is Locke's account (often referred to as *'reductionist account'*):

> For I think we may as rationally hope to see with other men's eyes, as to know by other men's understandings. So much as we ourselves consider and comprehend of truth and reason, so much we possess of real and true knowledge. The floating of other men's opinions in our brains makes us

---

[37] We will expand on this in due course when we discuss 'epistemic vigilance' (Section 8.4.2) and 'epistemic trustworthiness' (Section 8.4.3).

not one jot the more knowing, though they happen to be true. What in them was science is in us but opiniatrety.[38]

In Locke's account, your information, although it is 'floating in our brain', does not make us know the time, even though it happens to be true. According to this strict *reductionist account*, epistemic trust is never justified. Since, as we have shown, most of the time direct evidence is either not available or too complex for an individual to understand, and since epistemic trust is clearly prudentially superior to the direct evidence in many (if not most) situations, this complete rejection of epistemic trust is not in line with our views on this issue.

Reid's (so-called *non-reductionist)* view is slightly more tolerant of testimony as a source of knowledge. According to Reid,

> one is justified in accepting testimony to p if and only if one has insufficient reason to disbelieve p.[39]

Although Reid (like Locke) rejects epistemic trust, he leaves a loophole in his account: we may trust your information that it is twelve o'clock only if we have insufficient reason to disbelieve you. In other words, we may trust you, but only on condition that we have no sufficient reason to distrust you. Whether sufficient reason to disbelieve such knowledge would include conflicting testimony is less clear, although one can imagine a case where the weight of testimony concerning not p might be greater than that of testimony concerning that p. More likely, however, such sufficient reason would be constituted by possession of non-testimonial knowledge. Hence, Reid treats testimonial knowledge as an eminently defeasible form of knowledge.

A more tolerant position has been advocated by Burge, who argues that the default position is what he calls the *'acceptance principle'*. According to this,

> [a] person is a priori entitled to accept a proposition that is presented as true and that is intelligible to him, unless there are stronger reasons not to do so.[40]

Although bearing some similarity to the position offered by Reid in terms of recognising rejection principles for testimony, this is a more permissive position: as long as you present your information in a way that lets it

---

[38] Locke 1690, Book I, chapter 3, #24.
[39] Reid T, 1764, 'An Inquiry into the Mind on the Principles of Common Sense', cited in Faulkner 2003, p. 37.
[40] Burge 1993, p. 469.

appear true and as long as the information is intelligible to us, we may accept the information that it is twelve o'clock. This position grants what is called "*fundamental authority* to the opinions of others".[41] Origgi, who views "fundamental authority as an extension of the necessary self-trust that we grant to our past, present and future judgements",[42] considers granting fundamental authority as legitimate. We do not agree with her on this. To us, this argument does not legitimate granting fundamental authority because our own judgements are far from always being reliable. It is a position of credulousness, which is no more justified than complete rejection of epistemic trust. We are often confronted with stories that appear perfectly reasonable, even though they are pure fiction, and often even meant to deceive us.

So far, we have three positions: (a) the complete rejection of epistemic trust (Locke), which we ourselves have outright rejected; (b) the rejection of epistemic trust but with an exit option (Reid); and (c) an account on which epistemic trust is almost the default position, bordering on credulousness (Burge). To us, none of these accounts is acceptable. What we favour instead is Faulkner's position that

> one is justified in accepting testimony to p if and only if one has sufficient reason to believe that p – testimony in itself provides no such reason.[43]

In other words, even if your testimony does not count as evidence per se we may still be justified to accept your testimony provided we have sufficient reason (apart from your testimony) to believe that it is indeed twelve o'clock. Contrary to Burge's account that grants the informant fundamental authority, this account grants *derivative authority* to the propositions of others.[44] Granting derivative authority means that we have sufficient reason to believe that you are trustworthy with regard to this particular item of information.

Given this, we consider that epistemic trust is in principle justified, provided we have sufficient reasons to believe that the source is trustworthy, that is, trustworthy with regard to this particular item of information. This position amounts to granting derivative authority to the testimony of others. What remains to be shown is what counts as

---

[41] Goldman 2001, p. 86.
[42] Origgi 2004, p. 66.
[43] Faulkner 2003, p. 37 claims that this is in fact Locke's position. It is irrelevant in the present context and beyond the scope of this book to discuss whether this claim is warranted.
[44] Origgi 2004, p. 65.

sufficient reasons, or in other words, under what conditions it is epistemically responsible (for laypeople) to trust experts.[45]

To start the discussion, we want to introduce the concept of 'street-
level epistemology' as an alternative to a somewhat stricter approach that
might be characterised as 'traditional philosophical epistemology'.

8.4.1   Traditional Epistemology versus Street-Level Epistemology

The philosophy of knowledge (epistemology) traditionally "focuses on
particular beliefs or types of belief and the criteria for truth or what
philosophers call 'justified true beliefs'".[46]

That is to say, epistemology focuses on under what conditions 'I know
that p' is justified as one of its most fundamental concerns.

Since we can rarely 'know that p', and since (in everyday life) we are
more interested in knowing under what conditions it is responsible to
trust a specific belief acquired through testimony than in knowing under
what conditions a general belief is a 'justified true belief',[47] Hardin
proposes "an account of epistemology of individual knowledge or belief,
of street-level epistemology, to complete the rational theory of trust".[48] In
this 'street-level-epistemology', "we cannot speak of the justification of
belief X tout court; rather, we must speak of the justification of belief X by
person A".[49]

Traditional epistemology assumes that we can rationally choose to
accept or refuse a testimony. Street-level-epistemology avoids this "arti-
ficial image, that depicts the hearer as a rational chooser who has the
option of accepting or refusing a chunk of information that is presented
towards her by a speaker. In most cases, we just do not have that
choice."[50] This last sentence is very important. The patient who is told
by her physician that her 'lump' is a pleomorphic adenoma and that she
should have it removed cannot choose between accepting and refusing
this information. This information refers to what is called 'esoteric
knowledge' (or 'privileged knowledge') to which she has no direct access,

---

[45] Of course, the same applies to one expert trusting another expert and to choosing between
different experts.
[46] Hardin 2002, p. 115. This is not to say that this is the only concern of epistemology, just
that it is a primary focus.
[47] Baurmann 2010, p. 187.
[48] Hardin 1993, p. 505.
[49] Hardin 2002, p. 116.
[50] Origgi 2008, p. 36.

i.e. information that she cannot adequately check herself. All that the patient can do (apart from refusing treatment) is to try to assess the epistemic trustworthiness of the physician in general (but not his trustworthiness with regard to his statement about the patient's tumour). Of course, she can seek a second opinion. But this is not going to solve her problem. At best, the second opinion confirms the first; in which case she may feel more comfortable but she will still have to trust. At worst, the second opinion contradicts the first; in which case she will have the additional problem of deciding whom she wants to trust.

In other words, whereas traditional epistemology deals with whether trusting testimony is *rational* (or can be rational), street-level-epistemology is more concerned with the conditions under which trusting testimony is *responsible*. It deals with epistemic responsibility, which is, according to Origgi, "a matter of adjusting our way of interpreting what other people say to our epistemic needs".[51] And whereas traditional epistemology deals with the *truth content* of a statement, street-level epistemology is not so much concerned with the truth-value of statements but with the *content relevance*, that is, with the relevance (or the interest) which a statement has for the recipient.

Truth and relevance of a statement do not always coincide. Take, for example, the simple statement given by the physician that 80 per cent of all tumours of the parotid gland are benign pleomorphic adenomas. This statement is based on the best possible epidemiological evidence. Recognising that medical knowledge is notoriously contingent, this statement comes as close to truth as can possibly be ascertained at the moment. And yet, the patient is not interested in it for as long as she does not know whether her tumour belongs to the 80 per cent. It is only once the physician tells her that, based on what she has told him and based on his exam, he believes her tumour to be a benign pleomorphic adenoma that this information becomes relevant to her. The truth-value of the second statement is definitely no higher (in fact, it is lower) than that of the first statement, but the content is now relevant for the patient because it refers to *her* tumour (and not just to 'such tumours in general'). Equally, the pathologist's opinion that the cells aspirated from her tumour are benign is relevant for the patient, since it tells her what is most important for her (even though it may not be true because aspiration cytology typically misses about 2 per cent of all malignant parotid lesions). So, again the responsibility of trusting testimony trumps the

---

[51] Origgi 2008, p. 42.

truth-value of the testimony when it comes to matters of content relevance.

According to this view, the 'pragmatic' value of a statement depends on the context. Whereas the statement that '80 percent of all tumours of the parotid gland are benign pleomorphic adenomas' is *not* relevant for the patient (and hence has no pragmatic value for her as long as she does not know whether her tumour belongs to this category), the same statement *is* relevant (and is epistemically valuable) for the medical student preparing for his exams. Therefore, by shifting from a focus on the truth content of a statement to content relevance (i.e. the relevance, which a statement has for the recipient), street-level epistemology allows us to justify epistemic trust.

With this in mind, we can now turn to consider two strategies that we commonly use to make sure that we have sufficient reasons to believe that the source is trustworthy (with regard to this particular item of information): epistemic vigilance and the assessment of epistemic trustworthiness.

8.4.2 Epistemic Vigilance

As recipients of information, we have two options. We can mistrust (i.e. neither trust nor distrust) the 'producer' of the information, in which case our epistemic situation (our 'pool of useful knowledge') will remain the same, or we can trust the producer of the information. If the information is true, our epistemic situation will improve; if it turns out to be false, our epistemic situation will deteriorate.[52] Since, as rational persons, we want to increase our knowledge we will also want to trust, given the alternative to trusting would be to remain ignorant. Yet, since 'trust implies risk', we also want to make sure that we trust responsibly. In order to reduce the risk of accepting the wrong information or of trusting the wrong producer of information, we use a form of prudence, or what is generally called 'epistemic vigilance'. Under what conditions it is responsible to accept testimonies depends on a number of factors. To illustrate these factors, we will use an example from the world of music, which we will present in four variations.

First, let us assume that at a party someone mentions that he owns a violin made by Jacobus Stainer.[53] Of course, you know that most so-

---

[52] Baurmann 2010, p. 192.
[53] J. Stainer from Absam, Tirol (1618–83) was the most prominent luthier of his time outside Italy.

called Stainer violins are copies (or fakes, depending on how you look at it). Nevertheless, under the circumstances you see no reason to challenge his statement. Second, assume that you are interested in buying the violin and that the owner (who is a private violin amateur) is willing to sell it. Would you still accept his testimony that this violin is a 'Stainer'? You certainly would not. One may ask 'why not?' (after all, it is the same fiddle and the same person). The answer is that epistemic trust depends on the situation. Whereas the first situation was one of non-committal small talk, the second situation is that of serious business.[54] Our epistemic threshold is usually rather low in small talk situations but considerably higher in business situations. Third, assume that the man offers the same violin as the work of an unidentified luthier from Mittenwald. Would you buy it? Probably yes, if it suits your purposes, is in good condition, and the price is right (i.e. right for an unspecified Mittenwald violin). Again, one may wonder why you would buy it under these circumstances (after all, it is still the same fiddle and the same person). The answer is that epistemic trust depends on the 'topic' of the testimony (or the claim that is made in the testimony). The claim that this is a violin by Stainer is much less likely to be true than the attribution to an unidentified Mittenwald luthier. Our epistemic threshold is usually inversely proportional to the truth probability of the claim. To take a simpler example, if someone claims to have won a local five-mile run, we are more inclined to believe him than if he boasts of having finished tenth at the London marathon. Finally, for the fourth variation, let us assume that (a year later) you are offered the same violin, this time by a renowned violin dealer, who sells the violin with his certificate that it is a violin by Jacobus Stainer in good condition. Would you buy it? The answer is 'yes', provided you had the money and that the price was 'right' (i.e. reasonable for a Stainer violin). What has made you change your mind is the fact that you believe the dealer to be 'trustworthy'.

What these variations exemplify is that we base our willingness to accept testimonies on an appraisal of the situation and the topic of the information, as well as on our assessment of the source of the information.[55] What has changed through the four variations is the risk

---

[54] Particularly given an authentic Stainer violin may cost up to or even above £100,000.

[55] In the words of Faulkner: "We are likely to believe speakers talking about everyday events, giving us directions, or telling us the football scores. However, we tend to be sceptical of speakers talking about politics, the greatness of their exploits, or the statistics that favour their opinion. On some quite specific topics, we may be utterly sceptical or conversely credulous" (Faulkner, 2002, p. 356).

you run if you accept the testimony that the violin is by Stainer. A violin by Stainer is easily worth twenty to thirty times as much as a fiddle from Mittenwald. In the small talk situation, you lose nothing if the statement is false. If you buy the violin as a 'Mittenwald' and at the price of a 'Mittenwald', you cannot lose much as long as the instrument is in good condition. If, however, you pay the price of a Stainer and it turns out to be by someone else, you will lose a fortune. So, you had better make sure you have the best possible certificate of authenticity before you buy the violin.

Hence, when it comes to epistemic vigilance, both the *situation* of the information transfer and the *topic* of the information are important features. They act as necessary filters, with which we adjust our epistemic vigilance. However, the most important single filter is the trustworthiness of the epistemic source, to which we now turn.

8.4.3   Assessing Epistemic Trustworthiness

Our epistemic trust is not blind. According to Baurmann,

> it is for the recipient a rational decision to accept the truth of information, which he cannot verify himself, if he can presume the competence, incentives, and disposition of the witness. In principle, the recipient can verify the presence or absence of these facts (competence, incentives, and disposition of the witness), even if he cannot verify the truth of the information.[56]

In other words, even though we cannot verify the truth of a testimony, we can assess the epistemic trustworthiness of the witness. We agree with Baurmann that epistemic trustworthiness (like trustworthiness *tout court*) depends on the competence and disposition (what we would call 'commitment') of the witness. However, we disagree with Baurmann with regard to his claim about incentives. Incentives do not *define* trustworthiness; they are a means of *assuring* someone's trustworthiness. Positive incentives are typically used to increase someone's interest in being trustworthy. Gaining the patient's trust (and thereby keeping him as a patient) is an incentive for the physician to be trustworthy. Similarly, negative incentives (i.e. sanctions) are used to dissuade people from being untrustworthy. If "we are more likely to believe friends, family, and lovers than strangers",[57] this is because we know that friends, etc., have a stronger incentive to be

---

[56]   Baurmann 2010, p. 193, our translation.
[57]   Faulkner 2002, p. 256.

trustworthy (in order not to lose our friendship) than strangers. Knowing someone's incentives to be trustworthy is also a means of assessing their trustworthiness. Knowing the positive and negative incentives, which someone has to be trustworthy, influences our willingness to trust them. Given the importance of this to understanding trust, we will return to the role of incentives presently as well as in Section 12.4.

As we previously discussed in Section 5.2, the expectation in trust always encompasses both competence and commitment. Of course, this applies to epistemic trust as well, but whereas 'commitment' in the context of epistemic trust does not differ from 'commitment' in the context of trust in general, 'competence' takes on a specific meaning in the context of epistemic trust. We therefore focus on competence in this chapter as the more relevant concern for epistemic trust.[58] As we have seen, testimony can refer to either first-hand or second-hand knowledge. Since we cannot ascertain the truth of the testimony (irrespective of whether it is first- or second-hand), we want to make sure that whoever supplies the information uses reliable tools (or procedures) to acquire his knowledge. Colloquially, we might say, since we cannot know whether what you say is true, we want to at least know how you came to know it. To quote Schwab: "epistemically responsible trust is epistemic trust in others who employ reliable belief-forming processes".[59]

We agree this definition is correct but it needs some fleshing out. As we have said earlier, trust implies uncertainty, whereas reliability is based on evidence (such as from past, faultless performance).[60] The patient trusts her doctor (which involves uncertainty), but the doctor uses reliable methods (therefore speaks with certainty). There are two notable problems with this 'reliabilist approach'. The first problem is that no belief-forming process (no test and no trial) in medicine is 100 per cent reliable. So, we will often have to be content with relative, rather than absolute, reliability. The second problem is that there are multiple levels of trust and reliability leading to (almost infinite) regression. We can consider these two problems in turn.

8.4.4 No Belief-Forming Process in Medicine Is 100 Per Cent Reliable

Many clinical tests or exams have one thing in common: they are sensitive (i.e. good at detecting pathology) but not very specific (i.e. not

---

[58] We will, however, discuss the role that commitment plays in the justification of trust in the chapter on the justification of trust in physicians (in particular in Section 9.2.2).

[59] Schwab 2008, p. 305.

[60] See page 83.

very good at differentiating between different pathologies). The diagnosis of angina is a good example to illustrate this.[61] Typical symptoms and signs of angina (or tonsillitis) are sore throat, fever, and coated tonsils. Causative agents include streptococci (about 20 per cent), other bacteria (40 per cent), and viruses (40 per cent). Whereas streptococcal angina (SA) must be treated with an antibiotic because of the risk of late complications, all other forms of tonsillitis need no antibiotic treatment because they are harmless and self-limiting. Clinical examination does not routinely allow us to differentiate between the different types of angina. So, if all patients are treated, 80 per cent of the patients receive an antibiotic that they do not need (and this costs money and may cause complications, as well as contributing to the over-use of antibiotics on a global scale). On the other hand, not treating any patient exposes 20 per cent of them to the risk of a late complication. What we would like is a test that is 100 per cent sensitive (i.e. one which identifies all cases of SA) and at the same time 100 per cent specific (i.e. one which eliminates all other cases). Unfortunately, no test fulfils this requirement. So-called quick tests correctly identify about 80 per cent of all cases of SA but are falsely positive in at least 10 per cent of non-SA (i.e. they say that it is SA, when in fact it is not). If we remember that virtually nothing is 100 per cent certain in medicine, this is a good performance. Only taking a bacterial culture is better than quick tests (with a sensitivity of >90 per cent, and a specificity of almost 100 per cent). Overall, we could say that the SA quick test qualifies as a very reliable belief-forming process, and bacterial culture as a maximally reliable belief-forming process. In principle, confidence in both quick tests and culture is justified.

Now, one may ask, why confidence in quick tests (which are only *very* reliable) is justified if cultures are *maximally* reliable? The answer is that cultures, although somewhat more reliable, take much more time (a few days versus a few minutes of the quick test) and cost a lot more.

Given (a) that the cost (both in time and money) to benefit ratio is so much superior for the quick test, and (b) that the quick test is only marginally inferior to taking cultures, it may still be epistemologically responsible to prefer the quick test.[62] Similarly, on occasions,[63] it may be

---

[61] The example serves the purpose of illustration. The details need not be correct in every aspect.
[62] Schwab 2008, p. 307.
[63] See, e.g. the example on page 105.

better to trust than to distrust because the overall costs (in the broad sense of this term) are lower.

In the example of the patient with the pleomorphic adenoma, the patient is justified to trust her physician when he tells her that her tumour is benign on the grounds that the ultrasound he used is a reasonably reliable method to distinguish between benign and malignant tumours. It may not be quite as reliable as magnetic resonance imaging, but it is available on the spot, much cheaper, far less unpleasant for the patient, and easily sufficient to make a responsible therapeutic decision.

8.4.5   There Are Multiple Levels of Trust and Reliability

The patient who trusts her doctor not only trusts him to use reliable diagnostic tools; she also trusts him to base his decisions on reliable theoretical knowledge. At a first approximation, we might say that knowledge gained from, for example, *The Lancet* is more reliable (or at least more likely to be reliable) than knowledge picked up at some local conference.[64] Ultimately, the reliability of theoretical knowledge depends on the level of evidence on which it is based. The higher the level of evidence, the more reliable (and hence the epistemically more responsible) is the information.[65] However, since evidence always has to rely on other evidence, this opens a road to regression.[66]

Indeed, the second problem with the 'reliabilist approach' to epistemic responsibility is that there are multiple levels of trust and reliability.[67] The patient trusts her physician to use a reliable test. The reliability of the

---

[64] For those unfamiliar with the example, *The Lancet* is one of the world's most respected medical journals.

[65] This is the credo of evidence-based medicine (EBM), according to which only 'Randomised Clinical Trials' confer level I evidence. Unfortunately, even supposedly high evidence is not necessarily true. Often the epistemic trust in the RCTs is not justified. The selective reporting of studies with positive results and the suppression of negative results lead to false evidence and undermine the credibility of (and the confidence in) EBM and eventually even in medicine 'tout court' (see, e.g. Elliott 2011). We will come back to this in Section 12.3.

[66] Without some sort of fundamental basis of absolute knowledge, there will be a potential infinite regression in our evidence base. One proposed solution to this is to appeal to other sources of evidence in a way that creates a circular 'loop' of knowledge. It has been argued that all our fundamental sources of belief and knowledge are circular and rely upon each other (see Alston 1986), although the specifics of the problem go back at least as far as Descartes and, more generally, to Ancient Pyrrhonean scepticism. There has since been a significant amount of debate as to what to do about epistemic circularity; for example by Schmitt 2004.

[67] Schwab 2008, p. 305.

test is based on its past performance. Yet, reliability presupposes competent execution of the test. So, the physician has to trust the lab technician's competence, which includes using reliable equipment. Of course, this list can be extended almost endlessly. And there is yet another aspect of this problem of regression: how do we know that a test is reliable? Usually we do so by comparing it with another test of 'proven reliability' (what we call the 'gold standard'). Unfortunately, even this gold standard is rarely beyond any reasonable doubt. We do not have an answer to the problem of infinite regression, which lurks behind the reliabilist approach. However, we think that at a 'street level' (to use Hardin's term once more) this need not concern us. In the words of Schwab: "If a belief-forming process produces reliable predictions that is precisely what tells us it is responsible."[68]

Epistemic vigilance and assessing epistemic trustworthiness are therefore means to make sure that we have sufficient reasons to believe that the informant is trustworthy, i.e. trustworthy with regard to this particular item of information.

8.5   Summary and Conclusions

In this chapter, we have stipulated that only information which is relevant to the receiver counts as testimony. Contrary to this, irrelevant information (which probably applies to 99 per cent of all media contents, for example), arguments (which we are free to accept or not), and the provision of pieces of evidence do not count as testimony. By resorting to the concept of street-level epistemology, that is, by shifting from the truth content of a statement to the content relevance (the relevance which a statement has for the recipient), we have been able to justify epistemic trust. Between the extreme positions of complete rejection and almost a priori acceptance of epistemic trust, we have argued that it is responsible to grant *derivative authority,* i.e. to accept testimony to p if and only if we have *sufficient reason* to believe that p. To determine what might count as 'sufficient reason' we have presented two strategies: 'epistemic vigilance' and assessing the 'epistemic trustworthiness' of the trustee. Now that we have established that, and under what conditions, epistemic trust is justified, we can turn our attention to whether and, if so, how patients' trust in physicians can be justified.

---

[68]   Schwab 2008, p. 306.

9

Justification of Patients' Trust in Physicians

In the preceding chapter, we argued that epistemic trust is justified provided we have good reasons to believe that the source is trustworthy, that is, trustworthy with regard to a particular item of information. We called this 'granting the informant derivative authority'. Since epistemic trust is a constituent, non-eliminable, part of trust in physicians,[1] adopting a more restrictive or a more liberal position for the whole (trust in physicians) than for a part (epistemic trust) would lead to contradictions. So, it appears reasonable to adopt the same position with regard to the justification of patients' trust in physicians. In other words, we want to argue that trust in physicians is justified if we have sufficient reason to believe that they are trustworthy. This claim may seem something of a platitude, but it is far from it, as 'trust' and 'trustworthiness' are not identical, even if they are closely related. Therefore, not only will unpacking this claim give us further important insight into the nature of trust; it will also lay the groundwork as to why there has been an apparent decline in patients' trust of physicians.

Two types of justification for patients' belief that physicians are trustworthy (i.e. for the patients' trust in physicians) are usually cited in the literature: (1) the physician's status as professional ('status trust') and (2) the physician's trustworthiness as assessed by the patient ('merit trust'). Accordingly, in this chapter, we will limit ourselves to an analysis of these two types of justification. This analysis is designed to show that, *in principle*, trust in physicians is justified, since both professionalism and individually assessed trustworthiness grant derivative authority. In Sections 12.1 and 12.2, we will return to consider 'status trust' and 'merit trust' again, only this time with a critical analysis of the two types of justifying trust and the underlying principles and limitations

---

[1] How can you trust a physician at all if you do not trust what he tells you?

fully in place, in order to find out why *in fact* fewer and fewer patients appear to believe that trust in physicians is justified.

Until fairly recently, justifying trust in physicians was easy. A physician's professionalism was accepted as sufficient reason to justify trust. Physicians *qua* professionals enjoyed what Buchanan calls 'status trust'.[2] More recently, however, 'professionalism' and 'professional status' have come under suspicion.[3] Professional status is no longer accepted as guarantor of trustworthiness.[4] Patients increasingly insist on limiting their trust to only those physicians whom, based on their own assessment, they believe to be trustworthy, that is, those who merit their trust. This shift away from 'status trust' towards a 'merit-based conception trust' (or, more simply, 'merit trust') has been hailed as a major step forward in the patient–physician relationship,[5] comparable to the move from paternalism to a greater respect for individual patient autonomy and shared decision-making. This sounds so plausible that people tend to overlook how difficult it is to define 'merit' (i.e. 'trustworthiness'), let alone how daunting a task it is for the patient to assess a physician's trustworthiness.

From this brief overview, it follows that a discussion of the justification of trust in physicians presupposes a clear understanding of the four key terms involved: *'trustworthiness'*, *'competence'*, *'commitment'*, and *'professionalism'*. Although all four terms are used liberally in the literature, they are all under-explored and in need of elaboration. Therefore, we will devote the first section of this chapter to the definition of 'professionalism' and the second section to an in-depth analysis of the term 'trustworthiness' and of its two constituent parts 'competence' and 'commitment'.

9.1   Professionalism and 'Status Trust'

"Not so long ago, the question of trust in the medical profession simply did not arise; Doctors functioned in a quasi-ecclesiastic atmosphere of patient awe and confidence."[6] What Clark refers to in this quotation is

---

[2] Buchanan 2000, p. 189.
[3] We will explain why 'professionalism' is no longer accepted as token of trustworthiness in Section 12.1.
[4] Pellegrino 1991, p. 69.
[5] Buchanan 2000, p. 208.
[6] Clark 2002, p. 14.

'status trust',[7] i.e. trust that is granted to individuals simply because they belong to a specific profession,[8] irrespective of any individual merit.[9] In general, we trust someone if we believe him to be trustworthy. Therefore, as the argument for status trust goes, if we trust someone simply because he is a professional, this implies that we take 'professionalism' as a guarantor of trustworthiness. This raises the question why we do this. One answer might be that we believe that particularly trustworthy characters become professionals. This answer may have been correct, at least up to a point, in the distant past.[10] Yet, without being overly cynical, we think that one would have to be exceedingly naïve to believe this to hold on a general level today. An alternative answer might be that we believe that the profession somehow instils trustworthiness in the professional, much as other roles cultivate or embed certain attitudes, such as how a copyist becomes very precise and conscientious. Again, this does not sound entirely plausible. So, we have to look for yet another answer. And the best way to do so is to analyse and define the term 'professionalism'. Unfortunately, very much like 'trust', 'professionalism' defies an easy definition. So, rather than (vainly) searching for an analytic definition, let us make some appeal to everyday usage and see how those directly involved (i.e. patients and physicians) use the term.

To our knowledge, only Chandratilake has investigated how the *public* views doctors' professionalism. In his survey, 953 people responded to a 55-item online inventory of professional attributes. The survey shows that people "recognise doctors as professionals by their good behaviour, high values, and positive attitudes".[11] However, this only describes how people see professionals, but it does not define what 'professionalism' is in the eyes of the public.

Physicians, on the other hand, have defined their profession themselves:

---

[7] An alternative interpretation would be that Clark refers to 'faith'. We will briefly address (and refute) such an interpretation on page 177.

[8] In principle 'profession' is a generic term, which may be used in reference to any occupation requiring specific knowledge or skills. It was only in the nineteenth century when society started to regulate important activities such as medicine and the law that the term assumed a more limited sense (Cruess and Cruess 2010, p. 713).Today, we are witnessing the opposite: with legislation regarding the exercise of all kinds of occupations, the number of occupations which consider themselves 'professions' continuously rises.

[9] Buchanan 2000, p. 191.

[10] In further support of this claim, we do not actually mean that only or mostly particularly trustworthy characters became professionals but that people believed this to be the case.

[11] Chandratilake 2010, p. 364.

> Physicians have been granted by society a high degree of professional autonomy . . ., whereby they are able to make recommendations based on the best interests of their patients without undue outside influence. . . ., the medical profession has a continuing responsibility to be self-regulating . . . [to] ensure quality of care provided, competence, and professional conduct of the physician. . . . Ultimate control and decision-making authority must rest with physicians, based on their specific medical training, knowledge, experience, and expertise . . . physicians who have erred must be appropriately disciplined.[12]

Even if this World Medical Association (WMA) declaration is perhaps somewhat skewed towards physicians' rights at the expense of their duties, it is perfectly in line with definitions proposed by others.[13] It contains the important elements that are currently used to define a profession, namely: (1) the possession of highly specific and complex knowledge and skills requiring significant amounts of training, (2) the duty to serve the interests of society as well as the duty for self-regulation and policing, (3) the right to autonomy and decision-making control without external influence, and (4) the provision of serious consequences in case of failure to comply with these duties or of unethical behaviour.[14] Although none of these features is unique to professions, together they define 'professions' and separate them from other 'jobs' or 'trades'. In particular, the provision of sanctions in case of unethical behaviour or failure to comply with professional norms sets professions apart from other occupations, which may otherwise be equally demanding or difficult.

The 'possession of highly specific and complex knowledge and skills' corresponds to 'competence', and the 'duty to serve the interests of society as well as the duty for self-regulation' corresponds to 'commitment'. So far, the justification of status trust does not differ from that of merit trust: both 'status trust' and 'merit trust' refer to the trustworthiness of physicians. What sets the two apart is that, whereas in 'merit trust' trustworthiness is assessed by the truster and sanctions are imposed by external institutions, in 'status trust' self-regulation and policing by the

---

[12] WMA 2009, p. 1, our insertion.

[13] For example, by Rhodes 2001 and by Cruess 2004.

[14] Granting physicians the right to autonomy and decision-making control without external influence in exchange for the duty to serve the interests of society, as well as the duty for self-regulation and policing of defaulting physicians, is often described as a social contract between the state, the public, and the medical profession. In the United Kingdom, it was first set down in 1858 Medical Act, which established the General Medical Council (GMC) (see Dixon-Woods et al. 2011, p. 1452).

professionals are supposed to ensure trustworthy behaviour.[15] In other words, in 'status trust' professionalism is seen as a guarantor of trustworthiness, obviating the need for each patient to assess the merit (i.e. the trustworthiness) of the individual practitioner. As long as the patient accepts professionalism as a guarantor of trustworthiness, professionalism offers a sufficient justification of trust. However, an increasing number of patients are reluctant to grant physicians the privilege of self-regulation and policing and to accept professionalism as a guarantor of trustworthiness.[16]

We are now in a position to say that 'status trust' refers to trust which is bestowed upon physicians *qua* members of a 'profession' because professionalism is accepted as a guarantor of physicians' trustworthiness. Provided the patients accept the underlying principles, professionalism offers sufficient justification of trust. However, patients are increasingly unwilling to grant physicians the autonomy of decision-making. Also, as we will argue in Section 12.1, it is the failure of the medical profession to fulfil the duty for self-regulation and the policing of offending members which eventually brought down 'professionalism' and 'status trust'.

9.2   Assessing Trustworthiness and 'Merit Trust'

Much like 'reliance' and 'reliability', 'trust' and 'trustworthiness' are like "two faces of the same coin".[17] Indeed, we cannot define one without referring to the other. However, the relationship between the two concepts is not symmetrical. It does not mean that one is not thinkable without the other. We can very well trust someone who is not trustworthy (even if this may not be advisable). And, since we can choose whether we want to trust someone, we can decide not to trust someone, even if we believe that someone to be trustworthy.[18] Moreover, it is very well possible to fake both trustworthiness and trust, just as caring behaviour in principle indicates commitment, and yet it offers no proof that the commitment will be realised.[19] We have probably all fallen prey to

---

[15] See, e.g. Holtman, who says: 'The foundational sociological and philosophical work on professionalism in medicine has crystallised around the idea of a social contract in which the medical profession is granted the privilege to self-regulate in exchange for its fulfilment of a fiduciary responsibility toward patients' (Holtman 2008, p. 234).

[16] We will come back to this in the section on the 'discrediting of professionalism and physicians' loss of professional authority' (Section 12.1).

[17] Stirrat and Gill 2005, p. 128.

[18] Hall et al. 2001, p. 616.

[19] Buchanan 2000, p. 194.

"the untrustworthy who parade as trustworthy ('you know you can trust me!')", and we all can remember situations when we have been "living up to what another presents as her trust in one, when that is not really trust but reliance on her evident power to punish those who fail her ('I am trusting you and don't you forget it')".[20] Before we go on to define 'trustworthiness', which is the principle goal of this section, we will point out those features that 'trust' and 'trustworthiness' have in common. This helps us avoid repeating what has been said before and at the same time underlines the close relationship between trustworthiness and trust.

Just as trust can never be general but must always be specified with regard to the object of trust (the trustee) and the content of your trust (i.e. what you expect of the trustee),[21] someone is only trustworthy to a specific truster with regard to a specified issue. Hence, *trustworthiness is not transferable*. To see what we mean by this, consider the following view from Iltis:

> Trust is a relationship that depends on the actions and beliefs of all the parties involved, and assessments of trust made by one patient are not necessarily transferable to others.[22]

The fact that, to us, you might appear to be trustworthy does not necessarily imply that someone else will come to the same conclusion, either because she has different standards of judging trustworthiness (or different demands on your commitment) or because your commitment to her is not necessarily the same as your commitment to us.

As there is no blanket trust, there is no wholesale trustworthiness.[23] By this we mean the belief, which some people hold, that a person is (or at least can be) trustworthy with regard to anything and towards anyone. However, such a belief is not reasonable. Nor is it plausible that the trustworthiness of doctors should, ideally, be unconditional (i.e. that a patient should be able to trust doctors with regard to anything). Trustworthiness is not simply 'out there'. Just as we have to specify with regard to what that we trust someone, we have to state with regard to what that we believe someone to be trustworthy; and like trust, *trustworthiness must comprise both competence and commitment*. Consequently, if we want to understand the role that 'trustworthiness' plays in 'merit trust',

---

[20] Baier 1991, p. 113.
[21] See page 45.
[22] Iltis 2007, p. 47.
[23] See page 41.

we need to have a clear understanding of what 'competence' and 'commitment' mean.

9.2.1 Defining Competence of Physicians

'Competence' is one of today's buzzwords.[24] It is on everyone's lips, and yet we believe that it is poorly defined and under-explored. But what exactly is a 'competent physician'? In this section, we will argue that competence of physicians has three components: (a) theoretical (science-based) knowledge, (b) practical (personal, experience-based) knowledge, and (c) skill or craftsmanship. Of course, this claim is not novel. In fact, it can be traced back to Aristotle, who used the terms *episteme, phronesis,* and *techne* to denote three components of 'knowledge'.[25] Moreover, we will argue that all three components are necessary and that together they are sufficient to define a physician's competence.

Here is a first brief definition of competence (with reference to professionals):

Competence represents the scope of what we can know and can do.[26]

In other words, 'competence' refers to the 'know-what' and the 'know-how', or roughly to 'knowledge' and 'craftsmanship'. This much is uncontested in the literature. However, it is much less clear what exactly 'know-what' and 'know-how' means. There is a strong tendency to equate 'know-what' with (what many consider "impartial, universal, and generalizable") epistemological knowledge at the expense of the "more messy practical experience".[27]

To illustrate what 'know-what' and 'know-how' mean, we will return to our original model case study of the patient with the lump in front of the right ear. After listening to the patient's story, asking a few pertinent questions, and palpating the lump the doctor tells the patient that this is in all likelihood a benign tumour of the preauricular salivary gland called 'pleomorphic adenoma'. Further, he tells her that the diagnosis can be confirmed with a fine-needle aspiration biopsy. Lastly (once the diagnosis is confirmed), he recommends her to have the tumour removed. Asked

---

[24] E.g. what used to be a 'tumour conference' is now a 'head and neck tumour competence centre'.

[25] See *Nichomachean Ethics,* 1139b18-36 (*episteme*), 140a1-23 (*techne*), and 1140a24-1140b12 (*phronesis.*)

[26] Sellman 2012, p. 115.

[27] Kinsella and Pitman 2012, p. 6.

by her relatives why she has agreed to the proposed surgery, the patient says that she trusts the competence of her physician. Pressed to explain what exactly she means by this she would probably roughly argue that she believes (1) that he has made the correct presumptive diagnosis, (2) that he is suggesting the best work-up, (3) that his recommendation to have the tumour removed is best for her, and finally (4) that he is considered a 'good surgeon'. Let us have a closer look at these four components of the folk understanding of 'competence'.

(1) We start with the question of *how the physician makes his diagnosis*. Why does he believe that this is a benign tumour of the parotid gland and most likely a pleomorphic adenoma? If asked, he would most likely give two reasons: the *first reason* is that he knows from the literature that tumours of this size in front of the ear are with few exceptions tumours of the parotid salivary gland; that at least 90 per cent of all parotid tumours are benign; and that about 80 per cent of all parotid tumours are pleomorphic adenomas. So far, this is epistemological knowledge. Yet, put less candidly, his 'diagnosis' would appear to be not much more than an educated guess, based on statistical probabilities. If this were all the physician had to offer, the patient's trust would hardly be justified. In fact, the patient might well have come up with the same probabilistic diagnosis if she had 'googled' the phrase 'tumour in front of the ear'.[28] However, his diagnosis is based on more than this epistemological knowledge. It is more than mere probability, because (and this is the *second reason* the physician would give) he also knows that benign tumours are usually mobile (whereas malignant tumours tend to be fixed to the surrounding tissues) and that pleomorphic adenomas have a firm rubbery consistency (whereas other benign parotid tumours are rather soft or doughy). Having read this, you too now also 'know'[29] that these tumours are 'mobile and firm', and yet you would probably be hard pressed to judge the fixedness and the consistency of such a tumour if you were to palpate one. Why is this so? The answer is that, in addition to the epistemological knowledge about these tumours, one needs 'experience' with how these tumours feel on palpation (which you presumably do not have unless you are a medical professional in this area). So, the physician has made his diagnosis based on his epistemological knowledge (of such lesions) and on his personal experience (with these tumours).

---

[28] To save readers the trouble, we have tried it and it works.
[29] 'Know' in the folk sense of the word.

(2) Next, we come to *what the physician does to confirm the diagnosis*, i.e. his recommendation to take a fine-needle aspiration biopsy. Again, the physician knows from the literature that a fine-needle aspiration biopsy is a reliable and relatively non-invasive (virtually harmless) procedure. So far, this adds nothing to our concept of competence. However, since the physician is no pathologist, he himself has to trust the pathologist to whom he sends the aspirate to make the correct diagnosis, and the pathologist has to trust the lab-technician to have handled the material correctly and to have presented him the correct slides. Of course, this is not the end of the 'trust-chain', but we will stop here.[30] So, in addition to being knowledgeable and experienced, the competent physician must be prudential with regard to his choice of collaborators. Since, as we will see later, the choice of collaborators has more to do with the physician's integrity (which is part of his commitment) than with his competence, we will address this issue presently in the section on commitment.[31]

(3) We now come to the *treatment recommendation*. Of course, the recommendation to have the tumour removed is again based on the physician's knowledge of the relevant literature. In this case, there are two main arguments in favour of tumour removal: (a) there is a small (albeit non-negligible) risk of malignant transformation if a pleomorphic adenoma is left in site for an extended period, and (b) the bigger the tumour is let to grow, the greater is the surgical risk should an operation become necessary later on. Let us assume that these two observations are based on sound empirical evidence. In this case, the recommendation to have the tumour removed is 'evidence-based'. And yet not every pleomorphic adenoma of the parotid gland must be removed, because the majority of pleomorphic adenomas never turn malignant and many do not grow (at least for a long time). So, the risks of a 'wait-and-see policy' (i.e. 'to leave the tumour in site and check it at regular intervals') have to be balanced against the risks of the surgical removal (e.g. the risk of a facial paralysis). Moreover, there are patient-specific factors (such as age, profession,[32] and co-morbidity) that have to be taken into account. To balance all risks and advantages properly again requires experience on the part of the physician.

---

[30] For a further discussion of the 'pyramid of trust', see page 101.
[31] See Section 9.2.2.
[32] Whereas a slight facial palsy might be perfectly acceptable for many patients, even a minimal palsy may be detrimental for a musician or an actress.

(4) Finally, we come to *the surgery*. Removing a parotid tumour is not trivial. It has unavoidable side effects (such as a scar and a numb ear lobe), and it carries certain risks, most notably the risk of a facial paralysis. To perform a parotidectomy requires a number of 'skills' on the part of the surgeon. (a) He needs a thorough understanding of the anatomy and the principles of the operation. (b) In order to locate the facial nerve where it exits the skull and to follow the nerve through the parotid gland, the surgeon must have a three-dimensional mental image of the course of the nerve. (c) Although a parotidectomy is a 'standard procedure', there may be unexpected variations that the surgeon must be able to handle. Finally, (d) manual dexterity is needed to dissect the nerve away from the tumour and to handle the tumour without tearing its capsule (which would 'seed' the tumour into the surrounding tissue, causing the tumour to recur). In other words, the patient who trusts her physician to be a 'good surgeon' has to trust his theoretical knowledge (about the operation) and his practical skills (while performing the operation).

So far, we have identified three different aspects of the physician's competence: (a) *theoretical knowledge* with regard to these preauricular tumours and to the treatment options, (b) *personal experience* with such tumours, and (c) *practical skills* (or craftsmanship). These three components of competence broadly correspond to Aristotle's three 'types' or 'approaches to' knowledge famously found in his *Nicomachean Ethics*,[33] namely *episteme, phronesis,* and *techne,* where

> *episteme* embodies scientific deductive knowledge . . . *techne* is concerned with the craft, the productive act, of the practitioner; and *phronesis* with knowing how to act in a situation in order to achieve the goals of professional practice.[34]

There is a vast amount of scholarly work on what *episteme, techne,* and *phronesis* mean in Aristotle's original writings. It is not our intention to enter into this scholarly philosophical discussion. Rather, given their established importance in describing key aspects of knowledge and ability, we will use them as useful umbrella terms covering the different components of physicians' competence. After a brief comparison of *episteme, techne,* and *phronesis,* we will flesh out what each term means

---

[33] Although famously attributed to the work of Aristotle, these types of knowledge were employed by earlier great philosophers, such as the use of *techne* and *episteme* found in Plato's Republic.

[34] Tyreman 2000, p. 120, our emphasis.

in (and how we can apply them to) medical practice in separate sub-sections.

To illustrate how we understand the three terms, we will use an example from outside of medicine: rock climbing. Assume you intend to climb the famous north face of the Eiger in the Bernese Oberland. Obviously, you need to have the necessary climbing skills but this is not, by itself, sufficient. You will not simply start climbing and 'follow your nose'. Before you even consider attempting this daunting climb you will want to 'know everything possible' about this almost vertical (or in part even overhanging) wall of rock. You will study maps with descriptions of the possible routes and memorise the critical parts. Mountaineering is also notoriously full of contingencies. You will have to recognise and react to unpredicted weather changes and other unexpected difficulties. In summary, you must 'know what' (e.g. the route, etc.) and 'know how' (to climb). 'Knowing what' means the theoretical knowledge, what you have learned by reading and talking to experts. This is *episteme*. To 'know how' is the craft or the skill, which you have been instructed by your mountaineering guides and practised during long hours. This is *techne*. Finally, you must be able to react to the unexpected. This ability is what you have gained through many hours spent in the mountains. This is *phronesis*.

This example demonstrates not only the difference between *episteme* (knowing the route) and *techne* (the skill to climb) but also the difference between *episteme* and *phronesis*. *Episteme* is the theoretical knowledge of a given route, whereas *phronesis* is the practical knowledge necessary to apply your knowledge and to react to the unexpected. The distinction between them is important.

There is a basic difference between knowledge and practical skills on the one hand and *phronesis* on the other hand. Whereas *episteme* and *techne* are primarily taught or instructed and can be practised actively (i.e. in the example, it is up to you to study the available information about the chosen ascent and to practise climbing), *phronesis* cannot be taught (at least not in traditional ways). *Phronesis* only comes through 'praxis' (roughly, 'practice' or 'doing', which, in the example, would involve spending long hours on increasingly difficult routes) over an extended period. Crucially, it is *phronesis* that distinguishes the merely knowledgeable and skilled from the genuine 'expert'.[35]

---

[35] Here, as well as in what follows, we are using this term in the 'folk sense' of referring to someone with 'a lot of experience'. It is beyond the scope of this monograph and it would

Let us return to the context of medicine. Discussions about physicians' competence are usually limited to knowledge and skills, i.e. *episteme* and *techne*. Or, as Davidoff[36] puts it very nicely: "knowing the right thing" and "knowing how to do things right".[37] Contrary to theoretical knowledge and skills (*episteme* and *techne*), *phronesis* has found little attention in the literature.[38] This is reflected in medical curricula (with their focus on knowledge transfer and training of skills) and in medical exams (which almost exclusively assess knowledge and to a lesser extent skills).

Whereas *episteme* is theoretical knowledge and *techne* is practical skills, *phronesis* can be seen as a combination of both knowledge and skill. But whereas *episteme* is about theoretical knowledge, *phronesis* is about practical knowledge (knowing how to act in a specific situation) or about judgement.[39] And whereas *techne* refers to the practical skills of medical practice, *phronesis* "brings reflection to bear upon the appropriate action to take, depending on the concrete circumstances".[40]

So far, we have (provisionally) defined '*episteme*' to denote the theoretical, scientific knowledge, which underpins most of today's medicine, '*techne*' to denote the craft of medical practice, and '*phronesis*' to denote the personal experience (or practical knowledge) needed to apply the theoretical knowledge to individual patients. Our next step is to elaborate on the three concepts and show how they apply to medical practice.

Episteme

The standard translation of '*episteme*' is 'knowledge'. Yet, this is too general. *Episteme* aims at

not further our argument to enter into the scholarly discussion of the definition of the term 'expert' (but see, e.g. Priaulx et al. 2016).

[36] Davidoff 2011, p. 16.

[37] Often, the concepts of '*episteme*', '*techne*', and '*phronesis*' are invoked to distinguish between 'medicine as science' and 'medicine as art', where 'science' has to be read as objective (and referred to as episteme) and 'art' as subjective (and referred to as either '*techne*' or '*phronesis*') (Hofmann 2003, p. 416). Whether medical practice is a science or an art is a popular subject for debates (not only among physicians). We think that the contenders would often be hard pressed to offer a clear definition of what exactly they mean by 'art' and 'science'. Yet, many of them even use the terms 'science' and 'art' in a normative sense and see their respective position as a moral stance. Not surprisingly, these debates can become quite fervid. Since we do not think that this debate is fruitful (certainly not in the context of defining competence), we will not pursue this subject.

[38] We will try to remedy this and to explain why this is so further down.

[39] Horton 2005, p. 16.

[40] Dowie 2000, p. 241.

theoretical truth, scientific knowledge of what we know . . ., [it] does not require knowledge of particulars.[41]

In the context of medicine, '*episteme*' would mean knowing whether clinical (diagnostic or therapeutic) interventions actually work. It means knowing what treatment is effective and what is (most likely) due to the placebo effect. Above all, *episteme* refers to the factual knowledge of a physician – what he knows about diseases, their diagnosis, and treatment.

The following (slightly abbreviated) quotation describes the epistemic credo, which underpins most of medicine today:

> In seeking to determine what is wrong with the patient . . . the physician deploys scientific knowledge, that is, the predominantly probabilistic laws and rules, the theories and principles, of the biomedical sciences. She appeals to statistically validated norms of human biological function, . . . the physician reasons hypothetico-deductively and inductively.[42]

We have included this quotation because (as we will argue further in Section 12.3) we believe that a growing uneasiness with this epistemic credo is one of the reasons for the decline of trust in medicine.

As a final point on *episteme*, we want to emphasise that it is not important for the physician to know as much as possible. Rather, he must know what is relevant in the particular situation. Moreover, it is important that what he knows is 'up-to-date', that is, have the best available knowledge at the time. Whether a physician's *episteme* merits the patient's trust, however, depends upon his epistemic vigilance[43] (i.e. whether he chooses trustworthy information) and upon his commitment to stay abreast of the development of medical knowledge.

Techne

'Techne' is usually translated as 'craft' or 'skill'. Intuitively most people associate both craft and skill primarily (or even exclusively) with manual dexterity. However, neither term is entirely appropriate. First, *techne* is not limited to skills in the sense of dexterity but entails a cognitive part as well. Second, it is not limited to motor skills but includes mental skills such as physical examination, history taking, or even conversational therapy.

The following example will show that *techne* entails practical as well as cognitive aspects. It is often erroneously assumed that the surgical craft is

[41] Davis 1997, p. 189, our insertion.
[42] Davis 1997, pp. 182–3.
[43] See Section 8.4.2.

purely a question of manual dexterity or skill. However, to perform an operation one must know what exactly the operation entails and what one wants to achieve. Exact knowledge of the surgical anatomy including a three-dimensional mental image of the operative site and knowledge of basic surgical rules must precede the surgical act. Whereas the operating surgeon must be in command of the cognitive and of the motor part of the skill in question, these two parts may very well exist separately.[44]

Apart from motor skills, there are also mental skills. Perhaps the most widely used skill of physicians is history taking. Anyone who does not believe that history taking is a skill need only observe a novice and an experienced physician at work. Whereas the novice will most likely grapple along some (memorised) checklist (and quite likely miss the important features), the experienced will, with a few well-placed questions (or even pauses), elicit the important information. Just as an operation has a rhythm, so has history taking. There are parts of an operation during which one can press forward (because nothing serious can happen at that stage), and there are parts during which one has to be careful. Much the same is true for history taking. So, there are not only motor skills but also mental skills.

Anyone who is about to undergo a surgical operation hopes that his surgeon will be skilled. And yet, overall, skills enjoy a rather low reputation. Many people see in them no more than a set of manoeuvres capable of (mindless) repetition. And yet, *techne* implies far more than just drill;[45] rather, it " . . . involves knowing-in-action, a reflective conversation with a unique and uncertain situation".[46]

Phronesis

Whereas the importance of knowledge and skill in the overall picture of competence should be obvious, that of *phronesis* may be a bit less so. As

[44] Here is an example of such a separation of the parts of a skill from the surgical experience of M.W.: I still know, e.g. how to perform a stapedectomy (the term refers to the replacement of the ossified stapes with a prosthesis), and I think that I could still teach it. Yet, I know that I could not perform the operation myself any longer, because my eye-hand coordination is not what it used to be and my hands are no longer as steady as they would have to be. One might say that I still possess the cognitive part but no longer the manual skill part of the *techne* of stapedectomy.

[45] Even dribbling in football, which is often seen as an example of a skill devoid of cognitive context, requires an interpretation of the situation and foresight. The example is from Hinchliffe 2002, p. 190.

[46] Hinchliffe 2002, p. 195.

a consequence, *phronesis* "has been largely under-explored, probably because of difficulties in describing and assessing it".[47]

Personally, we believe that *phronesis* is not only under-explored but also under-valued. For this reason, we will not only define what *phronesis* is but also explain why *phronesis* is important.

Phronesis is practical knowledge or 'experience'.[48] Like skills, 'experience' enjoys a rather poor reputation. All too often it is used (not only by physicians) to parade one's beliefs as truths when in fact they are only personal 'opinions' or 'biases'. However, until fairly recently and prior to the advent of well-established evidence-based medicine, all that doctors could rely on was 'their experience'.[49] What this meant was that if a doctor had seen a patient improve after treatment x, he concluded that the patient's improvement was caused by x and that x would work in the next patient as well. Of course, neither conclusion was justified. The first is a case of the *'post hoc, ergo propter hoc'* fallacy,[50] and the second is refuted by a simple probability calculus.

By *phronesis*, we mean a different kind of experience, i.e. the knowing of how to act in a specific contingent situation. Contrary to *episteme*, *phronesis* does not aim at discovering 'generalities' (what is true in general) but 'individualities' (what is true in a given situation or for a given patient). With ever more knowledge being 'evidence-based',[51] it becomes vital to manage this vast amount of knowledge. We might say that what *phronesis* does is knowledge-management. It means integrating individual clinical experience with "the best available external clinical evidence from systematic research".[52] To use an analogy: it is no good having a large database if you do not have powerful software to make use of it. That is why *phronesis* must be a constituent part of any definition of

---

[47] Tyreman 2000, p. 118.

[48] Other translations include 'practical wisdom' (Dowie 2000, p. 240), which is something of a loaded term and 'practical rationality' (Montgomery 2009, p. 191), which is too restricted to reason and so precludes other elements of *phronesis*.

[49] We do not mean by this that every doctor was working entirely in isolation and devoid of training or theoretical discourse, only that there was a lack of a systematic means of establishing the efficacy of any given treatment which meant that its success was instead based on the experiences of the doctor and his predecessors. There remains something of a challenge for medicine to determine through appropriate research whether all received treatment options are, indeed, efficacious, and whether such research is ethically justifiable. See Fried C 1974; Hughes et al. 2010.

[50] I.e. the erroneous conclusion that just because 'B' follows 'A', 'B' is (or even must be) caused by 'A'. It is an error, which pervades the thinking of both patients and physicians.

[51] See footnote 65 on page 117.

[52] Sackett et al. 1996, p. 71.

'competence'. Both *techne* and *phronesis* have a practical and a cognitive component. But whereas *techne* is reflected application of skills, "phronesis brings reflection to bear upon the appropriate action to take, depending on the concrete circumstances".[53]

To further underline the importance of *phronesis*, let us come back to the concept of the 'expert'. Knowledge and skills (*episteme* and *techne*) alone do not make you fully competent. They do not make you an expert. It is *phronesis* which makes the difference between a novice and the expert. Whereas the novice can (only) apply the instrumental skills, the expert also knows their worth as well as their limits. He knows what can be achieved by them (and what not), and how they are best employed.[54] So, this raises the question as to why *phronesis* enjoys so much less attention than *episteme* and *techne*. One (or probably the prime) reason for today's over-reliance on knowledge and skills at the expense of *phronesis* is the fact that *episteme* and *techne* can be taught and assessed, whereas *phronesis* can only be acquired through praxis and is difficult to assess. A further reason might also be because *phronesis* is difficult to measure and therefore is unpopular with bureaucrats, who are increasingly in control of medicine and "who generally hold the purse strings".[55]

Finally, it is worth emphasising why we think that *phronesis* is important, not only as a component of competence but in itself. We have two answers, and both relate to the ethics of medical decision-making. Our first answer is that today's (almost) exclusive reliance on scientific knowledge (*episteme*) has far-reaching ethical consequences, in that it blurs the distinction between 'what *can* be done' and 'what *should* be done' and leads to an overemphasis of 'what can be done'. Evidence-based medicine will tell us what is effective in principle. It does not tell us what must, should, may, or indeed should not be done for an individual patient. This gap between what has been shown to be effective in general and what should be done in an individual patient's situation is bridged by *phronesis*.[56] Our second answer is that, in today's medicine, there is an increasing conflict between responsibility (vis-à-vis the patient) and accountability (before the law).[57] Science-based medicine (in particular EBM) favours rule-governed decision-making processes, but rule-governed decision-making fails if there are competing 'goods' or

[53] Dowie 2000, p. 241.
[54] Tyreman 2000, p. 118.
[55] Tyreman 2000, p. 122.
[56] Davis 1997, p. 183.
[57] Pitman 2012, p. 131.

competing rules. Should the epistemic rule (e.g. that pleomorphic adenomas should be removed because of the small risk of malignant degeneration), or rather the ethical rule (that the patient should not be exposed to an unnecessary surgical risk), take precedence? Protocols, such as treatment guidelines or algorithms, aim at increasing accountability (and thereby decreasing personal responsibility) of the physician, whereas *phronesis* encourages taking personal responsibility.[58] The inexperienced physician will likely opt for the protocol, that is, choose the accountable way and advocate surgery, whereas the *'phronimos'* (the practically wise) will accept the responsibility himself and often advise a wait-and-see policy, knowing that, should the tumour at a later time cause problems, he may have a problem of accountability. Unfortunately, exercising such *phronesis* is ever more demanding in a context where juridical accountability increasingly trumps both the patient's interest and the physician's self-respect as a professional.[59] The competent physician must therefore have sufficient theoretical knowledge, sufficient practical experience, and good craftsmanship. We have purposely qualified knowledge and experience with 'sufficient' because knowledge and experience always have to be judged in the current context. Although it never hurts to know more and to be more experienced, it would be irrational to expect the physician to know everything (even with regard to a specific topic) and to have experience with every possible lesion and every imaginable situation. It suffices if he has enough knowledge and experience to arrive safely at the correct diagnosis, etc. Contrary to this with regard to skill, merely 'sufficient' is not enough. Someone who performs at the limits of his capabilities is ill equipped to handle unexpected difficulties.

At the beginning of this section, we claimed that the three components, *episteme, techne,* and *phronesis,* are both necessary and sufficient to define 'competence' in physicians. We think it obvious that all three conditions are necessary. If a physician lacks adequate theoretical knowledge, is not skilled, and does not have sufficient practical wisdom, he is simply not competent. It is more difficult to show that jointly they are sufficient. However, when considering that question it is worth simply reflecting what does a physician who (1) has enough true beliefs (with regard to the disease he is confronted with) to make the correct diagnosis and to know the best treatment, who (2) has enough experience to apply

[58] Frank 2012, p. 58.
[59] Schwartz et al. 2004, p. 178.

the general knowledge to the individual patient, and who (3) is a skilled surgeon, miss to be considered competent? In all the examples we have considered we could not detect an additional element that was required. We therefore think it is reasonable to conclude that the three components *episteme, techne*, and *phronesis* are jointly sufficient to define 'competence' in physicians.

As a final point on this topic, it is worth noting that we have worked through and presented a relatively detailed analysis of 'competence' for two reasons: (1) we believe that few people have an adequate understanding of 'competence' and therefore use the term far too liberally, which causes confusion and conflation when accounting for trust. And (2) we wanted to prepare the reader for a claim that we will make in Section 12.2, namely that it is nigh on impossible for a patient to assess a physician's competence.

9.2.2   Defining Commitment of Physicians

Defining 'commitment' is much more difficult than defining 'competence'. Competence, once one has acquired it, is stable. Of course, one may lose (some of) it over time, but one does not have it one day and lack it the next day (except for certain extreme cases, such as head injury or stroke). One cannot decide to be competent one day and not to be competent the next day. If occasionally we act in a way that might be described as 'incompetently' (despite being competent), this is not because we have suddenly lost our competence, but because on that occasion we are not sufficiently committed to – or familiar with – the task. Contrary to competence, commitment is fragile. No one is always motivated to 'give his best'. You can even decide not to commit yourself to a task you have the competence to do. This is because commitment depends on one's will, whereas competence does not.[60] Some people are committed to many things, others only to a few things; some are highly committed, others only vaguely.

Our commitment may be general, specific, or purposive.[61] *General commitment* refers to what someone would do anyway, irrespective of

---

[60]   Of course, it requires a will to become and remain competent, but at a given moment you are or you are not competent independent of your will and independent of whether your competence is required.

[61]   Sztompka speaks of anticipatory, responsive, and evocative commitment (Sztompka 1999, pp. 26–8). However, since we do not consider these terms particularly illuminating, we will not use them.

whether anybody trusts him to do it or not. These are commitments we take for granted. If, for example, we are engaged in a discussion, we expect you to devote your attention to us (and not simultaneously to discuss your weekend plans with your partner on your mobile phone). This type of commitment has nothing to do with whether we trust you or not but can be attributed to something else (in this case, with general manners). *Specific commitment* refers to the obligation the trustee implicitly accepts when he undertakes to do what someone trusts him to do. It is the commitment the patient expects of the doctor when he accepts to treat her. This is the commitment to which trust refers. Finally, *purposive commitment* aims at provoking or inducing trust. Purposive commitment is used to demonstrate one's trustworthiness. A GP who calls a patient to convey some results he has just received may be said to show purposive commitment. Children often use this type of commitment to induce their parents to trust them.

Given this distinction between types of commitment, when we speak of the physician's commitment in a trust-based patient–physician relationship, we refer exclusively to the physician's specific commitments: (a) his commitment to lifelong learning and to a periodic self-assessment process and (b) his 'commitment to the interests of his patients'.[62] The commitment to stay abreast of recent developments eventually reflects on the physician's competence. Therefore, and since it is comparatively easy to assess a physician's commitment to 'continuing medical education' (CME), this commitment has become a proxy to assess the epistemic and general trustworthiness of physicians.[63] We will briefly come back to this issue in the section on how we assess trustworthiness.[64]

Defining the physician's commitment to his patients' interests is a more challenging task. As we have said earlier, defining 'trust' as an 'expectation that the trustee will act in the truster's interest' is insufficient, because it focuses solely on commitment and neglects competence. Yet, even defining 'commitment' as an 'expectation that the trustee will act in the truster's interest' is flawed. If you have a close look at this definition, you will easily see that it is a wolf in sheep's clothing; it is just good old paternalism in (poor) disguise. We will not go into a detailed discussion

---

[62] Kassirer 2007, p. 383; as will become clear later, we have chosen this rather vague description on purpose.

[63] Many physicians display their Continuing Medical Education (CME) diplomas in their office. Some specialist societies even make the CME data of their members accessible to the public.

[64] See Section 12.2.

of all the arguments against paternalism; they are well known by now. Like paternalism, the 'expectation that the physician will act in the patient's interest' presupposes that the physician knows what is best for the patient. It wrongly assumes that there is no difference between what the patient and the physician perceive as best. Alternatively, one might say that it falsely assumes that 'best interests' and 'patient autonomy' are comparable, or that 'best interests' trumps if the two principles conflict.[65] It cannot take into consideration that the patient himself may have conflicting interests, or that there may be a conflict between the physician's commitments to different patients or between the physician's commitment to his patient and to his employer. Some alternative definitions of 'commitment', such as Mechanic's definition as "commitment to act as the patient's agent"[66] face the same problems.

It is easy to give examples of commitment: 'keeping confidentiality', 'supplying adequate (and unbiased) information', 'being responsive', and 'continuing the relationship (i.e. not abandoning the patient) if something unexpected happens' are just a few examples that come to mind. They all refer to the physician's commitment. But they only illustrate commitment; they do not define it. What we need is a definition of 'commitment' that takes into account the nowadays-accepted model of the patient–physician relationship that involves informed consent and shared decision-making. To find out what such a definition might look like, let us use another example. A man has to undergo major abdominal surgery. Unfortunately, he has already had two serious myocardial infarctions, which makes him (as the anaesthesiologist puts it) a 'high-risk' patient. The man himself knows that, apart from the surgical risk, there is the risk of a third (and potentially fatal) heart attack. Moreover, he knows that cardiac resuscitation always carries the risk of surviving with a neurological deficit. During the pre-operative discussion, he lets the surgeon know that he would rather not wake up after the surgery than having to live the rest of his life with a neurological impairment. The night before the surgery, the patient tells his wife that he fully trusts the surgeon and his team. What does he mean by that, in particular with regard to a potential cardiac reanimation? Let us consider this by first looking at the different interests: The surgeon's personal interest clearly favours reanimation, should it become necessary, because 'losing a patient on the operating table' (to use professional jargon) is about

---

a surgeon's worst nightmare. Unquestionably, he might also believe reanimation to be in the patient's best interest because he holds the belief that 'life is always better than death'. As to the patient, he has clearly said to the surgeon that 'he would rather not wake up after the surgery than having to live as a vegetable' (to use his words). However, this does not imply that he considers dying to be his primary interest; of course, he prefers to live (only not under any condition). So, what does the trusting patient expect the operating team to do in the event of a cardiac arrest? Here, we think the patient trusts the surgeon to fulfil his expectation – in other words, to abstain from any attempt at resuscitation. What this amounts to is that he expects the physician to respect his values, even if they clash with the physician's own values.

We can see this interpretation elsewhere. Ana Smith Iltis, for example, proposes the following definition of trust: "Trust should be understood as an expectation that the trustee will act in a way that the truster approves."[67] As a definition of trust, this is inadequate because it neglects competence. However, the phrase 'acting in a way that the truster approves'[68] catches exactly what commitment means. The committed physician does not profess to always act in the patient's interest but always to act in a way that the patient approves, thereby accepting that what a patient approves need not be in his (i.e. that patient's) interest. To avoid any misunderstanding, this does not mean that the physician must fulfil all of a patient's wishes. For example, if a wish of a patient is incompatible with what the physician is willing to do, it is in the interest of the patient to be referred to another doctor. This definition of commitment has the further advantage of being able to account for moral (or cultural) pluralism in society.[69] The difference between 'acting in the patient's interest' and 'acting in a way that the patient approves' will become very important in subsequent discussion of the problems of professionalism in status trust.[70]

It is all very well to be committed to do something but only as long as one is at liberty to do so. In other words, it is not enough that a physician is willing to 'act in a way that the patient approves' if he is not free to do so. Kitcher and Schacht (albeit in a rather different context)[71] refer to this

[67] Iltis 2007, p. 47.
[68] Or 'would approve', if he were in a position to do so.
[69] Iltis 2007, p. 58.
[70] See Section 12.1 (the discrediting of professionalism).
[71] Namely in the context of discussing Wotan's authority in Wagner's 'Ring trilogy'.

as having 'directive authority'.[72] We will come back to this in Section 12.4, where we will argue that many patients today fear that physicians are no longer independent professionals but 'corporate employees',[73] and who, as such, no longer have the directive authority to act (solely) with the patient's interest in mind.

We mentioned earlier that the competent physician must have 'sufficient' knowledge and experience, that is, sufficient in the respective context. The same applies to commitment. Commitment is not all-or-none but admits of degrees. Depending on the context, we can expect more or less commitment. The expected duration of the relationship, the risk involved, and the presence or absence of a withdrawal option for the patient are just three factors that influence the extent of the commitment we can justifiably expect.[74] The fact that the 'presence or absence of a withdrawal option' influences the amount of commitment we can expect might seem an unusual claim and so deserves a comment:[75] If, for example, a patient repeatedly consults his ENT doctor for a chronic nasal obstruction, but never heeds his advice, the doctor may end his commitment and tell the patient to see someone else. The same does not apply to the physician in the emergency room, where the patient has no 'withdrawal option'. Even if the patient is perfectly obnoxious, the doctor cannot refuse to treat him. However, this does not mean (and we want to emphasise this) that the commitment can be expected to be unlimited. The patient has to acknowledge that the physician's commitment may be limited by competing commitments. Accordingly, we are in no way "indulging in the delusion that it is the physician's fiduciary obligation always to provide all care that is expected to be of any net benefit to the patient".[76]

It should be clear from this discussion that 'commitment', like 'trust', is difficult to define. Most authors resort to giving examples rather than actually providing a definition of 'commitment'. To us 'acting in a way that the truster approves (or, depending on the situation, would approve)' is the best available descriptive definition of commitment.

---

[72] Kitcher and Schacht 2004, p. 27.
[73] Clark 2002, p. 22.
[74] Sztompka 1999, pp. 28–9.
[75] See page 159.
[76] Buchanan 2000, p. 189.

9.3 Summary and Conclusions

In this chapter, we have presented the two justifications usually cited as sufficient to warrant patients' trust in physicians: professional status and individual merit (both of which in fact refer to trustworthiness). Whereas in 'status trust' professionalism is taken as a guarantor of trustworthiness, in 'merit trust' the physician's trustworthiness (i.e. competence and commitment) is assessed individually. Since 'trust' refers to the patient's expectation that the physician is trustworthy, trust is justified if the patient's assessment leads him to conclude that the physician is trustworthy. However, there are limitations which account for the fact that 'merit trust' has not (fully) compensated the decline of 'status trust'.

We have defined 'professionalism' as 'acting trustworthily in exchange for autonomy of decision-making'; 'competence' in terms of *episteme* (theoretical knowledge), *techne* (craft or skill), and *phronesis* (practical knowledge or experience); and 'commitment' as 'to act in a way that the truster approves'. These are all key elements that play a role in an analysis of 'trustworthiness' and lay the groundwork for an account as to why trust in physicians is justified.

Lastly, we have argued that although *in principle* trust in physicians is justified, since both professionalism and individually assessed trustworthiness grant derivative authority, the reality is somewhat different. This is due to an increasing number of patients rejecting the concept of professionalism and, accordingly, who find it difficult (or even impossible) to assess physicians' trustworthiness.[77] Hence, they no longer believe that their trust in physicians is justified.

---

[77] We will discuss this in Section 12.2.

PART IV

Significance of Trust

10

Instrumental Utility of Trust

One of our starting assumptions was that the decline of trust in medicine is a negative development and a reason for concern. Yet, so far, we have not presented any arguments to underpin this claim. So, in order to resolve such a concern, this is precisely what we intend to do in both this and the next chapter. In particular, we will argue that we have two reasons to be concerned about the loss of trust: first, because trust has an instrumental value[1] (or usefulness) and, second, because trust is not just a useful commodity but also a moral good.[2] Accordingly, we will devote this chapter to the discussion of the instrumental value of trust and address the claim that trust has a moral value in the next chapter.

Of course, the strongest argument in favour of the usefulness of trust in medicine and health care would be convincing *empirical evidence* that trust improves patient welfare. Yet, and quite apart from the fact that this would only show *that* but not *why or how* trust improves patient welfare, this approach poses two problems: first, we must be able to measure trust,[3] and second, we need a reliable outcome variable.[4] Of course, it would be tempting to correlate the level of trust with overall treatment success. Yet, if we consider how difficult it is to prove the very efficacy of a treatment, it must be evident that this is clearly not feasible. So, we have

[1] Miller uses the term 'strategic value' in this regard (Miller 2000, p. 44). Although the term is very enticing, we prefer not to use it because, to our mind, it puts too much emphasis on the purposefulness of trust.

[2] Alternatively, one might say that trust has both an instrumental and an intrinsic value, where 'instrumental' stands for 'a means to an end', and 'intrinsic' stands for 'an end in itself' (O'Neill 1992, p. 120).

[3] For a comment on the problem of the measurability of trust, see footnote 1 on page 11.

[4] An outcome variable (also called 'dependent variable') is a measurable variable, which correlates with the level of the variable that we want to assess (in this case, trust). Survival time and survival rate are typical examples of outcome variables used to assess the efficacy of cancer treatments.

to look for alternative outcome variables. Alternative variables may be either specific (such as earlier cancer detection in trusting patients)[5] or more general (such as the willingness of patients to consult and stay with a physician).[6] They may refer to whether patients are willing to follow the physician's advice, even if this means to change one's life style,[7] or to comply with treatment regimens.[8] Even broader outcome variables are conceivable; for example, Jen et al. (2010) studied the relationship between trust and self-rated health. Their conclusion was that "the level of trust … is predictive of individuals' health".[9] Helliwell and Putnam (2004) set out to prove the hypothesis that 'trust is vital for a meaningful life'. According to them, their study showed that people who claim to trust easily report a higher life satisfaction.[10] Similarly, Birkhauer et al. (2017) report more beneficial health behaviours, less symptoms, and higher quality of life as well as more treatment satisfaction in highly trusting patients.[11] Conversely, Fiscella (1999) looked at the correlation between mistrust and outcome and found that mistrust correlates with a higher mortality rate.[12]

Much as we would like to believe all these results, we do not think that they prove that trust is useful for a number of reasons. One reason is we are concerned that equating 'correlation' with 'causation' means committing the logical fallacy of *post hoc ergo propter hoc*,[13] without some substantial additional work on making the causal connection. Moreover, the direction of the causation may well be inverse (healthier or happier people may be more trusting rather than the other way around). Also, the outcome variable (such as 'life satisfaction') and trust may both be caused by a third factor (such as wealth) rather than one being the cause of the other. Similarly, the higher mortality rate in distrusting people may be caused by non-adherence to treatment recommendations and unhealthier behaviour rather than to distrust per se. Finally, even if we can show that a high level of trust correlates, for example, with earlier cancer detection, this may show that trust is useful for the patient; however, it does not prove that trust per se is overall useful in the patient–physician

[5] Mainous et al. 2004, p. 35
[6] Lee and Lin 2008, p. 44
[7] Bonds et al. 2004, p. 1.
[8] Gilson 2006, p. 361.
[9] Jen et al. 2010, pp. 1024–5.
[10] Helliwell and Putnam 2004, p. 1442.
[11] Birkhauer et al. 2017, p. 1.
[12] Fiscella 1999, p. 409.
[13] See footnote 50 on page 133.

relationship. Given that (at present) there is no convincing empirical evidence for the usefulness of trust (conceived in terms of positive patient welfare outcome), we have to look for alternative arguments.

Many metaphors have been used to describe trust. We particularly like the one by Jon Elster, who calls trust "the lubricant of society".[14] We think the association of trust with a lubricant is very appropriate. As anyone who suffers from arthrosis[15] can testify, we often only become aware of the importance of the synovial fluid that lubricates our joints once it is lacking. The same is true for trust. Trust is so omnipresent that we take it for granted – until it is lost, and until we find out how difficult it is to restore. In the words of Annette Baier:

> We inhabit a climate of trust as we inhabit an atmosphere and notice it as we notice air, only when it becomes scarce or polluted.[16]

The example points at the two most common ways of assessing the value of trust. We can list *the advantages of trust* (i.e. describe or measure what it does as long as we have it) or, alternatively, we can assess the *consequences of the loss of trust.* However, we think that there is also a third way. Let us briefly leave considering 'trust' directly and look at an everyday situation to illustrate what we mean. An umbrella is unquestionably useful on a rainy day because it protects us against rain (the advantage). Without it, we will get wet if we are surprised by a shower (consequences of loss). However, an umbrella loses much of its attraction if we wear a rain-jacket, which not only protects against rain but also against wind and cold. Similarly, trust may be relegated to 'second best' if we can find a better alternative.

We will consider each of these three ways of assessing the usefulness (or instrumental value) of trust in turn and start by looking at the advantages of trust. To do so, we will present *three* arguments in favour of trust, all of which are derived from our definition of trust, namely the role that trust plays with regard to the handling of uncertainty, of complexity, and of risk. All three arguments will not only show *that* trust is useful but will also explain *why* (or in what way) trust is useful. We will then look at the consequences of the decline of trust and argue that the measures taken to compensate for the loss of trust are inadequate and only transfer the need to trust from a first-order object (e.g. physicians) to

---

[14] Elster 2007, p. 344.
[15] Arthrosis is a degenerative disease of the joints causing stiffness and pain.
[16] Baier 1986, p. 234.

a second-order object (e.g. those responsible for making or implementing regulations). Finally, we will analyse the only model that is commonly propagated as superior to the traditional trust-based model, namely the 'contractual model'. We hope to show that an exclusively contractual model is not feasible in the patient–physician relationship context. Moreover, like the measures taken to compensate for the loss of trust, the contractual model itself cannot entirely dispense with trust. We will end with the conclusion that, in the final analysis, trust is an inevitable part of the patient-physician relationship.

10.1   Advantages of Trusting

Just to show *that* trust is useful is not enough for a comprehensive analysis. We also have to specify *why* trust is useful. To show why trust is useful in the patient–physician relationship, we need to know what characterises the traditional patient–physician relationship. By 'traditional', we mean a relationship into which each partner enters with an open mind, i.e. without preconceived ideas of what exactly he wants and of how to proceed.[17] Once we have done this, we can analyse the role which trust plays in the relationship. Admittedly, the relationship between patient and physician is very complex, but *uncertainty* with regard to the physician's competence and disposition, *complexity* of medicine and medical decision-making, and *risk* are unquestionably decisive features of the patient–physician relationship. As should be obvious, these are exactly the type of features that figure prominently in our definition of trust. We will argue that trust is useful with regard to each of these features, (1) because it helps patients cope with uncertainty and risk and because it reduces the transaction costs caused by the inherent risk, (2) because it reduces uncertainty by inducing trustworthiness in physicians, and (3) because it reduces complexity.

(1) *Trust is useful because it helps the patient to cope with uncertainty and risk and reduces transaction costs.* Uncertainty and risk are common to human relationships. We can either accept them and learn to 'live with'

---

[17]   *Vide* the following example: When the patient enters the surgery, the physician starts the conversation with an open question, such as 'What brings you to me?' To this, the patient answers 'For a week or two I have had an earache which has been gradually getting worse.' From here on in the conversation continues in a non-predetermined way. Eventually, patient and physician will agree upon how to proceed. The alternative to this traditional model is the 'contractual model', in which a goal and a means of achieving that goal are agreed upon in advance. We will come to this in Section 10.3.

them or we can try to reduce them by checking information, seeking additional advice, monitoring behaviour, and occasionally even setting up legal safeguards. Setting up such a system of surveillance has its costs, which are usually referred to as 'transaction costs'.[18] According to our definition, trust implies the conscious acceptance of risk. This acceptance of risk has a double beneficial effect: it helps us to cope with the uncertainty (i.e. live with it), and it helps us to reduce the transaction costs by "refraining from taking precautions against an interaction partner, even when the other ... could act in a way that might seem to justify precautions".[19] A particularly good example of how trust helps us cope with uncertainty is the 'no alternative' situation that we discussed earlier.[20] In this situation, trust helps us conquer our fear, which is very often not a specific fear but rather the 'fear of the unknown', i.e. the uncertainty. Here is an example derived from one of the author's (M. W.'s) own experiences: "When I had to go to my first military training[21] (even though this was fifty years ago, I remember it vividly), I had no idea what to expect. I do not think that I was 'afraid' properly speaking, but I know that I was very tense. Knowing that some of my best friends would be in the same unit and trusting that they would help me if ever I got into any 'difficulties' (again, I had no idea what difficulties) helped me cope with this tension."

In other words, simply knowing that (whatever may happen) one will not be alone and that someone will help (if necessary) helps us cope with the unknown. To avoid any misunderstanding, trust does not 'spirit away' the uncertainty, but it helps us to live (i.e. to cope) with it. Coping strategies are very important not only in general life but especially in medicine. In particular, patients with chronic intractable disorders often have to learn to cope with their symptoms, and trust in their physician[22] is one means that may help them to do so.

(2) *Trust is useful because it induces trustworthiness.* Trust not only helps us cope with uncertainty and reduce transaction costs; it also effectively reduces the uncertainty regarding the physician's contingent behaviour by inducing trustworthiness in the physician. We have previously

---

[18] Cohen and Dienhart 2013, p. 5.
[19] Elster 2007, p. 344.
[20] See page 65.
[21] In Switzerland, military service is (at least on paper) mandatory for all male citizens.
[22] For example, just to have the physician's mobile phone number (and the permission to use it should a crisis come on) will help the patient with recurrent anxiety.

argued[23] that demonstrating one's trustworthiness induces trust. There is plenty of support for this view; for example, Mahatma Gandhi is usually credited for saying that 'trust begets trust', although the saying can be traced back to Plutarch,[24] and we think that instinctively most of us act accordingly; that is, we trust those who trust us.[25] Here, we argue that there is yet a third causative interaction between trust and trustworthiness: 'trust induces trustworthiness'. In other words, the fact that you trust me motivates me to deserve your trust.[26] We think that anyone who has children remembers situations when he or she demonstratively trusted the child, hoping that this would induce the child to honour one's trust (and behave trustworthily in a situation in which it might otherwise perhaps not have done so). Nickel has the following explanation for this observation:

> It seems clear that motivation through awareness of an obligation, or an obligation-ascription, may serve as an important part of the explanation why trust reinforces reliability in this way.[27]

This strategy of 'purposive trust' is also illustrated by the following quotation from a man who worked in an area (warfare) in which trust plays a very particular role:[28] "The chief lesson I have learned in a long life is that the only way to make a man trustworthy is to trust him; and the surest way to make him untrustworthy is to distrust him and show your distrust."

(3) *Trust is useful because it reduces complexity.* Complexity is a key feature of medicine and medical decision-making and no patient can even remotely hope to understand everything involved in making a diagnosis and deciding on an optimal treatment plan. In our initial

---

[23] See page 137 on 'purposive commitment'.

[24] "Trust begets trust, and love [begets] love" (Moralia, p. 79 in the translation by Shiletto AR, published in 1898 by Chiswick Press, available from www.gutenberg.org/files/23639/23639-h/23639-h.htm).

[25] In fact, Glaeser et al. have shown in a series of trust experiments (as far as this can be empirically measured) that those who trust are more likely to be themselves trustworthy than those who mistrust. In other words: "To determine whether someone is trustworthy, ask him if he trusts others" (Glaeser et al. 2000, p. 840).

[26] This is a view also shared by Pettit 1995, p. 216. We are aware that Kiyonari et al. have shown that trust does not seem to engender trustworthy behaviour (Kiyonari et al. 2006), but their experiments were one-shot trust games, whereas we are speaking of long-term relationships.

[27] Nickel 2007, p. 316.

[28] Henry L. Stimson was US Secretary of War from 1911 to 1913 and from 1940 to 1945, as well as Secretary of State from 1929 to 1933.

model case example, the patient with the pleomorphic adenoma is over-whelmed by a myriad of questions. What can it be? Do I have to be worried? Will it go away on its own or do I need treatment, etc.? Although the patient has a simple lump in front of her ear, she is baffled by the complexity of the problem. By trusting her physician, that is, by deferring to his authority, she reduces this complexity. To avoid any misunderstanding, as with uncertainty, trust does not actually reduce or even eliminate the complexity of the problem but it does make the situation appear to be less complex.

So far, we have supplied three reasons for the usefulness of trust: the help it offers the patient to cope with uncertainty, risk, and complexity, the reduction of transaction costs, and the fact that trust itself is a means of inducing trust. All these reasons directly bear upon specific features of our account of trust. Again, we see this as a positive feature of our account because, just as with explaining the decline of trust, existing definitions of 'trust' cannot explain its usefulness to the same degree as none of them refers to these issues. With an account of the usefulness of trust in place, we turn to look next at what happens if trust declines and we resort to mistrust.

10.2   Consequences of the Decline of Trust

Of course, we lose all the above-mentioned advantages of trust with the loss of trust, but we also want to argue that we lose considerably more than this utility. If trust declines, something else has to fill the vacuum created by this decline. Regulations, controls, and systems of stricter accountability are set up and procedural standards are introduced with the objective of reducing uncertainty and complexity, replacing or improving trustworthiness, and reducing the inevitable risk.[29] If these provisions were sufficient to compensate for the loss of trust then we would have no reason to be concerned about the decline of trust. However, we will argue that regulatory measures do not adequately compensate for the loss of trust[30] and, moreover, that they cannot do so without having to fall back on trust themselves.

Here is an illustration of what we are getting at. A few years ago, three pit-bull terriers (which were not on a leash) fatally injured a small child

---

[29] Manson and O'Neill 2007, p. 162; and Kohn 2008, p. 65.

[30] This is not in contradiction to the statement on page 176, where we argue that regulations and standardisations of medical education have improved the quality of health care. Regulations may increase quality, but this is not necessarily reflected in increased trust.

near Zurich. There was an outcry in the population and a call for better (i.e. more) regulations from politicians across all political parties. The consequence is that now *all* dog owners (not just the owners of combat dogs or other 'dangerous breeds') have to attend a four-hour theoretical course and then practical training amounting to at least four times 60 minutes.[31] Probably, the exercise does have positive effects, but we are afraid that it will not prevent irresponsible dog owners from letting their dangerous dogs off the leash. In other words, these regulations do not solve the problem. We still have to trust dog owners to behave responsibly. Here is a less polemical way of saying the same thing:

> Whenever anything goes wrong in society, we hear the same rhetoric: more transparency and stricter regulation. And the result as a rule is more formal procedures and additional chicaneries.[32]

This is exactly what happened in health care as well. Trust has been (and is still being) replaced by increased regulation, as well as by the development of procedural standards (at all levels, from local hospital to national health authorities)[33] based on encoded knowledge.[34] The proclaimed purpose of these regulations and standards is 'risk reduction'. Unfortunately, this is achieved (if it is achieved at all) at the price of increased costs and a lot of red tape, causing tremendous frustration.[35] An illustrative example, particularly in the present context, is the proliferation over the last few decades of ethics committees, not all of which seem to be concerned with actual ethical scrutiny lending itself to the advancement of (ethically) good conduct but, rather, with a 'going through the motions' of making sure that something has the committee's approval. De Vries and Kim are perhaps not far off the mark in this regard with their claim that "bioethics is a field born from *mis*trust".[36] We have already considered the problem of risk perception and risk reduction in Section 5.3. Suffice here to repeat that only if we know what the risk is, what the probability of its occurrence is, and how we can prevent it, do we have a chance of preventing it.[37]

---

[31] See: www.tierrecht.ch/hundehaltung.html.
[32] This is an abbreviated translation of "Läuft in der Wirtschaft oder in der Politik etwas grundsätzlich schief, erklingt immer die gleiche Remedurrhetorik: 'höhere Transparenz' und 'strengere Regulierung'. Und in aller Regel folgt ihr die immer gleiche Massnahme: formellere Verfahren mit zusätzlichen Schikanen" (Hirschi 2014, p. N4).
[33] Alaszewski and Brown 2007, p. 1.
[34] See page 192 for an explanation of the term 'encoded knowledge'.
[35] Wildavsky 1989, p. 4.
[36] De Vries and Kim 2008, p. 377, their emphasis.
[37] Wildavsky 1989, p. 5.

Otherwise, we are just falling into the trap of over-activism. Sending all dog-owners to dog training is a prime example of overreaction and does not prevent irresponsible owners of combat dogs to let their dog run loose.

To give some substance to these claims, we will consider four arguments why regulations (i.e. guidelines, controls, systems of stricter accountability, and procedural standards)[38] do not compensate for the loss of trust. These are: (1) regulations do not necessarily reduce uncertainty; (2) procedures take precedence over outcome; (3) trust is not made redundant but only transferred from first-order object to second-order object; and (4) an increase in ('objective') trustworthiness does not necessarily lead to an increase in trust but may even lead instead to a further loss of trust.

(1) *Regulations do not necessarily reduce uncertainty.* We previously discussed protocols, etc. from the physician's standpoint.[39] In particular, we argued that because of the increasing need to account for their actions and decisions, physicians shy away from taking responsibility by following external regulations such as protocols, guidelines, etc. Now let us turn to the standpoint of the patient or, more particularly, to the mistrusting patient. Very often, these patients are reassured if they are told that what they are recommended is based on accepted guidelines or hospital protocols. Not being familiar with such regulations and how they are generated, the patients will believe that the regulations remove uncertainty worries because they offer a reasonable certainty that they will receive the optimal treatment. However, this is (at least very often) an illusion. Only a minority of guidelines are based solely on high-level evidence (RCTs, etc.), simply because, very often, there is no such evidence. More commonly, they are based on uncontrolled studies or 'expert opinions'. And even in the case of guidelines based on high-level evidence, there remains the uncertainty whether they are useful for a given patient.[40] Lastly, it must be noted that often guidelines primarily serve to standardise procedures and to set minimal – rather than optimal – standards,[41] in which case following them strictly may well be inferior to what a competent physician has to offer.

---

[38] Of course, We are aware that 'protocols', 'recommendations', guidelines',' hospital standards', etc. are not the same. Here, we are using the term 'regulations' to include any external influence on the physicians' decision-making.

[39] See page 135.

[40] See page 191.

[41] M.W. has been involved in the development of guidelines for the management of head and neck cancer patients, which served exactly this purpose (Wolfensberger et al. 2002).

(2) *Procedures take precedence over outcome.* This reflects another problem with regulations in that, eventually, *the procedure,* i.e. 'how' something is achieved, *becomes more important than 'what' is achieved.*[42] This
manifests itself where people become more anxious to fulfil the regulations than to care for the outcome because, rather than being held
responsible for the outcomes, they are called to account for *"following
prescribed procedures".*[43] Litigation cases can also succeed or fail depending on whether the physician can document that he has followed the
required 'patient information protocol'.[44] Sadly enough, the 'quality
indicators' (so dear to managers) are more often than not chosen because
they are measurable and not because they truly reflect quality.[45]

(3) *Trust is not made redundant but only transferred from first-order
object to second-order object.* The belief that trust can be replaced by the
above-mentioned measures is a fallacy. In effect, *these measures simply
transfer trust* from a first-order object (e.g. physicians) to a second-order
object (e.g. those responsible for making or implementing the
regulations).[46] We doubt whether it is indeed preferable to trust the
'regulators' rather than the physicians themselves. Although this may
sound like a physician's bias, we think there are good arguments to
support this claim: first, we take it as reasonable to believe that doctors
have more incentive (are more motivated) to be trustworthy (and hence
trusted) than those who are responsible for any kind of regulations (be
they peer-groups, politicians, or hospital administrators), on the grounds
that physicians are in a direct relationship with (and personally answer-
able to) the patient, whereas regulators are much more removed and
hardly ever personally accountable. Second, we think it is ultimately

---

[42] Luhmann, cited in Hirschi 2014, p. N4. This is also something that was noted in the
Francis Report into failures of care at the Mid Staffordshire NHS Foundation Trust in the
United Kingdom. In the Report's opening letter to the Secretary of State, the chair of
the Public Inquiry, Sir Robert Francis QC, noted that there was "A culture focused on
doing the system's business – not that of the patients", and that the Trust's "failure was in
part the consequence of allowing a focus on reaching national access targets, achieving
financial balance and seeking foundation trust status to be at the cost of delivering
acceptable standards of care." Available at: http://www.midstaffspublicinquiry.com/
report.

[43] O'Neill 2002a, p. 132; emphasis in original.

[44] Just from personal experience, M.W. has been called in as an expert in several litigation
cases, in which this turned out to be the clinching factor.

[45] O'Neill 2002b, p. 54.

[46] Manson and O'Neill 2007, p. 162. This is also referred to as shift from the micro-level to
the macro-level by De Vries and Kim 2008, p. 378.

more beneficial to patients to have trustworthy doctors than to have trustworthy regulators. Although this might sound somewhat concerning, it is not meant to present the view that all regulators are inherently untrustworthy but, rather, that much of what patients might require from regulators can be captured in other ways, such as competence. Yet it remains extremely important that patients' doctors are trustworthy, as this cannot be replaced in any other way. Finally, regulations are general rules and may not always be applicable to individual patients, whereas the physician's decision always concerns his individual patient.[47]

(4) Finally, *regulations and controls are claimed (by those who set them up) to increase trustworthiness by reducing the risk of the trustee behaving untrustworthily.* Contrary to this, we claim that *they make trust redundant,* and that they themselves *in fact contribute to the erosion of trust.*[48] We have two arguments to underpin this claim. (1) If the other person (in this case your doctor) has no option to behave unprofessionally because he is so tightly reined in by rules and controls, you may not feel any need for trust. In such cases, trust becomes redundant and, for some people, the purpose of ever more regulations (the 'hidden agenda') is not to increase trust (as they claim) but precisely to make it redundant. Of course, this is what some people want. (2) Although there may be genuine positions based on views about the quality of explicit contracts that some people have argued might take the place of trust,[49] we are concerned that they ultimately do the patient a disservice. Regulations do not increase trust. Consider this: assume that you are faced with a serious diagnosis. Would you rather sit in consultation with a doctor who takes his time and the responsibility to explain and discuss the treatment options and to answer your questions, or a doctor who tells you 'that's what we will do; it's the rules'. Chances are that you lose whatever trust you had in your doctor before this type of encounter. We admit that this is a very simplified picture and, of course, there are intermediary scenarios that might make your response less clear. Nevertheless, we know from experience

---

[47] Although there may be some exceptions to this, such as decisions about public health concerns, where there may be an overriding reason to consider the welfare of entire groups of patients at a time. This sort of situation, however, is far from a standard patient–physician relationship.

[48] A position also considered by Smith 2005, p. 305.

[49] For example, Alan Buchanan, who favours a contractual patient–physician relationship model over one based on trust (Buchanan 1988). See further also our discussion in Section 10.3.

that some doctors may take the opportunity to eschew the personal responsibility of decision-making and hide behind imposed rules.[50]

To sum up, the measures used to compensate for the vacuum created by the decline of trust do not adequately compensate for the loss of trust: first, because they do not reduce uncertainty; second, because procedures often take precedence over outcome; third, because trust is not made redundant but only transferred from first-order object to second-order object; and fourth, because an increase in ('objective') trustworthiness does not necessarily lead to an increase in trust but may even lead to an erosion of trust. It follows that we cannot do entirely without trust, unless (and this is important) there is an alternative model of the patient–physician relationship that is superior to the one based on trust. The only candidate for such a model that has been offered and discussed in the literature is the 'contractual model',[51] which we will discuss in the next section.

10.3 The Contractual Model as Alternative to the Trust-Based Model

Before we move on to discuss the contractual model, let us briefly reiterate the key features (or perhaps we should say, the key problems) of the patient–physician relationship: asymmetry with regard to knowledge and skills, uncertainty with regard to the physician's behaviour, and agent risk as well as agent costs.[52] In the previous section, we argued that trust is valuable as a way of coping with these problems. Yet, even if trust is valuable it may not always be the best possible option. Per our definition, to trust means to take a risk, and this risk may be too big. Too much (or poorly placed) trust may even be detrimental. So, for a fair assessment of the value of trust, we must balance its advantages with its downsides, and since *il meglio è nemico del bene*[53] we must make sure that there is no better alternative.

---

[50] This has been the practice experience of M.W. See also page 154 for a detailed discussion of the difference between accountability and responsibility.

[51] This is not to be confused with a 'regulatory model'. In the 'regulatory model' (which we have discussed in the previous section), regulations are imposed from outside, whereas in the 'contractual model', a spelt-out agreement is set up jointly by patient and physician.

[52] See page 148.

[53] 'Better is the enemy of good' which is historically an Italian proverb but is usually attributed to Voltaire, who used it in the first stanza of his 'Conte Moral' *La Bégueule* (1772) and in the second volume of his *Dictionnaire Philosophique* (1764).

Buchanan (among others) argues strongly in favour of basing the patient–physician relationship on a 'principal/agent' (i.e. contractual) model rather than on the traditional trust-based model.[54] Very briefly, what a principal/agent relationship amounts to is the following: a principal (in this case, the patient) commissions an agent (here, a physician) to render a certain service, which the agent then provides. So far, this hardly differs from a trust-based relationship. There is the same asymmetry between the two sides and the principal is at the same disadvantage as regards assessing the agent and monitoring the progress of the commissioned service. So, we might ask, what is the advantage of setting up a contract?[55] We think that (at least in theory) the main advantage of a contract is that it reduces (a certain type of) uncertainty and the thereof resulting risk by spelling out goals as well as standards and limits that will apply. Moreover, contracts are (again, in principle, but not necessarily in reality) enforceable, which gives the principal a certain feeling of security. Despite these undisputed advantages, we will present four arguments why we believe that contracts may complement, but cannot replace, trust, as follows: (1) to set up a contract, the goal, and the means to be used to achieve this goal, must be known in advance. This is not usually feasible in the patient–physician relationship, because the patient–physician relationship is characterised by contingency and is far too complex to be accommodated by a contract. (2) Somewhat paradoxically, the principal/agent model 'reduces the agency of the agent' and leads to 'ethical minimalism'. (3) The contractual model neglects important emotional aspects of the patient–physician relationship and (because the agent can unilaterally terminate the contract) increases the patient's anxiety. (4) The contractual model further reduces trust and (like regulations and controls) ultimately transfers trust from a first-order to a second-order object.

(1) According to Quill, a contract is defined as an "explicit bilateral commitment to a well-defined course of action".[56] This implies that *to*

---

[54] Buchanan 1988, pp. 321–2.

[55] To avoid any misunderstanding: by 'contract' we mean a spelt-out advance agreement, which specifies the main points of the commission and establishes "monitoring and regulating bodies, managing litigation and maintaining a legal framework that is concerned with specifying conditions for co-operation and responding to breaches of the agreement" (Smith 2005, p. 302). Agreements, which are reached interactively in the process of shared decision-making and informed consent and during the therapeutic relationship, are not contracts under this definition.

[56] Quill 1983, p. 228.

set up a contract "both a goal and the means of achieving this goal are agreed on in advance".[57] This, in turn, presupposes that the goal and the means to achieve this goal are known. Here is an example from outside medicine. Assume you commission an architect to design and build a house for you. Even if you have no clear-cut idea what type of house exactly you want, you will have some starting points, such as the number of rooms, the style of the house, etc. Given this, the architect will then start designing, and through various stages, i.e. in an iterative process, you will eventually reach the point at which you will say 'this is the house I want you to build'. Maybe you had a preliminary contract for this planning phase. But even if you did not, there was not much need for you to trust the architect, because you were monitoring the process as it went on and could have stopped it at any stage (at comparatively little loss). Yet before you commission the architect to do all the fine planning and to actually build the house, you will certainly want to set up a contract, detailing among other things price, quality standards, materials to be used, time frame, as well as what happens if he fails to deliver to your satisfaction and on time. Of course, despite the best possible contract, the architect may (try to) cheat you without your being able to detect it, for example, by buying and using cheaper materials than he said he would use. So, you will still have to trust him to some, albeit perhaps lesser, extent. In other words, the contract may reduce the need for trust but it cannot fully eliminate it. Of course, one may argue that contracts are legally binding and that they can be legally enforced. Yet again, you will have to trust those who have to enforce the contract.

With this architectural example in place, let us return to medicine. Assume that for several weeks you have had a headache. You eventually decide to see a doctor with a clear goal in mind: to get rid of the headache. Unfortunately, headache is not a disease but a symptom. Moreover, it is a symptom that may be caused by just about anything which is wrong inside (or even outside) your head (that is why 'headache' is often referred to as a physician's 'pain in the neck'). Unfortunately, 'God has put the diagnosis before the treatment'.[58] So, before the doctor can even consider treating your headache, he must try to find the underlying diagnosis. In most cases, this means stepwise ruling out possible causes, and so on. We do not think that we have to continue this description. In

---

[57] Quill 1983, p. 229, our emphasis.

[58] The deep meaning of this maxim is that one should only treat symptoms if a competent search for a diagnosis has failed. Sadly enough, this maxim is all too often not heeded.

most cases, *the patient–physician interaction is too complex and too contingent to be easily accommodated by a contract.* 'Advanced healthcare directives' offer a good example: except perhaps for 'do not resuscitate', most stipulated patient's wishes are open to different interpretations[59] and, because advance directives cannot specify every possible contingency, they cannot supplant trust in whoever has to act on these directives.[60] This is not to say that contracts can play no role in the patient–physician relationship. They can supplement trust, but they cannot make trust completely redundant.

(2) A major difference between the trust-based and the contract-based model concerns the *commitment of the agent.* The difference is this. Whereas in the former, the physician has the ethical duty to put the patient's interest above his own and, moreover, is expected 'to go the extra mile' for his patient, in the latter each is (as per contract) entitled to have his own interest at heart, to promote his own interests, and to limit his engagement to what he is required to do by the contract.[61] It is in this regard that Pellegrino aptly talks of the *'ethical minimalism'* of legalistic or contractual relationships.[62] In Section 12.4, we will argue that one of the reasons for the decline of trust is that patients fear that physicians increasingly adopt a business attitude, caring more for their own (pecuniary) advantage than for the patient's benefit. We believe that relying too much on trying to regulate everything with a contract will only increase this 'business attitude'. It is therefore not in the patients' interest to seek to adopt a purely contractual model.

(3) Following on from our second argument, we think that most patients and physicians will agree that the relationship between patient and physician is not purely a 'business relationship' but has an (conscious or unconscious) *emotional component.* This component cannot be taken care of by a contractual arrangement. It may develop over time (much as trust may develop over time, even in a contractual relationship), but it does so despite the contractual nature of the relationship rather than thanks to the contract. Moreover, there is a major difference between the

---

[59] This is borne out by both authors: in M.W.'s experience as a surgeon and as head of the clinical ethics consultation team at his hospital in Basel this has often proved to be the case. It has also been discussed at length by, among others, A.W. in Wrigley 2007a; Wrigley 2007b.

[60] Pellegrino 1991, p. 75.

[61] Buchanan 1988, p. 322.

[62] Pellegrino 1991, p. 79.

trust-based and the contractual model regarding the *possibility of terminating the relationship*. Whereas a traditional patient–physician relationship cannot (with possibly few exceptions)[63] be unilaterally terminated by the physician, a contract can be terminated by either side on the 'exit conditions' fixed in the contract. Since it is of great importance for the patient to be sure that the physician will stand by him and will not abandon him, this is a vital disadvantage of the contractual model.

(4) Recall that, in the previous section, we argued that regulations and controls do not increase trust, and that knowing that compliance can be enforced by a contract also does not increase trust. In fact, the ultimate upshot of a purely contractual approach means that "if there is no opportunity for one partner to deceive the other there is no need for trust to develop".[64] Therefore, at best, contractual agreements may increase confidence but what they cannot do is increase trust.[65] The same applies to ombudsmen or similar arbitrators, who are purportedly "appointed with the goal of monitoring physicians' behaviour and thereby increasing trust".[66] Moreover, like regulations, contracts *simply transfer trust from first-order to second-order objects* (i.e. from the physician to those who set up and enforce contracts). So, we are left with the paradox that "elaborate measures to ensure that people keep agreements and do not betray trust must, in the end, be backed by trust".[67]

Again, we had better place our trust in physicians rather than in those who set up and enforce contracts, because the former have a personal interest in being trusted, whereas the latter have not (or at least less so).[68]

10.4 Summary and Conclusions

We do not believe that the contractual model is superior to the traditional trust-based model of the patient–physician relationship. To avoid any misunderstanding, we are not claiming that contracts play no role (or even that they cannot play a role) in health care. In fact, to draw on but one example, when patients are admitted to the University Hospital of Basel, they sign a form which outlines their rights (as well as their duties)

---

[63] For example, if a patient makes demands that are clearly outside the physician's duty.
[64] Barrera 2007, p. 509.
[65] Seligman (1997), cited in Harrison and Smith 2004, p. 377.
[66] Pellegrino 1991, p. 70.
[67] O'Neill 2002b, p. 6.
[68] For our arguments as to why we believe that this is so, see page 154.

during their stay. This may well be considered a (albeit subsidiary) contract. However, its purpose is to assure the patient that he is not entering a 'legal vacuum', where he would never get any legal protection (if need be), rather than to replace trust. Moreover, it refers primarily to procedural aspects rather than to the patient–physician relationship properly speaking. In this sense (or situation), we agree that contract and trust can *coexist* and may even complement each other. To be absolutely clear, our claim is that contracts cannot *replace* trust in the patient–physician relationship.

Trust is useful because it helps patients cope with uncertainty and risk, because it reduces the transaction costs caused by the inherent risk, because it induces trustworthiness in physicians, and because it reduces (apparent) complexity. Moreover, because neither regulations and controls nor contracts can compensate for the loss of trust or replace trust in the patient–physician relationship, trust is, in the final analysis, inevitable.

11

The Moral Value of Trust

Now that we have established the instrumental usefulness of trust, we come to our second claim regarding the value of trust, namely that trust is a moral notion and that it is the moral significance of trust which makes its loss particularly serious. We are well aware that this is a difficult and potentially contentious claim, since, as Lagerspetz and Hertzberg put it, "mainstream theorists invariably adopt an instrumental [i.e. non-moral] perspective [of trust]".[1] Or, as Hardin argues, "trust might be fully explicable as ... a product of rational expectation without any moral residue. I treat trust as an un-moralised notion."[2] To avoid any misunderstanding, we do not claim that we have a moral duty to trust.[3] All we claim is that trust is a moral good, analogous, for example, to friendship.[4] Moreover, we think that it would clarify matters if we did not use the term 'trust' for expectations or beliefs we may have regarding others, which do not pertain to morality.

To support our claim, we will present two arguments: the first argument is indirect; it refers to the contention, already presented in Section 5.5, that the feeling of betrayal caused by a breach of trust is a reactive attitude that is justified only in the case of moral issues. The second argument purports that the truster's belief in a moral obligation of the

---

[1] Lagerspetz and Hertzberg 2013, p. 42, our insertions.

[2] Hardin 1996, p. 28.

[3] Even a discussion of (let alone giving an answer to) the question whether we have a moral duty to trust would be way beyond the scope of this book. It would, however be interesting to discuss this in further work.

[4] There have been numerous philosophical discussions of the moral value of friendship, made famous by Aristotle's discussion of different kinds of friendship in his Nicomachean Ethics, but with plenty of contemporary discussion (see, for example, Blum 1980 and Badhwar 1993). There have even been discussions of the direct connection between trust and friendship (see Alfano 2016).

trustee to be trustworthy can be justified. To do this, we will have recourse to what Nickels calls the 'obligation-ascription thesis'.[5]

11.1 Feeling of Betrayal Implies that Trust Is a Moral Concept

In Section 5.5 we argued that we have to distinguish between non-moral and moral expectations, and that only in the case of a moral expectation (such as trust) are we entitled to react to the non-fulfilment of our expectation with a feeling of betrayal.

The following example will help us explain the difference between what we call non-moral[6] and moral expectations (such as trust). Assume that you agree to lend us £10,000 under the condition that we return the loan within a month. Of course, you would not do so unless you had reason to believe that we will return the money. This belief may take two forms: (a) the belief that *we will return* the money or (b) the belief that *we ought to* return the money (i.e. that we have a moral obligation to return the money). Here is to what the first belief amounts: if you have good reasons to believe that we *will* return the money, your expectation is purely instrumental. Your belief is that you "simply believe there is a high probability that the expected will occur".[7] This is a case of a 'non-moral'[8] expectation. If the expected does not occur (i.e. if your belief that we will return the money was mistaken), you can only blame yourself for the bad judgement that led to the formation of the belief in the first place. Luhmann calls this 'internal attribution'.[9] Consequently, you can feel disappointed but you cannot feel betrayed (because it is not our fault). Alternatively, here is to what the second belief amounts: if you expect us to return the money because you believe that we have a *moral obligation* to do so, this is a case of a 'moral expectation'. If we do not return the loan, the blame, ceteris paribus, shifts to us.[10] Luhmann calls this 'external attribution'.[11] In this case, you feel betrayed. And you are entitled to feel betrayed because we did not fulfil our moral obligation. Whereas in the first case, you have made an error of judgement, in the second case *we*

---

[5] Nickel 2007, p. 309.
[6] To avoid any confusion with 'amoral' and 'unmoral' we will use the term 'non-moral' to refer to the absence of any moral connotation of a term.
[7] Wallace 2008, p. 158.
[8] Hollis 1998, p. 11, and Cohen and Dienhart 2013, p. 1, call this 'non-moral trust'. However, we prefer not to use this term because it unnecessarily confuses the issue.
[9] Luhmann 2000, pp. 97–8.
[10] Of course, this is only true if your belief that we had a moral obligation was justified.
[11] Luhmann 2000, pp. 97–8.

have let you down. Crucially, for our purposes, trust is just such a case of a 'moral expectation'.

Of course, the same can be applied to the patient–physician relationship. Assume that a patient (thinks she) has reason to believe that her physician is 'a good doctor' (perhaps because he has repeatedly appeared on television or in the tabloid press).[12] If the physician fails to meet her expectations, the patient may be disappointed but she can only blame herself (and maybe she will revise her view of the value of television appearances as a quality indicator). If, however, the patient believes that the doctor has a moral duty to treat her competently and to be committed to her interests (in short, to be trustworthy), i.e. if she trusts him, she will justifiably feel betrayed if her trust is breached. To her, it will be as if the physician had promised her something and then broken this promise.

Obviously, there appears to be a relationship between trust and betrayal. We are not alone in considering that 'trust' and 'betrayal' belong together. As Lagerspetz and Hertzberg put it:[13] "By invoking the language of trust and betrayal, we do not simply identify facts, possibilities, or risks that exist 'out there'. Instead, we take up a certain perspective... this perspective is an ethical one."[14]

In other words, you feel betrayed if someone does not keep a promise, if he lies, etc. (which are moral concepts), but not if he shows up late (showing up late is not a moral concept, unless he has promised to be on time). Whereas we merely feel disappointed or perhaps annoyed if a non-moral expectation is not met, we are justified to feel betrayed or resentful if a moral expectation is not fulfilled. In the words of Baier, "it is uncontroversial that the betrayal of trust ... is a grave moral wrong".[15] From the fact that a breach of trust results in a feeling of betrayal we derive that trust is a moral notion.

This inference might meet with some surprise; after all, why should a feeling signify that something is a moral issue rather than a non-moral one? Such a question has played a hugely important role in meta-ethical debates concerning emotivist and other non-cognitive approaches to moral judgements.[16] We do not intend to engage in any depth with

---

[12] The implicit cynicism is intended but nothing more should be read into the choice of example!

[13] Lagerspetz and Hertzberg 2013, p. 37.

[14] Lagerspetz and Hertzberg 2013, p. 39.

[15] Baier 1994, p. 245.

[16] Meta-ethics is the area of philosophy that considers the foundations of ethics and morality. Non-cognitivist meta-ethical positions (also sometimes called 'anti-realist'

such meta-ethical debates but recognise the need to support our position given the emphasis we place on the feeling of betrayal when it comes to treating 'trust' as a moral concept. We will do this by appeal to *reactive* attitudes. In doing so, we are not making a non-cognitivist meta-ethical claim that moral judgements are reducible to or identical with expressions of our emotions, such as emotivists do. Instead, we are endorsing the view that certain kinds of feeling are associated with moral judgements in a particular kind of way that we would not experience if it concerned a non-moral matter, but that this does not imply that we need be non-cognitivists about morals.

The feelings of betrayal and resentment are often referred to as *reactive attitudes*. For us, as for Ruokonen, the fact that we respond to a breach of trust with a 'reactive attitude', such as betrayal, shows that we take the trustee first and foremost to be a responsible (i.e. autonomous, rational, and reflective) agent and therefore subject to moral evaluation, so implying that trust is a moral concept.[17] However, to some people our resorting to a reactive attitude to justify the moral significance of trust may seem dubious. Reactive attitudes are emotions, and as such are 'philosophically problematic', because much of the pertinent discussion on reactive attitudes refers to the moral value of 'disgust' (often referred to as the 'appeal to disgust' or, more casually, the 'yuck factor').[18] So, if we want to support our claim that the feeling of betrayal proves the morality of 'trust', we will have to 'rehabilitate' reactive attitudes. To do this, we will present three arguments: (1) we will show that there is a significant difference between general (i.e. non-relational) reactive attitudes and relational ones. (2) We will argue that reactive attitudes are a vital part of our everyday life. And

---

positions) deny that moral claims are truth-apt and also hold that moral judgements do not express cognitive states of mind, such as beliefs. Instead, they view moral claims as expressing non-cognitive attitudes similar to desires or states of approval or disapproval. Cognitivist (or 'realist') meta-ethical positions deny these non-cognitivist views and instead consider moral claims to be truth-apt and moral judgements to be beliefs. Probably the most famous account of non-cognitivism is the emotivist position that takes moral judgements as not expressing beliefs but emotions or sentiments instead (see Ayer 1936 for an early account of emotivism). Anyone interested in the meta-ethical debates underpinning such questions should read Miller 2003.

[17] Ruokonen 2013, p. 10.

[18] Since (as we will show) we do not use the term 'reactive attitude' in this sense, we will not discuss it any further. For a defence of the position that "there are indeed situations, in which properly directed disgust is indispensable to a morally accurate perception at what is at stake in the law", see Kahan 1999, p. 63. For a good refutation of the position that disgust is suited to do moral work, the interested reader is referred to Kelly and Morar 2014.

(3) we will analyse how non-moral reactive attitudes are distinguished from moral ones and show that resentment and betrayal are genuine moral reactive attitudes.

(1) Let us start with the *difference between non-relational (or general) reactive attitudes and relational reactive attitudes*. Assume that you experience a feeling of disgust at the thought of cloning humans.[19] This reactive attitude is clearly non-relational. This holds true even if you are disgusted with a scientist friend who has declared his intention of cloning humans because your disgust is still caused by the idea of cloning itself and not by your friend's behaviour towards you. When Strawson coined the term 'reactive attitude' in 1962, he had a particular conception in mind that was different from the non-relational one:

> I want to speak . . . of the non-detached attitudes and reactions of *people directly involved* in transactions with each other; . . . of the attitudes and reactions of offended parties, of such things as . . . resentment . . . and hurt feelings.[20]

Contrary to the reactive attitudes of the disgust type, this type of reactive attitude is relational. We hold that the feeling of betrayal caused by a breach of trust belongs to this (relational) type of reactive attitudes: it can only arise within the relationship of the truster and the trustee. It is caused by the other's behaviour towards me.

(2) Most people will probably agree that our *(reactive) attitudes toward one another are a vital part of our everyday life*,[21] and that this (relational) type of reactive attitude "cannot be eliminated altogether, because doing so would involve exiting interpersonal relationships altogether".[22] Just imagine *Don Giovanni* without Donna Anna, Donna Elvira et al. giving vent to their feelings (i.e. 'reactive attitudes') regarding Don Giovanni's immoral behaviour; or, better still, imagine what would happen if everybody behaved like Don Giovanni and nobody reacted to it.

(3) At the beginning of this section, we argued that we feel betrayed if someone does not keep a promise but only feel annoyed if he shows up late, and, furthermore, we have claimed that the reactions differ because the first is a moral expectation, whereas the second is a non-moral one.

---

[19] The example is taken from Kass 1997.
[20] Strawson 1962, p. 5, our emphasis.
[21] Hildebrand 2013, p. 1.
[22] Goldman 2014, p. 1.

So, in our view, there are both moral and non-moral reactive attitudes. Yet, so far, we have not provided any support for this claim. In order to do so, to explain how we can *distinguish moral from non-moral reactive attitudes,* we must first turn to a quotation from Rawls:

> In general, it is a necessary feature of moral feelings, and part of what distinguishes them from the natural [i.e. non-moral] attitudes, that the person's explanation of his experience invokes a moral concept and its associated principles. His account of his feeling makes reference to an acknowledged right or wrong.[23]

In other words, our feeling of annoyance if someone shows up late is non-moral because 'being late' does not refer to an accepted moral concept of right and wrong. Contrary to this, the feelings of guilt, shame, resentment, indignation, etc. are all caused by a transgression of moral principles.[24] This implies not only that we can distinguish 'moral' from 'non-moral' reactive attitudes but also that 'trust' is a moral concept, because we react[25] to it with a feeling (i.e. a reactive attitude) of resentment (or betrayal).[26]

With these three arguments (conceiving reactive attitudes as relational, reactive attitudes being inescapable, and defining reactive attitudes as moral if they refer to an underlying moral concept), we hope to have effectively countered objections raised against the use of reactive attitudes to show that trust is a moral notion.[27]

We admit, however, that the reactive attitude of betrayal may be a rather trivial indicator of the morality of trust. Moreover, we agree with Nickel that "there is something dissatisfying about a proof which draws on a secondary, reactive attitude, such as betrayal, resentment, disappointment".[28] It would be much more satisfying to be able to establish that the 'belief in a moral duty to be trustworthy' is justified. As such, this is precisely what we intend to do in the next section.

---

[23] Rawls 1971, p. 421, our insertion.

[24] Rawls 1971, p. 424.

[25] Crucially, we all consistently react this way. If someone does not react this way, this shows that he did not trust, rather than that trust is not a moral concept.

[26] We use the term 'betrayal' rather than 'resentment', because most authors use this term in the context of trust (e.g. Baier 1994; Lagerspetz and Hertzberg 2013). Yet, 'betrayal' could always be replaced by 'resentment'.

[27] We admit, however, that not everyone agrees with this: Wallace, e.g. argues that Rawls' approach excessively moralises the concept of 'reactive attitudes' (Wallace 2008, p. 158).

[28] Nickel 2007, p. 318.

11.2   Justification of the Belief in a Moral Obligation to Be Trustworthy

In the introduction to this chapter, we argued that trust is a moral concept if it is based on the belief that the trustee *has an obligation to do* what the truster expects him to do, rather than on the belief that he *will do* what the truster expects him to do, provided (and this is important) that this belief is justified. There are two arguments that have been put forward to account for why such a belief is, indeed, justified: one refers to *general morality or socially accepted norms* of behaviour; it posits a general moral duty to be trustworthy. The other relates to the concept of trust as *'obligation-ascription'*.

Let us start by examining the first argument: the *claim there is a general moral duty to be trustworthy* (i.e. to do what we are trusted to do), where 'moral' may refer to 'universal reasons for action' as well as to 'local reasons embodied in social norms'.[29] Typically, we spell out moral concepts by couching them in terms of moral rules or commands, such as 'do not lie' for 'honesty' or 'do not harm others' for 'non-maleficence'. The answer to the sceptic's query why he should be honest or refrain from harming others is that 'reasonable people' (or people in the Rawlsian 'original position'[30]) would agree to do so. Of course, the same answer could be given to the question why one should be trustworthy. Intuitively this sounds reasonable. Yet there is a snag with this argument. Let us look at three typical trust situations. (a) Patient 'A' trusts his physician to be honest. (b) Patient 'B' trusts his physician to call him as soon as he has the results from the biopsy. And (c) patient 'C' trusts his physician to assist him in committing suicide. So, what is the difference? In the first case, trust refers to something that is generally considered morally right. In the second case, trust refers to something that is ceteris paribus morally neither right nor wrong. And in the third case, trust refers to something that many people (and societies more broadly) consider immoral. Of these three trust situations, the appeal to a 'general moral duty to do what we are trusted to do' applies only to the first case. There is no reason why we should have a moral duty to do something which is morally irrelevant or even (potentially) morally reprehensible. Consequently, the appeal to general morality is insufficient to justify our belief that the trustee has a moral duty to do as expected in all cases of trust. What we want is

---

[29] Hollis 1998, p. 11.
[30] Rawls 1971, p. 11.

a justification of the belief that the trustee has an obligation to be trustworthy irrespective of what the truster trusts the trustee to do.

The concept of *trust as obligation-ascription,* proposed by Cohen and Dienhart, offers such a justification. On this account, the duty to be trustworthy is derived from an *invitation to acknowledge an obligation:*[31]

> When A trusts B to do x, A invites B to acknowledge and accept an obligation to do x. When – or if – B accepts the invitation, B takes on that obligation. In that way trust creates an obligation and forms a trust relationship.[32]

Here is an example to help explain what this means. A patient offers you her trust and invites you to acknowledge and accept an obligation to be trustworthy. Unlike a moral duty to be trustworthy that is grounded in 'universal reasons for action' or 'local reasons embodied in social norms',[33] this conception of trust as a form of 'moral contract' does not depend on what we expect the trustee to do. If you acknowledge and accept the obligation to be trustworthy (in return for the patient's trust), you impose the obligation to be trustworthy upon yourself. If, in return for the patient's trust, you accept her invitation (i.e. acknowledge the obligation) to be trustworthy and then fail to fulfil this obligation (without a good or overriding reason), you thereby commit a serious moral wrong. And, since you, as trustee, have accepted the obligation to do x, it does not matter what x is. In other words, this account of the obligation to be trustworthy applies to all three examples mentioned above. Obviously, in most instances the offer and the acceptance of trust are implicit. However, we do not think that this invalidates the argument. Every physician starts from the premise that a patient who consults him is, in principle, willing to trust him and hence expects the physician to accept his offer of trust. It is important, however, that the trustee is aware of the obligation he has accepted, i.e. what exactly he is expected to do.[34]

So, to sum up, we have argued that trust is a moral good because a breach of trust leads to a feeling of resentment or betrayal. Such feelings are understood as reactive attitudes, which are only warranted in cases pertaining to morality, and arise because the belief in a moral obligation of the trustee can be justified by the concept of obligation-ascription.

---

[31] As Cohen and Dienhart acknowledge, their account is similar to Nickel's 'obligation-ascription thesis' (Nickel 2007, p. 309).

[32] Cohen and Dienhart 2013, p. 1.

[33] Hollis 1998, p. 11.

[34] See page 46.

11.3   Summary and Conclusions

Whereas most people agree that trust has an instrumental value, there is a considerable debate about whether trust is a moral notion and hence is of moral significance. To defend our position that trust is morally significant we have presented two arguments. (1) A breach of trust typically leads to a feeling of betrayal, a reactive attitude, which is only warranted in cases pertaining to morality. And, (2) the argument that the belief in a moral obligation of the trustee can be justified by the concept of obligation-ascription.

PART V

The Decline of Trust

12

Reasons for the Decline of Trust

Now that we have a solid conceptual foundation, know how trust is justified, and have established the significance of trust, we wish to finish off our discussion of trust in the field of medicine and health care with its particular emphasis on the physician–patient relationship by considering the important practical question of trying to explain why trust has declined. In this chapter, what we hope to show is that from our account of trust we can explain this decline. Then, in our final chapter, we will go on to analyse how the understanding we have gained in this chapter about the decline of trust can also help us answer the question of how trust may be regained.

We will argue that the following five developments, which all have occurred in society and in health care over the past decades, are primarily responsible for the decline of trust:[1]

(1) The discrediting of professionalism
(2) The insistence on (and difficulty of) assessing physicians' trustworthiness
(3) The disavowal of the basic tenets of scientific medicine
(4) The commodification of medicine and the re-conceptualisation of physicians as dependent employees
(5) Changes of risk perception and risk acceptance

While we recognise there are limits to the amount of detail and support we can lend to both establishing these as genuine phenomena and to linking them to a decline in trust, we hope to be able to offer some convincing argument and indicate where any further investigation might be warranted. In particular, we will argue as follows: first, the discrediting

---

[1] Of course, there may other reasons as well, but we believe that these are the most important ones.

of professionalism leads to a loss of 'professional authority' and a decline of 'status-based trust' because it impairs the justification of trust and, hence, unless it is compensated for by an increase in 'merit-based authority' and 'merit trust' (i.e. trust based on perceived trustworthiness), leads to an overall decline of trust. Second, since trustworthiness is difficult to assess, the sort of compensation needed is often insufficient to prevent an overall decline of trust. Third, the disavowal of the basic tenets of scientific medicine undermines physicians' 'medical authority',[2] again leading to a decline of trust. Fourth, the commodification of medicine leads to a decline of trust partly because patients doubt physicians' commitment and partly because it is perceived to compromise physicians' 'directive authority' (i.e. their independence of decision-making). Finally, fifth, the increase of risk sensibility and the decrease of the preparedness to accept risks cause a decline of trust because people are less willing to accept trust-inherent risk. The first four of the explanations refer to the loss of (different types of) physicians' authority, while the fifth concerns what O'Neill aptly calls an "unrealistic hankering for a world, in which safety and compliance are total".[3]

As we have shown previously, common definitions of 'trust' (such as 'trust means expecting caring, honesty, or responsiveness', 'the trustee will act in the truster's interest or act as the truster's agent',[4] or 'individuals and institutions will meet their responsibilities to us')[5] all refer solely to the trustee's commitment or agency and neglect important features of trust, such as competence, the fact that trust has to be justified, and the fact that trust always implies risk. Consequently, such definitions can only explain why the commodification of medicine and the re-conceptualisation of physicians as dependent employees (with the resulting doubt about the physicians' commitment to their patients) can lead to a loss of trust. They cannot, however, explain why the discrediting of professionalism, the insistence on (and difficulty of) assessing physicians' trustworthiness, the disavowal of the basic tenets of scientific medicine (all of which undermine the possibility to justify one's trust), and changes of risk perception and risk acceptance should

---

[2] For a discussion of the difference between 'professional authority' and 'medical authority', see page 188.

[3] O'Neill 2002b, p. 19.

[4] This is also true for Hardin's 'encapsulated interest' theory of trust i.e. 'trust means that my interests are encapsulated in your interest' (Hardin 2002, pp. 3ff).

[5] For more examples as well as for the references for these definitions, see pages 23ff.

lead to a decline of trust.[6] This is insufficient. What we want is a definition of 'trust' which has the necessary explanatory power to help us understand why any (or in fact all) of the five afore mentioned recent developments in society and health care can be held responsible for the decline of trust. Therefore, apart from identifying the reason for the decline of trust, this chapter also serves to demonstrate that (contrary to the above-mentioned definitions) our definition of 'trust' is indeed able to explain the decline of trust and, thereby, that it offers a significant contribution to the ongoing debate about trust in the patient–physician relationship.

Just as a reminder, here is a summary of our definition of 'trust': (a) trust is an expectation regarding the competence and commitment of the trustee; (b) this expectation must be realistic[7] and (c) justified; (d) trust presupposes a situation of uncertainty and risk; (e) trust is a free choice and implies the conscious acceptance of the trust-inherent risk;[8] (f) a breach of trust causes a feeling of betrayal on the part of the truster; and finally (g) trust refers to a relationship between competent and autonomous agents. In this definition, anything that negatively affects the perception of physicians' competence or commitment (his trustworthiness), as well as anything that negatively affects the willingness to accept risks, will cause a decline of trust. Hence, if you do not believe that someone is competent and/or committed, you will not trust him. If you do not feel that your trust is justified, you will not trust. Nor will you trust if you are not willing to accept the trust-inherent risk.

Before we individually address the five explanations for the decline of trust in separate sections, we want to briefly offer some reasons why we reject three alternative explanations that would seem to provide easy answers to the question of the decline in trust. These are (1) the allegation that the decline of trust is caused by an objective overall deterioration of the quality of health care, (2) the claim that the changes in the patient–physician relationship (such as we described in the two case histories at the very beginning of the book)[9] reflect the changed self-perception of today's patients rather than a decline of trust, and (3) the suggestion that what we call a loss of trust is, in fact, a loss of faith in physicians.

---

[6] In other words, these definitions lack what we have called the 'explanatory power' (see page 23).

[7] For details, see page 47 (trust presupposes capability).

[8] For details, see page 86.

[9] See pages 4ff.

The first of these alternative explanations is the assumption that *physicians (or the healthcare system in general) are no longer as 'good' as they used to be*. This would be the simplest explanation for the decline of trust in physicians. Of course, the physician's (in the case of the authors, only one of whom is a physician, this would be M.W.'s) ego baulks at this thought. But quite apart from any personal feelings, we think that there are two good arguments against this assumption. First, taking into account how highly regulated and standardised medical training, life-long continuing education, and practice are today, it is unlikely that the overall quality of performance has indeed declined. In fact, it is much more reasonable to assume that the quality has improved. Second, the loss of confidence is not limited to medicine. It similarly affects most other social institutions (such as Higher Education, the Church, and the Supreme Court), with the exception of those institutions that never enjoyed much confidence to begin with (such as the press).[10] A decline of trust in so many different social institutions is highly unlikely to be due to a simultaneous deterioration of performance in every area, even if this were not already made an untenable position by reflection upon advances in training, education, and practice. So, simply on the grounds of prob-ability alone, we think there must be another reason (or several other reasons) that involves "something beyond the level of performance".[11]

The *self-perception of patients* has unquestionably (and, we might add, fortunately) changed greatly over the past three to four decades. Whereas forty years ago the patient was just that, a 'patient' in the original etymological sense of the word as a passive recipient of treatment, today's patient defines him- or herself as an autonomous partner in the patient–physician relationship, who wants to take control and participate in the process of decision-making and who has access to an almost unlimited amount of information. We agree that this changed self-perception of today's patient alone can explain at least some of the changes observed in the patient–physician relationship. However, the fact remains that it is patients themselves who have declared that they lost trust in physicians, as evidenced by the empirical data presented in Chapter 2. So, it is not a change in self-perception as much as an overt position taken by patients. Furthermore, since there is no reason why a patient should not trust just because she is well informed and autonomous, there must be additional explanations for the decline of trust (albeit that being well

---

[10] Corso 2010.
[11] Norris 2009, p. 35.

informed and autonomous might be factors when combined with other concerns).

Lastly, there is the question as to *whether what we call 'status trust' is in fact simply a form of 'faith'*. We introduced the section on 'status trust' with a quotation from Clarke, who claimed "not so long ago, . . . doctors functioned in a quasi-ecclesiastic atmosphere of patient awe and confidence"[12] and we subsequently argued that the 'quasi-ecclesiastic atmosphere' referred to 'status trust'. An alternative interpretation which is suggested by the term 'quasi-ecclesiastic' is that patients did not trust physicians but rather had faith in them. At an early stage of our research into writing this book, we did briefly consider this interpretation. However, we dismissed it for the following reason. In faith

> there is a leap . . . beyond rational evidence, . . . a leap from knowledge to . . . faith, . . . a leap over the confines of common sense and reason.[13]

Such an account of faith does not properly capture what is happening in the patient–physician relationship. Rather, the patient's expectation regarding the physician's behaviour is perfectly rational and justified by the belief in the physician's trustworthiness, irrespective of whether this belief is based on a personal assessment of trustworthiness or on the acceptance of the physician's professionalism as guarantor of his trustworthiness.

12.1 The Discrediting of Professionalism: Physicians' Loss of 'Professional Authority'

Having offered a brief rejection of three possible alternative explanations to the decline of trust in medicine, we can now turn to each of the five major possible reasons in turn, starting with the discrediting of professionalism as a general development within society. In Section 9.1, we defined 'professionalism' and pointed to the fact that, increasingly, its role as guarantor of trustworthiness has been challenged.[14] In this

---

[12] Clark 2002, p. 14.

[13] O'Brien 2014, in the chapter on Kierkegaard. It is worth noting that the term 'leap of faith' is usually attributed to Kierkegaard, although he did not use the term himself.

[14] In fact, the disavowal of 'professionalism' can be seen in a much wider context. Traditionally, the legitimacy of values was based on subordination of the individual to established authorities (be they natural, social, or other). Today's idealisation of individualism (which can be observed in all Western societies and at all levels of society) legitimatises values primarily or even solely by the interests of the individual and subordinates the social order to the wishes of the individual (see Dogan 1998, p. 88).

section, we will present the major criticisms levelled against 'professionalism'. Moreover, we will address a claim which regularly comes up in discussions about the decline of trust, namely that the scandals which have shaken medicine and their subsequent exploitation by the (tabloid) press are responsible for the decline of trust:

> Public trust in health care in the UK is believed to have been shaken by the recent *intense media scrutiny about scandals over medical competence* such as the enquiry into paediatric cardiac surgery in Bristol, the conviction of the GP Harold Shipman, and the removal of organs from children at Alder Hey Hospital.[15]

We will argue that the scandals are not per se responsible for the decline of trust, but that they are responsible for the demise of professionalism.

There are general as well as specific criticisms against 'professionalism': a *general criticism* of the construct of 'professionalism' itself holds that it is *too vague* (for example, because it utilises descriptive accounts such as the 'commitment to excellence'), *over-simplifying* (so that, for example, it is charged with ignoring cultural or ethnical differences),[16] and that it is guilty of *ignoring the negative consequences of trust* (such as overutilization of care and increasing costs or iatrogenic deaths) as well as the *'dark' sides of trust* (such as the abuse of the power that trust grants physicians).[17]

Alongside this, the monopoly it grants physicians is seen as both an ethical and an economic problem. It poses an ethical problem because it allows physicians to decide what constitutes relevant medical knowledge and reasoning, and it poses an economic problem because the fact that it lets physicians decide what work-up or treatment they consider necessary may seduce doctors to recommend unnecessary (i.e. costly or even harmful) tests or treatments.[18] Of course, this problem is particularly relevant in countries where physicians are primarily paid on a 'fee-for-service' basis, as is the case in countries such as Switzerland.

The first *specific criticism* against 'professionalism' concerns the *paternalistic attitude* aspect of the concept, that is, the professional's fiduciary

---

Whereas, traditionally, a person enjoyed 'authority' because of her social position, today such a priori deference to others has become all but obsolete.

[15] Calnan and Sanford 2004, p. 92, our italics. Similar views are expressed e.g. by Ahern and Hendryx 2003, p. 1136, Imber 2008, p. 107, and Pellegrino 1991, p. 77.

[16] Veatch 1991, p. 162.

[17] Buchanan 2000, p. 190.

[18] Erde 2008, pp. 11–12.

obligation to act in the 'patient's best interest'. For the critics of professionalism, the claim

> that it is constitutive of the physician's role to act in the patient's best interest either falsely assumes that this will always be compatible with respecting the competent patient's autonomy or acknowledge the possibility of a conflict but implies that the duty to act in the patient's best interest overrides the duty to respect the patient's autonomy when the two conflict.[19]

Let us unpack this. We think that most people will agree (a) that a competent and reasonable patient is in the best position to decide what is best for him, and to act accordingly, and (b) that the physician has a duty to respect the patient's autonomy.[20] As long as the patient's estimate of his best interest coincides with the physician's estimate of what is best for the patient, the physician can, indeed, 'act in the patient's best interest' and, at the same time, respect the patient's autonomy. However, it is certainly false to assume that patient and physician will always agree as to what is best. And if the two disagree, the physician will have to choose between acting 'professionally', which, under this definition of what it is to act professionally, would mean acting in what he believes to be 'in the patient's best interest', or respecting the patient's autonomy. In the first case, he violates the duty to respect the patient's autonomy; in the second case, he violates his professional duty. In other words, as long as the patient's and the physician's estimate of what is best for the patient converge, there is no problem with professionalism, but there is no need for it either: respecting the patient's autonomy is sufficient. And if the two do not agree, professionalism becomes paternalistic and, hence, for those who strongly adhere to the moral importance of respecting autonomy, inacceptable. In this situation, it may be tempting to try to save the concept of 'professionalism' by redefining the professional duty of the physician as 'the duty to respect the patient's autonomy', i.e. to act in the way the patient desires. This may intuitively sound right, and yet, we do not wholly agree. First, we do not think there is a need to stipulate a moral duty which is so widely and generally held, namely to respect the other's autonomy. Second, to reduce the physician's duty to respect the patient's autonomy is a step in the wrong direction. Much as we agree that 'respecting autonomy morally trumps best interests', we do not think we should completely eliminate the

---

[19] Buchanan 1991, p. 94.
[20] Buchanan 1991, p. 94.

'physician's duty to act in the patient's interest' (or, as we have argued previously,[21] to act in a way that the patient approves, or could approve) for two important reasons: (a) because not all patients can (or want to) act autonomously, and (b) because it releases the physician from the duty to think about what (in his estimate) would be best for the patient. In other words, it may tempt some physicians to resort to some form of ethical minimalism, in the sense Pellegrino suggested, whereby the physician may work to their own advantage as well, rather than attempting to 'go the extra mile' for their patient.[22]

A *second specific criticism* that sits alongside the first, major specific criticism holds that cost-containment issues, as well as the duty to other patients, make it impossible for the physician to always act in an individual patient's interest.[23] We agree with this. Only, we think that it has always been an illusion to believe that physicians can act 'without undue outside influence' (that is, entirely independently). Physicians are still people who are social agents and so always acted within society, having to balance the individual patient's interests with those of society or those of other patients. To take just one example from the past, we might consider their role in quarantining patients with infectious diseases, especially, for example, when dealing with serious contagions, such as bubonic plague or typhoid. The historical quarantining that offered little or no treatment but only isolation from others was not in the interest of the afflicted patient but in that of society. In recent times, discussions about rationing, cost containment, or managed care have simply raised the awareness of the physicians' dependence on their wider social concerns.[24]

Finally, there is a *third specific criticism* that concerns the *insistence of professionals on self-regulation and policing*.[25] Indeed, the physicians' argument that they are trustworthy because they are professionals is circular as long as it is the physicians themselves who define 'professionalism' (it reminds one of the famous quip 'you can trust me, I am a doctor'). So, this reproach is certainly justified.

Indeed, it is the *failure of the medical profession to police their members that has brought on the demise of 'professionalism'*. Recall that, in Section 9.1, we adopted a definition of 'professionalism' as a social contract between physicians, patients, and the state, which grants physicians the

---

[21] See page 140.
[22] We have discussed this point about minimalism in greater depth on page 159.
[23] Veatch 1991, p. 161.
[24] We discuss this further in Sections 12.4 and 13.3.
[25] Erde 2008, p. 7.

right to autonomy and decision-making control without external influence, in exchange for the duty to serve the interests of society, as well as the duty for self-regulation and policing of defaulting physicians. Indeed, as Emily Jackson points out, "other health care workers will often be better placed than patients to spot unusually poor results, or inadequate care".[26] Unfortunately, reliance on a model of pure self-regulation is vulnerable to abuse by physicians unwilling to comply with the standards set by the profession.[27] At a local level, it is usually the case that peers can informally 'take aside and admonish' a colleague whose conduct they consider substandard (be that medically or ethically). Moreover, they can apply some additional pressure to encourage a change in conduct by no longer referring patients to that colleague. While this system may work with 'minor offenders', it is doomed to fail if it is confronted with an offender who does not care for the respect and trust of his colleagues and who ruthlessly pursues his own interests, because neither the profession nor the National Health Service (NHS) were provided with the necessary administrative power to sanction defaulting members.[28] It was only in the early 2000s that the United Kingdom's General Medical Council (GMC) introduced new guidance, requiring doctors to report poor practice by colleagues to the GMC. This is in marked contrast to earlier guidance, where 'disparaging colleagues' was counted as serious professional misconduct for which a doctor could be disciplined.[29]

Despite the fact that there have always been defaulting physicians (the 'bad apples' as Dixon-Woods et al. 2011 call them), the GMC's organisational and governance structures remained virtually unchanged up to the end of the twentieth century and physicians remained self-regulating. So, given such a long history, we might well ask what was the final straw that brought down self-regulation by the medical profession? The common answer to this question is that it was medical and healthcare scandals and their exploitation by the mass press which finally forced the state to intervene and to curtail the self-regulation of the medical profession.[30] However, we are all the time bombarded with reports about 'scandals',

[26] Jackson 2013, p. 157.
[27] For this and the following arguments, we are indebted to Dixon-Woods et al. 2011.
[28] Freidson and Rhea 1963, p. 169.
[29] Allsop 2006, p. 230.
[30] To name but a few of a long list of such scandals, we have, for example:
the concerns raised in the Francis Report into failures of care at *the Mid Staffordshire NHS Foundation Trust* in the United Kingdom (available at: http://www.midstaffspubli cinquiry.com/report);

many of which are perfectly irrelevant or have no consequences (albeit that they might still make a bad impression upon the general public). So, we need to ask what differentiates these (resultless) 'scandals' from the sorts of relevant scandals that have led to such pressure for change over regulating the profession? According to Lull and Hinerman, we are justified to talk of scandals, "when private acts that disgrace or offend the idealised, dominant morality of a social community are made public and narrativised by the media, producing a range of effects from ideological and cultural retrenchment to disruption and change".[31]

The cases to which we have referred above certainly fulfil this condition. However, they were not the first cases of very serious misdemeanour in the media age,[32] and yet they were the first to propel the state into action. We have two explanations for this change of attitude on the part of the state. (1) Society itself has moved "from a population of grateful subjects to a population of demanding citizens".[33] (2) The sheer number and the extreme severity of the cases occurring within a short period of time "had a problem-amplifying effect that became increasingly difficult for any of the parties to the social contract to ignore".[34] Although this explains why patients lost trust in the physicians' self-regulatory power and why the state had to intervene and take over (at least much of) the regulation of the medical profession, it does not explain why these scandals should have made people lose trust in physicians *qua* physicians. What these scandals and the reports about them have done is to demystify physicians – to alert people to the fact that physicians are fallible, that science and medicine are fraught with

---

the Alder Hey Children's Hospital in Liverpool, United Kingdom's retention of children's organs without parental permission (see www.gov.uk/government/publica tions/the-royal-liverpool-childrens-inquiry-report);

or the actions of a lone physician in the case *of the Harold Shipman murder inquiry* (see https://assets.publishing.service.gov.uk/government/uploads/system/uploads/attach ment_data/file/273227/5854.pdf).

[31] Lull and Hinerman 1997, p. 3.

[32] An example of just one particularly appalling case was that of Dr John Bodkin Adams, who, in 1956, was accused of having murdered up to 160 patients after having made them change their will in his favour. However, he was later acquitted, apparently not least because "the Attorney General seems to have been particularly concerned that, were Adams to hang, ostensibly on the evidence that some elderly patients had died while in his care, there might have been a doctors' revolt, which would have damaged the still fragile National Health Service" (see www.strangerinblood.co.uk/html/case.htm).

[33] Dixon-Woods et al. 2011, p. 1587.

[34] Dixon-Woods et al. 2011, p. 1486.

uncertainty and risk, and that physicians may have competing (including personal) interests and accountabilities. In this way, these scandals have certainly (albeit perhaps indirectly) contributed to the decline of trust.[35] And, of course, the scandal reports alerted patients to the fact that there are crooks among the medical profession (as in any other part of society, it is just that expectations of good conduct may often be higher for those involved in professional occupations, as well as for the profession 'as a whole'). As a consequence, although there was never any evidence that many (let alone, most) doctors at the time of the scandals were 'bad',[36] people came to believe that it was not merely a few doctors who were bad but that the whole profession consisted of bad doctors, or even that the profession produces bad doctors. In other words, scandals pointed to (a few) 'bad apples', but the public believed that the entire orchard was bad – that, indeed, the profession itself produced bad doctors. The reality, however, was that the profession is not pathogenic but instead only overly or excessively tolerant of managing individual problem cases.[37] This is an issue which we will briefly come back to in Section 13.1, where we will discuss whether such regulation is indeed effective at preventing further scandal and whether it is able to contribute to a restoration of trust between the patients and their physicians.

There is doubtless more to be said on this matter by considering more nuanced accounts of 'professionalism'. However, without going into a more detailed discussion, we agree with Buchanan that, overall, the simple fact of being a professional does not by itself adequately justify trust.[38] This does not rule out, of course, that some patients still accept 'professionalism' as a guarantor of trustworthiness, either in general or at least in certain situations. Yet, overall, the number of people trusting physicians just because of their professional status has (unquestionably and justifiably) declined. This, in turn, leads to a decline of physicians' professional authority. However, it does not necessarily lead to an overall

---

[35] In Section 13.2, we will come to another type of scandal, namely scandals about 'wrong surgery', which perhaps played an even greater role in the decline of trust.

[36] In fact, the Chief Medical Officer in 2006 commented that "There are around 130,000 registered doctors in active practice ... The vast majority practise medicine of very high quality. The "scandal" doctors were "freeloaders", who used the claims of virtue of the profession to pursue their own self-interests to the detriment of the wider group" (Chief Medical Officer 2006).

[37] Dixon-Woods et al. 2011, p. 1454.

[38] Buchanan 2000, p. 189.

decline of trust, just as long as the demise of status-based trust can be compensated for by an increase of merit-based authority and merit trust.[39] In the following section, we will argue that a complete compensation for the loss of professional authority is difficult to obtain because of the inherent difficulties of assessing trustworthiness. It remains that, even if professional status is still considered a sufficient justification of trust by some patients and/or in certain situations, as a concept (as it is conceived today) it is no longer adequate to serve as justification of trust.

12.2   The Difficulty of Assessing Trustworthiness: Physicians' Loss of 'Merit-Based Authority'

According to our definition, trust is an expectation regarding the competence and commitment of the trustee. This expectation (and hence trust) is justified if and only if we have sufficient reason to believe that the trustee is competent and committed (i.e. trustworthy). This, however, presupposes that it is possible to assess the trustee's trustworthiness and, as we will go on to discuss, this is often far from an easy thing to do in 'real life'.

Given the complexity of trustworthiness in the medical context, it is an illusion to believe that an individual patient can even approximately assess a physician's all-out trustworthiness. Fortunately, this is often not necessary. In many cases, it is sufficient to know that a physician is competent with regard to a limited topic (such as a dentist's competence in pulling a wisdom tooth) or sufficiently committed in a specific situation (such as the obstetrician's willingness to deliver a baby, even if the baby is born at 2 a.m. on a Sunday morning). Usually we can obtain the necessary information by asking a few pertinent questions.

A wider appraisal of a physician's trustworthiness, however, is much more difficult to come by. Mechanic and Meyer, for instance, argue that in a long-term patient–physician relationship we may iteratively come to an overall judgement of a doctor's trustworthiness.[40] We doubt whether this is quite correct or, at least, enough to establish trust. The familiarity which usually develops in this situation doubtless engenders a feeling of reliability, and hence confidence, but not necessarily trust.[41] As we have outlined in Section 6.2, it is well recognised that "trustworthiness and

---

[39] Buchanan 2000, p. 189.
[40] Mechanic and Meyer 2000, p. 657.
[41] Trust presupposes uncertainty and risk, whereas in reliance and confidence, risk, although it may be inherent, is not conceived (see page 83).

trust are not reducible to reliability and reliance".[42] Reliability refers to faultless (or, depending on the context, at least 'sufficient' or 'good-enough') past performance, hence to the past. However, since trust refers to the future, you are therefore interested in the physician's future trustworthiness. Moreover, trustworthiness is a much richer concept, not least because you expect that the trustee will act in a way that you approve.[43] The fact that a physician has acted reliably in the past means that he will (probably) behave the same way in the future. Yet, in the future, you may have a different (more demanding) expectation, perhaps because you suffer from something much more serious. We admit that the transition from reliability to trustworthiness may be fluent. Still, we think that we should not equate reliability with trustworthiness. While we agree that familiarity-based confidence often (and justifiably) warrants trust, we are not convinced that it amounts to a general assessment of trustworthiness.

Rather than vainly trying to assess a physician's all-out trustworthiness, most patients instead look for specific features, which they believe are indicative of trustworthiness. Caring behaviour and compassion on the part of the physician are often also seen as indicative signs of the trustworthy physician.[44] Yet, although caring behaviour per se may indicate commitment, it does not guarantee that the commitment will be realised.[45] Other important features include, for example, the 'availability' of the physician[46] and receptive and expressive communication skills.[47] Again, availability may indicate commitment, and communication skills are what we expect from a competent physician, but none of them suffices to guarantee trustworthiness.

If you ask patients why they trust their doctor, you will quite often get an answer along the lines of 'because I believe he is a good person'. Of course, this answer somewhat begs the question. A more accurate interpretation of what these people mean is (first) that they believe they can judge the character of another person intuitively and (second) that trustworthiness is an essential virtue of a good person. In other words, if the doctor is (or at least appears to be) a 'good person', he must (so many people believe) be a 'good physician'. This second belief is

---

[42] Jones 2012, p. 62.
[43] See page 139.
[44] Thom 2001, p. 323.
[45] Buchanan 2000, p. 194.
[46] Gerretsen and Myers 2008, p. 595.
[47] Thom 2001, p. 327.

commonly called the 'consilience assumption'.[48] However, we think that neither of the two assumptions is justified: the first, because many (if not even most) of us are not very good at judging other people's character, and even those who are will usually need to be well acquainted to make an accurate judgement. The second, and perhaps more concerning criticism, is that there is no reason why anyone should have specific competences just because they have a good character.[49]

Recall that we previously argued that 'most of the time and on most topics we all have to rely on testimony from others'.[50] Unsurprisingly, one of the main reasons why we were interested in establishing this epistemic point is that it also applies to trustworthiness. If we cannot base our trust on our own perception of the physician's merits, we are left with the option of referring to someone else's testimony. Of course, this leads us back to 'epistemic trust'. Since, as we have argued,[51] epistemic trust is only responsible if the information is based on a reliable belief-forming process, and since we usually cannot know what belief-forming process was used by the informant, epistemic trust in external information on a physician's quality is (at least very often) not sufficient to justify trust in physicians.

Knowing that someone is trustworthy justifies one's trust in her. However, in reality it is often difficult or even unfeasible for a patient to assess a physician's trustworthiness, (a) because our own perception of a physician's trustworthiness is often inadequate and (b) because relying on external information amounts to epistemic trust, which on its own is often not sufficient to justify trust in physicians. If the loss of professional authority (and hence status trust) is not (or at least not fully) compensated for by a corresponding equivalent gain in merit-based authority (and hence merit trust), there inevitably results an overall decline of trust. As we have argued in Section 11.2, at an interpersonal level (i.e. between a patient and his or her physician), trust can be justified with the help of the obligation ascription. At a general level (i.e. trust of patients in physicians per se), however, trust in physicians may indeed not be justified. Since this is a conclusion which we find hard to accept, we will come back to the topic in the final chapter.

---

[48] The term 'consilience' refers to the principal that calculating a result by two different methods should lead to the same answer. The word consilience was coined in 1840 by William Whewell in 'The Philosophy of the Inductive Sciences'. It was popularised by the biologist E.O. Wilson in his book *Consilience: The Unity of Knowledge'* (Wilson 1998).

[49] Schwab 2008, pp. 313–14.

[50] See page 105.

[51] See page 115.

12.3 The Crisis of Modern Medicine: Physicians' Loss of 'Medical Authority'

Physicians in addition to having lost much of their 'professional authority' are also losing their 'medical authority',[52] by which we mean the authority they have originally won through the success of science-based medicine, because ever more people have become disenchanted with science and scientific medicine.[53] We will refer to this disenchantment as 'the crisis of modern medicine'.[54]

Somehow, we tend to assume that physicians always possessed (almost unlimited) medical authority. But this is not true. Up to the turn of the twentieth century, medicine had little to offer. Most treatments were either ineffective or even nocuous (just think of bleeding or purging). Physicians understood very little about diseases. They may have genuinely cared for their patients, but they rarely cured them. So, even if they commanded respect, they had no genuine medical authority.[55] It was only with the rise (and society's acceptance) of the paradigms of science-based medicine and the consequent understanding of many diseases, the improvement of diagnostic acumen, and the development of effective treatments that physicians rapidly gained genuine medical authority.[56] This medical authority reached its zenith around 1960.[57] From then on it started to decline steadily.[58] In the words of Schlesinger, "[t]he authority of the medical profession ... can be depicted as a grand historical arc, rising to great heights by mid-century but faltering badly as the century drew to a close".[59]

---

[52] We will explain the difference between 'professional authority' and 'medical authority' presently.

[53] Some people (e.g. Calnan and Sanford 2004) use the term 'orthodox medicine' to differentiate it from various forms of 'alternative medicine'. Others (e.g. Le Fanu 2011) talk of 'modern medicine' to differentiate it from 'pre-scientific' medicine. We prefer to use 'scientific (or "science-based") medicine' as an explanatory term. 'Orthodox' is somewhat judgemental (Sampson 1996, p. 191), and 'modern' would open up the debate as to whether today's medicine is still 'modern' or 'post-modern' (Sampson 1996, p. 194), a topic we prefer not to address.

[54] Ernst 2009, p. 298.

[55] Heritage 2005, p. 84.

[56] Kitcher and Schacht use the term 'epistemic authority' (Kitcher and Schacht 2004, p. 27), which in fact it is. We stay with the term 'medical authority' because it is the more commonly used term and to avoid confusion with 'epistemic trust'. See also McCullough 2009, p. 1.

[57] This was what McKinlay and Marceau call the "golden age of doctoring". McKinlay and Marceau 2002, p. 383.

[58] McCullough 2009, p. 1.

[59] Schlesinger 2002, p. 186.

Before we go on, we want to emphasise that 'professional authority' (as described in Section 12.1) is not identical with the 'medical authority', of which we are talking here. 'Professional authority' refers to the assumption that someone is trustworthy because he belongs to a profession. 'Medical authority', on the other hand, refers to a type of epistemic authority, which the corpus of science-based medical knowledge confers to those who practice scientific medicine, provided (and this is important) that people believe in this knowledge.[60] To believe in scientific medicine means that one approves of its paradigms and that one believes that it works.[61] Let us give an example to illustrate the difference between the two types of authority. We (i.e. the authors) do not believe in homoeopathy. So, for us, homoeopathic knowledge does not confer medical authority. Nevertheless, a homoeopath may practice homoeopathy in compliance with the regulations set up by the 'Society of Homoeopaths' and therefore deserve the professional authority conferred on him by this society.[62]

If medical knowledge confers authority, it is a perfectly reasonable question to ask in response, how it is possible that 'medical authority' can decline at a time when medical knowledge appears to increase relentlessly. If this holds, it would seem as if we were asserting something seemingly self-contradictory. Here is what we think explains this apparent paradox. Until the 1960s, most people believed in scientific medicine. Since then the number of people who have become sceptical of scientific medicine has steadily increased. Concomitantly, 'alternative (or complementary) medicine', which played only a negligible role during the rise of scientific medicine, has gained a substantial following over the last few decades.[63] For these people, the body of medical knowledge, irrespective of whether it increases or not, no longer legitimises medical authority.[64] Hence, "modern medicine is deemed to be in a crisis".[65] There are three charges brought forward against modern medicine that we think are

---

[60] Imber, in a recent article, aptly argues that "trusting a physician depends first on trusting a person, then trusting a person's skills and training, and *finally trusting the science that underwrites those skills*" (Imber 2017, p. 317). In other words, if you do not trust (or, as we would say believe in) scientific medicine, you will not trust your doctor.

[61] See Section 6.2.2 for our more detailed account as to what it means to believe in scientific medicine.

[62] "The Society of Homeopaths is a professional body whose members are trained to high standards and agree to practise according to a strict code of ethics and practice." See: www.homeopathy-soh.org/.

[63] Sierpina 2006, p. 906.

[64] Brown 2008, p. 360.

[65] Ernst 2009, p. 298.

responsible for this crisis:[66] (1) the slackening of progress, (2) a methodological bias and reductionism, and (3) the overreliance of physicians and, in particular, of evidence-based medicine on generalised and encoded scientific knowledge (*episteme*) at the expense of the physician's individual expertise (*phronesis*), together with a devaluation of the patient's role in the patient–physician relationship.

(1) *Lack of progress*: One of the simplest reasons for the increasing frustration people have with medicine is that, although the amount of knowledge in medicine increases, true therapeutic progress has slowed down over the last few decades and is not meeting the expectations it raised during the period of unprecedented success after the Second World War.[67] Le Fanu, in his book *The Rise and Fall of Modern Medicine*, lists thirty-five important discoveries or developments in medicine since 1940.[68] If we group these events by decade, we find seven events each for the 1940s and 1950s. Then the number drops to six (1960s), five (1970s), and two each for the 1980s and 1990s.[69] To aggravate matters, progress has slowed down despite a massive increase of investment in both research and health care.[70] Yet even given this, we do not think that slacking progress is an adequate reason to no longer acknowledge what medicine has achieved and is still achieving. There must be more to the 'crisis of medicine' than just disillusionment because of diminishing progress. Take the example of vaccinations. Despite the fact that vaccinations belong to medicine's top success stories,[71] "measles is [still] one of the leading causes of death among young children *even though a safe and cost-effective vaccine is available*".[72] Even if one sought to attribute the measles case to problems associated with developing nations rather than attitudes towards medicine, there are clearer

---

[66] To avoid any misunderstanding: We argue that these charges are responsible for the crisis, not that these charges are necessarily justified.

[67] Fitzpatrick 2001, p. 132.

[68] Admittedly, the list given by Le Fanu is debatable (as any such list is), but it certainly contains many things that immediately come to mind and which anyone with a reasonable ability to reflect upon the history of medicine might expect to be there: e.g. penicillin, renal dialysis, cataract surgery, cortisone, polio vaccination, contraceptive pill, hip replacement surgery, kidney and other organ transplants, Computerised Tomography, Helicobacter as the cause of gastric ulcers, and triple therapy for AIDS, etc.

[69] Le Fanu 2011, p. 3.

[70] Starr 1984, p. 410.

[71] Amit et al. 2017, p. 768.

[72] WHO 2015, our emphasis, available from www.who.int/mediacentre/factsheets/fs286/en/. At the time of writing (2019) this has gained renewed significance.

examples available that do suggest a crisis in medicine. Why, in developed countries, are physicians "struggling to secure the confidence and co-operation of individuals who appear obstinately disinclined to accept strong scientific evidence about childhood vaccination"?[73] One potentially promising answer is to be found in a spreading of cultural relativism, anti-scientific thinking, and even a general distrust of rationality.[74]

As to the second and third charges, many of the arguments brought forward against 'scientific medicine' concern 'medical science' rather than 'scientific medicine' properly speaking. By 'scientific (or science-based) medicine' we mean clinical medical practice based on the paradigms of the natural sciences. Its purpose is to treat patients. By 'medical science' we mean all those endeavours which aim at increasing medical knowledge. Since medical science primarily aims at improving medical practice and since scientific medicine heavily relies on the findings of medical science, there is evidently a considerable overlap. Nevertheless, we will treat the arguments separately. We will start with the arguments against medical science, namely the reproach of methodological bias and reductionism. Following this, we will address the arguments against scientific medicine, in particular the accusation of physicians' overreliance on science.

(2) *Methodological bias and reductionism*: One of these arguments pertains to the principle methodology used by medical scientists. At the heart of the critique of science-based medicine lies the upbraiding of an overreliance on what Davis calls "the epistemological credo of hypothetico-deductive and inductive reasoning".[75] In fact, this critique is twofold: (a) it is a critique of the principle per se and (b) it is a critique of the over-reliance on this single principle at the exclusion of other methods.[76]

The *first critique* is directed against the linear reductionist thinking, which holds that every disease has a specific cause (or aetiology) and, in principle, becomes treatable (or curable) once the aetiology is found, whereas in reality health and disease are part of a non-linear complex system, in which "properties of the whole cannot be predicted from the properties of the component units".[77] This argument is supported by the fact that 'mono-causal reasoning' (or 'linear thinking')[78] was very

---

[73] Sweeney 2002, p. 131.
[74] Sampson 1996, p. 194.
[75] Davis 1997, p. 183.
[76] Sellman 2012, p. 113.
[77] Frost 1997, p. 1045.
[78] Ernst 2009, p. 298.

successful with many acute diseases which do indeed have a single cause (such as infections), but much less so with chronic disorders (such as cardio-vascular diseases) where there is no single cause and, in particular, no linear cause–effect relationship.[79] Perhaps the simplest and most striking blow against the mono-causal thinking is the placebo effect: placebo often works, despite the fact that we have no or very little idea of what causes certain symptoms and how placebo works.[80]

The second critique refers to the bias in favour of one single method. By the end of the twentieth century, we had accumulated a huge amount of knowledge that (thanks to the informatics revolution) has become accessible to almost everyone. And yet, many urgent problems of medicine (such as the aforementioned cardio-vascular diseases or cancer) have not been solved. So, what do we do? The answer has been "more of the same, only harder".[81] One is reminded of the athlete who only increases but never changes his training impulses and is frustrated if he does not make any progress. Indeed, the "suspicion that we have exhausted the simple problems amenable to classic reductive scientific explanation"[82] could explain why therapeutic breakthroughs have become rather sparse.

(3) *The overreliance of physicians on science*: Many patients argue that physicians rely too much on science[83] and that too much emphasis is placed on rationality at the expense of emotional aspects. These patients complain that because of this technological pre-eminence, their role as narrator has all but disappeared.[84] This, in turn, has led to a feeling of disempowerment on the part of the patients. One of the goals of the 'disability right's movement'[85] is to increase the self-assertiveness of the sick and disabled and to re-empower patients.[86] Consequently, patients see themselves as consumers of health care without the need of deference to medical authority.[87]

Moreover, it is argued that science-based medical practice is too much based on knowledge about *generalities* at the expense of the

---

[79] Fitzpatrick 2001, p. 133.
[80] Charlton 1992, p. 436.
[81] Kegan and Lahey 2001, p. 233.
[82] Gillett 1995, p. 286.
[83] Schlesinger 2002, p. 193.
[84] Imber 2008, p. 109.
[85] Rodwin 1994, pp. 163ff.
[86] Schlesinger 2002, p. 196.
[87] Fitzpatrick 2001, p. 136.

individual.[88] The ultimate embodiment of the scientific method is the development and application of 'evidence-based medicine' (EBM) with its reliance on (and demand for) randomised clinical trials and meta-analyses. The problem of this approach in this context is that it creates knowledge about illnesses and their treatment 'in general' rather than about the illness of the sick individual.[89] For the sake of *methodological validity*, entire groups of the population are excluded from studies at the price of a loss of *practical relevance.*[90] Children are almost invariably excluded, as are old and often multi-morbid patients. Women are also very often underrepresented.[91] Hence, the results of such studies cannot be applied to these groups with any certainty. This 'criteria bias' reduces the transferability of knowledge gained in clinical studies to individual patients. It also explains why the results obtained in clinical studies are often not replicable in clinical practice.[92] This is why "many clinicians struggle to apply results of studies that do not seem relevant to their daily practice".[93]

Lastly, there is the concern that EBM replaces local knowledge (the physician's expertise) with encoded knowledge (national standards, Cochrane, NICE). Encoded knowledge is designed to improve outcome, reduce risks, and increase public confidence. Yet, "the effect of concentrating on cognitive rationality is leading to a system that functions efficiently in curing patients but which fails to meet the personal and emotional needs of patients and therefore does not inspire confidence and trust".[94]

---

[88] Sweeney 2002, p. 134.

[89] Tyreman 2000, p. 120.

[90] Knottnerus 1997, p. 1110.

[91] See, for example, the discussion of cases involving the exclusion of groups in Hughes 2010.

[92] We would like to note that we are not aware of any empirical evidence that the practice of EBM has improved medical practice, although one can extrapolate how this might be the case from scrutinising medical research and reflecting upon the likely practical implications of it. Take, for example, the famous early application of subjecting standard medical techniques to scientific scrutiny through properly conducted trials that applied to the standard surgical treatment for pectoral angina – internal mammary artery ligation. The discovery that this technique was not effective when compared to placebo would at least have saved many people suffering from angina from being sent for unnecessary surgery (Cobb et al. 1959). What we claim is lacking, somewhat ironically, is any systematic study as to how EBM might have improved medical practice.

[93] Knottnerus 1997, p. 1109. Knottnerus pointedly claims that we need more 'medicine-based evidence' rather than 'evidence-based medicine' if EBM is to work in clinical practice (Knottnerus 1997, p. 1110).

[94] Alaszewski and Brown 2007, p. 8.

Here is an illustration of what this means. From my (M.W.'s) personal experience (both as a physician and as a patient), I know that physicians tend to believe that they will gain the patient's trust by demonstrating their competence or knowledgeability, whereas patients are often more concerned about the physician's commitment and are much more willing to trust the physician who responds to their emotions of fear or worry.

We are neither in favour of alternative medicine nor of relativism and anti-scientific thinking, and yet we believe that there is more than a grain of truth in some of these arguments and we can understand why they appeal to many people, albeit sadly to the detriment of trust. Nevertheless, we are afraid that "from the belief that medicine can do anything, opinion is in danger of swinging to the equally untenable conclusion that it can do little or nothing".[95]

What we think this shows is that modern medicine is increasingly criticised for its methodological bias and reductionism and for the over-reliance of physicians on science at the expense of respecting the patient's needs. As such, the resulting 'crisis of modern medicine' and the consequent loss of medical authority of physicians offer a third explanation for the decline of trust.

12.4 The Commodification of Medicine: Physicians' Loss of 'Directive Authority'

In the previous section, we discussed why patients no longer trust physicians' *medical authority*. In this section, we turn to look at another form of authority that might also explain the decline in trust and argue that patients have come to increasingly doubt physicians' commitment and what is called their 'directive authority',[96] i.e. their agency and their freedom of decision-making. We present two arguments that explain these increasing doubts: (1) the commodification of medicine and (2) the re-conceptualisation of physicians as corporate employees.

(1) *The commodification of medicine*: In the first book of Plato's *Republic*, Socrates asks Thrasymachus "is the physician, taken in that strict sense of which you are speaking, a healer of the sick or a maker of money?"[97] This shows that the question whether medicine is a calling or a business is at

---

[95] McKeown 1976, p. 160.
[96] See page 140.
[97] Plato, Republic, section 341c. The translation is by B. Jowett, available from: www.gutenberg.org/files/1497/1497-h/1497-h.htm.

least two and a half millennia old. Thrasymachus' answer was "a healer of the sick", and we think that until fairly recently many people would have agreed with this. We are afraid, however, that today the answer might well be different.

Of course, physicians (even those referred to by Thrasymachus) have always been remunerated in one way or another. However, in the past, physicians (much as clergy) were often felt to be remunerated in recognition of their 'community service' under the implicit provision that these services are provided for the patient's good.[98] And, even if physicians were paid for their services, patients did not necessarily conceive the patient–physician relationship as a standard business relationship. However, with the commodification of medicine and the creation of health care as a 'big business' or, as Clark put it, with "professional health care more and more being reconceived as just another commodity in the free market",[99] patients fear that physicians increasingly adopt a business attitude, caring more for their own (pecuniary) advantage than for the patient's benefit. This fear appears to be particularly pronounced in China, where "the traditional moral principles [of Confucianism, Taoism, and Buddhism] were, to a large extent, shattered in the process of marketization in post-Mao era".[100]

However, not all patients conceive the commodification or, in this case, the blatant commercialisation of medicine as something negative. Among the most ardent supporters of such commodification are those who are patients of *private profit-oriented hospitals*, hospitals which cater to the rich and those who can afford to pay high insurance premiums. These hospitals guarantee unlimited access to specialists and provide any exam or treatment the patient or his physician thinks he needs. These patients conceive themselves (to use the terminology of 'principal/agent theory'[101]) as the 'principal' and the physician as the 'agent'. Accordingly, they believe that they can commission the physician to bring about a specific outcome, i.e. that they are entitled through this to expect this outcome. Those patients adopting this stance face two risks: The first risk is that their expectations will be frustrated because, even for them, there are limitations as to what medicine can do, and it is just as irrational to

---

[98] Sulmasy 1993, pp. 28–9.
[99] Clark 2002, p. 22.
[100] See e.g. Chan 2017, p. 2, our insertion and Yan 2017, p. 1. The decline of trust is more easily correlatable with the marketization process in China than in Western Countries because here this process was much more abrupt (Xin and Xin 2017).
[101] See Buchanan 1988.

commission someone to do something he is not capable of doing as it is to trust someone to provide something which is not within his reach. The second risk these patients face is the risk of overdiagnosis and overtreatment. However, since these patients see health care as a commodity and are used to getting what they order and pay for, they may not be overly concerned about this. As with any commodity, a typical belief towards it is that 'more (of anything) is always better'.

There is a wider issue here as well. This type of health care reflects the fact that "we live in a time when almost everything can be bought and sold".[102] Although it is not the purpose of this book to make moral judgements as to the nature and use of commercialised medicine, we are worried about the spread of the sort of mentality underpinning this commodification that we have briefly suggested here because it creates inequality where there should be none. This is because it is a delusion, even in affluent countries, to think that it is possible "to do that which is medically best for this patient, as if there were no other patients and as if the cost of doing what is medically best for this patient were zero".[103]

By offering "everything that is medically best" to a (rich) few, it puts the burden of rationing to the (less well-off) rest of the population, partly because not everything offered is an inexhaustible resource or even a fungible commodity and so would not be available for use by others once it is used and partly because it diverts excess resources (of objects, people, time, etc.) away from other cases of genuine need.[104] Rationing is therefore unavoidable and in fact practised every day,[105] even if many people (including physicians, who may unconsciously practice it,[106] as well as politicians, who loath to make unpopular decisions[107]) tend to scotomise this fact. More than the commodification of medicine per se, it is the fact that the commercialisation of medicine puts the onus of having

---

[102] Sandel 2012, p. 5.

[103] Buchanan 2000, p. 193.

[104] There is a great deal of debate about commodification of resources in medicine. For a good summary of some of the general principles underlying the debate, see Wilkinson 2013, pp. 44–55.

[105] The simple fact that a physician has to limit the time he can devote to a single patient is a (albeit it harmless) form of rationing. For a discussion of 'rationing' as well as the options we have to handle it, see, e.g. Scheunemann and White 2011.

[106] Ward et al. 2008, p. 471.

[107] "Successive governments have tried to distance themselves from decisions about what the NHS should pay for, sheltering behind complex technical arguments." Mossialos and McKee 2003, p. 373.

their care limited upon those who are less affluent that ultimately undermines trust. We will come back to this in Section 13.3.

(2) *The re-conceptualisation of physicians as corporate employees.* This offers yet another possible explanation for increasing doubts. Over the past two to three decades, healthcare costs have literally skyrocketed.[108] The need for cost containment has led to the introduction of various types of 'managed care'. We are using this term in a very general way to include all healthcare models, in which physicians are financially accountable to third parties and in which (positive or negative) incentives are used to encourage physicians to reduce costs, basically by limiting access to care. As a consequence of this, many people fear that physicians are no longer independent professionals but "corporate employees",[109] who have lost their independence as sole arbiters of medical matters and are no longer in a position to act with only the patient's interest in mind. Or, to put it into terms we have been consistently using here, physicians (are perceived to) have lost *directive authority*. As such, the commodification of medicine and the physicians' loss of directive authority are perceived as undermining the physicians' commitment to the patients' interest and, hence, lead to a decline of trust.

12.5 Changes of Risk Perception and Risk Acceptance

So far, we have looked at changes which, at least in the perception of patients, undermine the physician's (various types of) authority. But this is not the whole story. Alongside this, we want to argue that there is also a broad change in the attitudes or behaviour of patients which, in turn, also leads to a decline of trust, namely the patients' increasing sensibility to risks (be they real or imagined) and their increasing aversion to risks (including the risk inherent in trust). Our position involves two claims: (1) that (contrary to common belief) risks have not increased but people's

---

[108] A recent McKinsey study from the United States shows that over the past twenty years the healthcare costs have increased by about a factor of five, whereas the gross domestic product has only increased by about a factor of two during the same period (Bradford et al. 2011). It is worth noting that even in cases of large-scale social provision of medicine, as is the case with the NHS in the United Kingdom, strict financial limits on treatment and drug regimens are being imposed based on advice from public advisory bodies such as the National Institute for Health and Care Excellence (NICE), which was set up directly by the government to provide guidance and recommendations on what are the most effective ways to utilise healthcare resources across England.

[109] Clark 2002, p. 22.

perception of what constitutes risks has changed;[110] and (2) that (again, contrary to what many people believe) risks can materialise without it being anybody's fault. It is this change of risk perception, together with the increased risk aversion (i.e. the unwillingness to accept risks as inevitable parts of life), that we will argue contributes to the decline of trust.

To be able to support these claims we have to come back to the definition of 'risk' and to the relationship between risk and uncertainty. In Section 5.3, we defined 'risk' as a function of the probability that a certain adverse event will happen and of the (negative) consequences of this event.[111] This implies that we must know the possible adverse events and their prevalence if we want to be able to calculate (or at least estimate) the risk. Here is an example. If you go skiing, you run the risk of a fall with the possible consequence of a fracture. Since each year about 20,000 serious skiing accidents happen on the slopes of the Swiss Alps,[112] and since each skier spends on average five days per year skiing, your (theoretical) risk of having a serious accident is about 0.001 per cent if you go skiing for a day. Of course, such a skiing trip is full of other uncertainties as well. Fortunately, not all of them are risks. Although there is no risk without uncertainty, uncertainty does not necessarily imply risk.[113] And, contrary to risks, uncertainties cannot be assessed and/or quantified.[114] Uncertainties are inherent; you cannot measure them; they are 'simply there'.[115] It is important to keep this in mind as we go on to consider how uncertainty has increased but risks have not.

(1) *Risks have not increased*: If you listen to the news or read the newspapers you must get the impression that life on earth in general and medicine in particular are becoming increasingly dangerous. Indeed, hardly a day goes by without some headlines telling us about new risks (to our health or otherwise). The reality, however, appears to be almost the opposite to this, where "public concerns have grown, in the face of declining 'real' risks".[116] For example, the fact that from 1900 to 2000 the life expectancy (in the Western

---

[110] O'Neill 2002a, p. 8.
[111] See page 53.
[112] The figure is taken from: www.unfallstatistik.ch/d/publik/artikel/pdf/artikel_26_d.pdf.
[113] See page 52.
[114] Smith 2005, p. 307.
[115] Luhmann 2000, p. 100.
[116] For the following arguments and data, we are drawing on the work of William R. Freudenburg (Freudenburg 1993,1996).

World) has increased from 48 to 78 years[117] clearly contradicts the belief that serious health risks have increased (at the very least, those that contribute to morbidity). We are living longer and healthier lives than our ancestors. In other words, serious health risk cannot have increased all the time. So why do many people believe that everything has become riskier and more dangerous? And why do so many people "exhibit a marked global risk-avoidant decision-making bias"?[118] As we have already argued, we can estimate the risk of something if we know the probability of adverse effects and their consequences.[119] However, this is not how most people estimate risks.[120] Instead, they rely on their 'intuition', which makes them susceptible to a number of 'biases'.[121] Here are two examples of such biases in risk estimation:[122] (a) the 'availability heuristics bias' refers to the fact that the more often we have encountered (or just 'heard of') a risk materialising, the higher we estimate the risk to be. In the past, we had to search actively for information, whereas today even information for which we do not care is literally forced upon us. So, the probability that we hear or read of cases of risks materialising has greatly increased. (b) The increasing focus on losses at the expense of gains (referred to as 'loss aversion bias') and the increasing focus on the risk of doing something rather than on the risk of abstaining from doing the same thing (the so-called omission bias) also lead to an increase of the risk sensibility. A good tangible example of this is the previously mentioned aversion to the measles vaccinations, where people focus on the (anecdotal) risk of the vaccination and completely block out the (very real) risk of measles.

Perhaps an even more apt explanation for the fallacy of the belief that risks have increased is offered by the theory of increasing 'social interdependence'.[123] Let us use Freudenburg's own example to illustrate this. One hundred years ago, approximately 50 per cent of the population were in one way or another involved in the production of food. People ate what they produced themselves or what was produced by people they

---

[117] Alaszewski and Brown 2007; Wildavsky and Wildavsky 2014, figure 1.

[118] Lorian and Grisham 2010, p. 29.

[119] Alternatively, one could say that the risk is a function of the probability and the consequences of the risk materialising.

[120] Of course, it is, particularly in the medical context, unrealistic to expect people to make such risk assessments (Millstone and van Zwanenberg 2000, p. 1307).

[121] Kusch 2007, p. 133.

[122] The examples are taken from Kusch 2007, p. 133, and from Sunstein 2007, p. 165.

[123] Freudenburg 1993, pp. 914–15.

knew and therefore trusted. Today, only about 2 per cent of the population are involved in the food production. The fact that we no longer know who produces our food and how it is produced and processed increases our fear that someone in the production process fails to do their job properly. This 'division of labour' has led to an increasing dependence on others, i.e. on people whom we do not implicitly trust.[124] Behind this development (which, of course is not limited to food production) lies one single factor: specialisation and the emergence of experts. Whereas lay-people know very little (or close to nothing) about lots of different things, experts know a lot about very few things. This has led to a divergence of expert and lay knowledge.[125] This "split between the experts and the public"[126] leads to mistrust. People constantly fear that scientists 'might have overlooked something' (or, worse, that they are purposely withholding something). This has led to a position whereby "Science is seen as a source of knowledge which paradoxically both reduces and contributes to uncertainty".[127] In other words, the experts increase safety, yet leave us with the fear, which is typically associated with uncertainty and reduces our tolerance to perceived 'risks'.[128]

Many people may remember that when mobile phones became popular, we had signs on all hospital wards prohibiting their use 'because of the risk of interference with medical equipment'. Yet (as M.W. vividly recalls from his own clinical experience), since there was no 'equipment to interfere with' there was no risk, and yet these signs remained for a long time. This type of 'risk', in which a cause-and-effect relationship is hypothetically possible but neither probable nor plausible, is often called a *phantom risk*.[129] Indeed, "most of the claims of harm to human beings from technology are either false or unproven".[130] And yet, they are perceived as risks and are responsible for the application of the 'precautionary principle'. According to the 'Wingspread Declaration', derived from the Wingspread Conference on the Precautionary Principle, this principle states that "when an activity raises threats of harm to human

---

[124] In fact, this 'social interdependence' (or 'social vulnerability') has increased from about 60 per cent in 1900 to almost 100 per cent today (Freudenburg 1993, p. 915, figure 1).
[125] Alaszewski and Brown 2007, p. 1.
[126] Sharlin 1989, p. 269.
[127] Alaszewski and Brown 2007, p. 2.
[128] Imber 2008, p. 114.
[129] Foster et al. 1999, p. 1.
[130] Wildavsky 1994, p. 228.

health or the environment, precautionary measures should be taken *even if some cause and effect relationships are not established scientifically*.[131]

To make matters worse, the simple fact that these mostly unnecessary precautionary measures are taken is something that confirms people's belief that there must be a risk.[132] We have often wondered why patients see risks lurking everywhere. For lack of space, we cannot go into any details,[133] but there is one explanation which we do want to mention, namely: if something is continuously reiterated it gets so ingrained in people's mind that they believe it to be true. So, for example, if you keep telling people that old mobile phones 'radiate', that this 'radiation' is harmful, and that your brand-new phone 'radiates much less', people will buy a new one, even if none of the above claims is true (or makes sense).

(2) *Risks can materialise without it being anybody's fault*. In everybody's lives, eventually, a (true) risk will materialise (i.e. what we fear will happen). How we react to this depends on whether it was a 'voluntary risk' or an 'involuntary risk'.[134] Here is what we mean by this: if you go climbing, you know that you run the risk of falling because you might, for example, slip on a loose rock, etc. This is a risk, which you accept voluntarily, and for which you can only blame yourself if it materialises. If, however, you fall because a rope you were provided with by the climbing instructor ruptures, this is an 'involuntary risk', i.e. one which you could not foresee.[135] It has been noted that in earlier times involuntary risks were accepted as part of life, whereas today, whenever an involuntary risk materialises, this is seen as a failure of someone or something for which someone has to take the blame.[136] While this is true in general, it is particularly true in medicine, as many patients today believe that they are entitled to a complication-free treatment and that if a complication arises, the doctor must have made a blunder. In fact, many people not only believe that they are entitled to a complication-free treatment, they even believe to have a 'right for health'. This statement may come as a surprise,[137] but we have only got to look at

---

[131] The Wingspread Conference on the Precautionary Principle took place in January 1998 in Racine, Wisconsin, USA. The citation (our italics) is from the summary of the conference, which is available from: www.sehn.org/wing.html.

[132] Wiedemann et al. 2006, p. 361.

[133] For a detailed analysis of this problem, see Kusch 2007, pp. 133ff.

[134] Sharlin 1989, p. 261.

[135] See also pages 44, 156, and 163 for the difference between 'internal' and 'external' attribution'.

[136] Sharlin 1989, p. 261.

[137] Frankly, we think that any claim to this being a right is mistaken. We may have a right to health care and to living conditions which promote health etc., but not to health itself.

the Constitution of the World Health Organisation to see that it is not as far-fetched as it looks. Here is a quote from the Preamble to the Constitution of the World Health Organisation: "The enjoyment of the *highest attainable standard of health* is one of the *fundamental rights* of every human."[138]

Of course, the erroneous inference proceeds along the lines that, if we have a right to health, there must be someone to provide this health. From there it is only a small step to expect the physician to provide this health and to forget that "the primary mission of the physician is to *render health care, not health*".[139] We easily forget that we can only trust the physician to provide this health care 'as best as he can' but not that he will guarantee our health.[140]

Since most people have at one time or another themselves suffered (what they believe to be) a complication, or at least know of someone who has experienced (again, what he believes to be) a complication, they conclude that most physicians blunder and are better not trusted.[141]

As we have argued earlier,[142] trust implies consciously taking a risk. If you are not prepared to accept the risk inherent in trust, you will not trust. Therefore, if you are not willing to accept that bad medical

---

The conception of a 'right to health', as we go on to discuss, we take as a misunderstanding of the (1946) WHO Constitution (available at: http://apps.who.int /gb/bd/PDF/bd48/basic-documents-48th-edition-en.pdf#page=1) which established the right to "the enjoyment of the highest attainable standard of health". This was subsequently also taken up by, for example, the Universal Declaration of Human Rights, Article 25 (available at: www.un.org/en/universal-declaration-human-rights/), and (almost verbatim) by the (1966) International Covenant of Economic, Social and Cultural rights, Article 12 (available at: www.ohchr.org/EN/ProfessionalInterest/Pages/ CESCR.aspx). Upon inspection, this claim of a 'right to health' is only expressed as a right to health care. If and when advances in genetic modification and selection in the future become an accepted part of medical practice and family planning, there may be further debate to be had as to whether there is any right or concomitant duty to prevent disease and disability and hence secure something closer to a 'right to health'. For some of the foundational philosophical concerns that might underpin such a rights claim, see Newson and Wrigley 2016; Wrigley 2006; Wrigley 2012.

[138] Available from: www.who.int/about/mission/en/.

[139] Sulmasy 1993, p. 32, our emphasis.

[140] This is another example of conceiving trust as outcome-related, a misconception of trust, to which we have repeatedly alluded, and which has found surprisingly little attention in the literature.

[141] According to the then EU Commissioner of Health, Androulla Vassiliou, physicians make errors which seriously harm the patient in every tenth patient and errors which are fatal to the patient in every 1,000th hospitalised patient. Moreover, she claims that 78 per cent of the European population consider 'medical errors a serious problem' (Schiltz 2008).

[142] See page 86.

outcomes are sometimes unavoidable, you will not trust physicians.[143] The increasing readiness to perceive risks where in fact there is no risk (only uncertainty), together with a decreasing willingness to accept risks, must inevitably lead to a loss of trust. Although there is no evidence that true risks have increased, maybe there are some of which we were just previously not aware. Even given this possibility, most of the perceived new risks are explainable as being nothing more than uncertainties, turned into risks by "unrealistic hankering for a world, in which safety and compliance are total",[144] and by the continuous reiteration and appeals to people's fears. Despite the fact that risks have not increased, and although risks can materialise without it being anybody's fault, people's changes of risk perception and their increasing risk aversion can reasonably be held to have led to a decline of trust.

12.6   Summary and Conclusions

We started this chapter by rejecting three commonly made allegations regarding the decline of trust, namely (1) that a decrease of the quality of performance of physicians is responsible for the decline of trust, (2) that the recent changes in the patient-physician relationship reflect the changed self-perception of today's patients rather than a decline of trust, and (3) that what we call a loss of trust is, in fact, a loss of faith in physicians.

Since, on our definition, trust is a *justified expectation regarding the trustworthiness (i.e. the competence and commitment)* of the physician, we then set out to identify recent changes in people's attitude and behaviour, which negatively affect the justification of trust, thereby leading to a decline of trust.

Obviously, most of the changes in people's attitude and behaviour do not relate to trust. We have, however, identified five changes, which not only can explain the decline of trust, but which must almost inevitably lead to a decline of trust.

(1) The discrediting of professionalism
(2) The insistence on (and difficulty of) assessing physicians' trustworthiness
(3) The disavowal of the basic tenets of scientific medicine (commonly referred to as 'crisis of modern medicine')

---

[143] Imber 2008, p. 239.
[144] O'Neill 2002b, p. 19.

(4) The commodification of medicine and the re-conceptualisation of physicians as dependent employees
(5) Changes of risk perception and increasing risk-averseness

The first four of these changes engender what may be summarised under the heading 'loss of physicians' authority': the *discrediting of 'professionalism'* has led to a decline of professional authority, a decline that cannot be fully compensated for by an increase in merit-based authority because of the *difficulty of assessing trustworthiness*. A *questioning of physicians' medical authority* (caused by the what is commonly referred to as the 'crisis of modern medicine') and increasing *doubts regarding the physician's agency and their directive authority* (caused by the commodification of medicine and a re-conceptualisation of physicians as dependent employees) further jeopardise the justification of trust. So, overall, the decline of trust is primarily the consequence of physicians' loss of (different types of) authority.

The fifth explanation is independent of physicians' authority but has to do with the risk inherent in trust. Contrary to what many people believe, it is not risks which have increased but uncertainty. Yet, people perceive this increase of uncertainty as an increase of risk; a risk which an increasing number of people are no longer willing to accept. Together, the changed risk perception and the increased risk aversion account (at least in part) for the decline of trust.

While these may not be all the possible explanations for the decline of trust, they are certainly sufficient to understand why trust has declined.

PART VI

Perspectives

13

Can We Restore Trust?

We started this book on trust with a quotation taken from what is in fact an impassioned plea to restore trust in the medical profession: Alice K. Jacobs' Presidential Address to the American Heart Association in 2004, entitled 'Rebuilding an Enduring Trust – A Global Mandate'.[1] As we used this as one of our initial motivations for addressing the issue of trust in medicine, it is fitting that we return to Professor Jacobs at the start of this final chapter to see the extent to which we have met some of the concerns she has voiced. In her address, Jacobs states:

> Trust is a vital, unseen, and essential element in diagnosis, treatment, and healing. So, it is fundamental that we understand what it is, why it's important in medicine, its recent decline, and what we can all do to rebuild trust in our profession.[2]

So far, we have presented a definition of 'trust' that should help us understand what trust is. We have put forward several different arguments as to why trust is important in medicine, both from an instrumental and a moral standpoint. And we have also identified five reasons that we believe are responsible for the decline of trust. So, what remains for us to do is to try to answer the question whether and, if so, how trust in the medical profession can be regained.

This may sound rather cautious and indeed it is. Appeals to restore trust appear very commonly, especially in publications by medical societies, councils, and suchlike.[3] However, most of them have one thing in

---

[1] Section 1.1: "one of the most critical issues facing our profession today is the erosion of trust".

[2] Jacobs 2005, p. 3494.

[3] To name but two recent cases: "Rebuilding trust – the real challenge for health system improvement" (Sturmberg 2015) and "Public's distrust of medicines needs urgent action, says Academy" (Hawkes 2017).

common: they are rather shy with presenting viable, concrete advice. Jacobs herself argues that in order to improve trust, physicians will have to improve their technical competency, interpersonal competency, and agency. Yet, the competence of today's physicians is undoubtedly higher than that of the physicians of forty years ago, when trust in physicians was high. Similarly, fifty years ago the patient–physician relationship was dominated by paternalism, which certainly called for less interpersonal competency than the presently favoured decision-sharing model. Jacobs may have a point, however, with regard to agency, which may be threatened by the commodification of medicine, and with regard to patient safety, which was rather neglected in the past. We will come back to these two points presently.

Before we address these points about agency and patient safety, we would like to get rid of a suspicion we harbour regarding the basis of a particular call for a restoration of trust, one which seems to stem largely from an older generation of physicians. Our concern is that there is still a distinct proportion of the profession who are dreaming of a time "not so long ago, [when] the question of trust in the medical profession simply did not arise; [when] doctors functioned in a quasi-ecclesiastic atmosphere of patient awe and confidence".[4] That is, when 'being a doctor' was considered synonymous with 'being trustworthy'. However, even a cursory look at the explanations for the decline of trust (which we presented in the previous chapter) should make it clear to all that 'it is not going to be' when it comes to restoring trust on this basis.

To aid our discussion of this concern, let us briefly recall these five explanations for this decline: (1) the demise of the traditional concept of professionalism, (2) the difficulty of assessing trustworthiness, (3) the discrediting of scientific medicine, (4) the commodification of health care, and (5) changing risk perception and increasing risk-averseness. We think that we can provide a relatively swift and cursory response to explanations (3) and (5). The fact that the average life expectancy has increased by approximately ten years over the past twenty years certainly testifies to the success of science-based medicine and its allied sciences (such as nutrition science). And yet, as we have argued, ever more people refuse to accept its underlying tenets and veer towards 'snake oil medicine'.[5] Similarly, as we have shown in Section 12.5, risks have not

---

[4] Clark 2002, p. 14, our insertions.

[5] It is worth noting that this tendency is more pronounced in people with high levels of 'health literacy' (i.e. people with a high ability to obtain basic health information, and to

increased, yet ever more people see risks lurking behind every corner. Of course, identifying phenomena and being able to account for the reasons behind them are two different things. Trying to account for changes in social attitudes such as these will inevitably involve a complex array of issues and deal, to a certain extent, in generalities. Even establishing any sort of genuine causal link would require a great deal of dedicated research. Yet some possible reasons for the explanations in question offer more support as an account and are more probable than others.

One interesting account as to these changes of people's attitudes is their attribution, at least in part, to a spreading of 'post-modern' relativistic, anti-scientific, and subjectivist thinking, and, more recently, even to a general distrust of rationality.[6] Although there is not a singular movement of thought behind such views, post-modernist thought has become more pervasive throughout society from the late twentieth century as a rejection of more traditional forms of 'realist' thinking, with its acceptance of universal or absolute facts, truths, and values, by replacing them with something akin to an 'anti-realist' approach that places emphasis on the cultural or subjective aspects of judgements about these issues.[7] The growing awareness of post-modernism as a cultural movement has allowed aspects of these views to take hold and spread as an approach taken by members of society more generally. Although there is a vast philosophical heritage behind various anti-realist positions that reject realist views that the truths of statements must correspond to an external and independent reality,[8] the nuanced philosophical debate that accompanies and explains the nature of them is not at the disposal of

---

process and to understand it). This is contrary to what one would expect because these same people generally adopt a more positive health behaviour (Amit et al. 2017, p. 768).

[6] Sampson 1996, p. 194.

[7] 'Post-modernism' as used here is a general term for a broad social movement of thought and culture but with an emphasis on certain philosophical underpinnings that are relevant to our discussion of trust. As it is used only in a loose sense, it is not something that can be captured in a neat and simple definition and the use of it here is doubtless open to dispute. Its philosophical basis is found in the work of many well-known thinkers, such as Heidegger, Foucault, Derrida and Rorty. For those interested in its nature and development, see Cahoone 2003.

[8] Anti-realist positions existed both prior to and beyond post-modernist movements. Their origins can be found in ancient philosophy, but in modern philosophical tradition, much stems from Rene Descartes 'method of doubt'. It is worth noting, however, both that precise definitions as to what constitutes realist or anti-realist positions are difficult to ascertain and that many philosophers tend to be selectively realist or anti-realist depending upon the topic (for example, about morals, aesthetics, properties, objects, etc.). There is plenty of modern discussion on the development of realist and anti-realist debate. See, for example, Wright 1992 and Miller 2006.

much of the general public. Therefore, although we have gained something of a positive outcome in terms of a greater awareness in society as to the very existence of philosophical views that underpin a social movement which incorporates and extols important anti-realist thinking (i.e. that we might question certain claims to there being an objective fact of the matter in various areas of life), there is a corresponding negative outcome that this approach to thinking has been applied by individuals to many – or even all – aspects of life without the resources to fully recognise its implications. The result is not only a rejection of universal acceptance of facts but the adoption of more extreme views, such as that there are no facts, that individuals themselves are the measure of the truth and falsity of all claims to facts, and, correspondingly, that there are no experts.[9] As such, anyone who has been significantly influenced by such views tends not to be amenable to any intervention on the part of physicians or healthcare regulators, whose authority and expertise have been the focus of their rejection. As long as the pendulum does not swing back to more rational and analytical thinking, there is probably no way we can regain these people's trust through rational methods alone (although whether methods designed to change people's perceptions and feelings through other, non-rational, means would be successful is an untested consideration).

Rather than pursue what we take to be potentially hopeless avenues of approach by trying to address pervasive and entrenched social attitudes that lend themselves to explanations (3) and (5), we believe that a closer look at explanations (1), (2), and (4) will help us give at least a qualified answer to the question as to whether and how the medical profession in general – and individual physicians in particular – may regain some trust. It is beyond the scope of this work to present an exhaustive list and analysis of all possible means of restoring trust, but what we intend to do

---

[9] Again, we reiterate that any of these positions can be part of genuine and important philosophical theory. It is the unreflective application of such views that we are attributing our concern to. Anyone who has for one moment reflected upon the recent phenomenon of 'fake news' or the constant rejection of 'expert views' in matters of politics will have witnessed the effects of this as a genuine position in society. However, one extreme version of this scepticism towards facts and expertise, 'denialism', is already a well-known phenomenon. This includes numerous (in)famous examples of rejecting empirical observation and method as a means of establishing reality and truth, such as Flat Earth societies, or, for more political ends, Holocaust, AIDS, and climate change denial. For a general discussion of denialism, see Specter 2009. For a discussion focusing on medicine and public health issues, see Diethelm and McKee 2009. For a discussion of the rejection of expertise, see Nichols 2017.

instead is to briefly discuss answers to the following three questions. (1) Can external regulations increase trust in the medical profession? (2) Can we overcome the difficulty of assessing trustworthiness (and thereby facilitate merit-based trust)? And finally: (3) Is trust in a managed care setting possible? What we offer is far from definitive but, despite being cautious and somewhat tentative about suggestions as to how we might restore trust, we at least feel confident in offering likely avenues or directions to pursue.

13.1 Can External Regulations of the Medical Profession Restore Status Trust?

Arguably, the most important reason for the decline of trust that we have identified is the disavowal of professionalism as a token of trustworthiness. As we discussed in Section 12.1, it was the medical profession's unwillingness and/or inability to fulfil their obligation to regulate the profession and to police defaulting members which brought about the demise of the trust-based old model of professionalism and its replacement with an (at least in greater part) externally regulated model.

There can be no doubt that the medical profession either was not or was only poorly equipped to fulfil their duty of policing themselves because they were not granted effective tools to enforce their rules and to sanction defaulting members. However, if this was all that was at issue, then it would have been sufficient to create such tools and to put them at the disposal of the profession. Yet there is at least some evidence that the profession as a whole was not too keen to police their own members. In fact, it appears that many of their rules of conduct were much more geared towards protecting their members and their own interests than to protecting patients.[10] This reluctance can be seen spreading out into a wider context, for example, in litigation cases, where physicians were notoriously reluctant to testify against their peers.[11]

Crucially, this model of professionalism was based on trust, namely the trust of society that the medical professionalism would (through self-regulation) fulfil its obligation to protect patients from incompetent or

---

[10] Moran and Young (2003), cited in Dixon-Woods et al. 2011, p. 1455.
[11] Gregory 2002. This is reflected in the folk saying that 'one hawk will not pick out another hawk's eyes'.

212 CAN WE RESTORE TRUST?

fraudulent physicians.[12] If physicians had honoured this trust by rigorously policing incompetent or fraudulent peers, it would have greatly enhanced people's trust in physicians in general. Yet, once a series of scandals had made patients aware that they could not trust physicians to police defaulting members, the entire trust-based construct of professionalism, and hence self-regulation, collapsed.

It was at this point in the United Kingdom that "a government White Paper (Department of Health, 2007) outlined the series of reforms that effectively signalled the end of self-regulation in British medicine" by imposing external regulations on physicians.[13] This raises two questions, the answers to which might potentially be universalised to wider contexts beyond the United Kingdom. (1) Can these external regulations restore trust in physicians? (2) Can these regulations indeed protect patients sufficiently? Or, in other words, do these external regulations contribute to a new definition of professionalism, one which will again serve as a token of trustworthiness?

To answer the first question, let us briefly examine the effect of regulations in a rather different setting, that of aviation. Aviation is generally considered one of the most tightly regulated businesses. We all know that pilots have to undergo regular medical check-ups, have to practice critical situations in the flight simulator, etc. Does this, therefore, mean that you trust the pilot? Based on our account of trust, the answer must be 'no'. Rather, you are *confident* that he will do his job competently and that he will know how to handle critical situations. To explain exactly why this is so we have to come back to the difference between trust and confidence, which we discussed in detail in Section 6.2.4. Instead of repeating our arguments, suffice it to remember that trust implies making a choice in the face of uncertainty about the motivations of others, whereas confidence is more like a "habitual expectation".[14] Confidence "implies a situation of relative stability and security where judgements about others are based on what is predictable, involving little risk for the person making the judgement".[15]

This is what regulations, be they in aviation or medicine, do; they bring in relative stability and security and thereby increase confidence. Much as

---

[12] As we have argued before (see page 180), this leads to a circular justification of trust: patients trust physicians to be trustworthy, because they trust them to protect them from un-trustworthy physicians.

[13] Dixon-Woods et al. 2011, p. 1457.

[14] Misztal 1996, p. 16.

[15] Gilson 2006, p. 36.

people are confident that the pilot will do his job competently, they are confident that physicians will comply with the (externally imposed) regulations. In other words, external regulations increase confidence but not trust. To believe that measures which aim at improving confidence will automatically encourage trust is wrong, because this is to misunderstand what trust is.[16] So, our answer to the first question is, no, external regulations do not and will not increase trust in physicians.

This brings us to the second question: Can these external regulations protect patients sufficiently? An empirical answer to this question is not yet possible because not enough time has elapsed since the introduction of external regulation for any meaningful statistics to be generated that might be used to indicate an answer one way or the other. We are, however, not entirely convinced that external regulations will bring a tremendous improvement. They may, perhaps, not so much raise but rather level the standard of competence among physicians by such means as re-certification, etc. To what extent their options of sanctioning will deter those intent on bending the rules, however, remains to be seen. Let's not forget that the notorious scandals alluded to earlier were not provoked by GPs who had not followed the latest guidelines on 'how to treat diabetes in the poly-morbid elderly patient', for example, but instead by those intent on serious moral transgression, including serial killers, rapists, illicit organ harvesters, etc.

In sum, whether external regulations will improve patient protection or not remains to be seen. It is quite clear, however, that external regulations will not reinstate 'professionalism' as a token of physicians' trustworthiness.

13.2 Can We Improve Merit Trust?

If physicians cannot hope to regain status trust, they will have to look for means of facilitating merit trust instead. At the beginning of Section 12.2, we argued that "given the complexity of trustworthiness in the medical context, it is an illusion to believe that an individual patient can even approximately assess a physician's all-out trustworthiness". The same applies to people's assessment of physicians' (and hospitals') trustworthiness in general. Recall also that in Section 6.1 we argued for a differentiation between mistrust and distrust, where *mis*trust is the suspension of trust and *dis*trust the negative expectation.[17] Patients

---

[16] See page 87 for a discussion of these arguments.

[17] See page 74.

who distrust physicians will probably be hard to persuade that they may be wrong. All those, however, who have simply suspended their trust because they cannot judge physicians' trustworthiness should, presumably, be amenable to signs of trustworthiness as evidence to warrant trust over mistrust.

There is a folk saying 'do good and talk about it'. What this means is that it is often not enough simply 'to do good', you also have to 'talk about it' in order to ensure or maximise the action's effect. In the present context, this means that although 'being trustworthy' is 'good per se', it will not earn you people's trust unless you make sure that people know that you are trustworthy. In other words, it is not so much trustworthiness per se that counts when establishing trust in social situations but *perceived* trustworthiness. It is important that the medical profession and the hospitals themselves provide the information patients need to judge their trustworthiness and not leave this to 'consumer reports'.[18] Failing to provide this information themselves could easily be misconstrued, for example, as a sign that this information is handed over reluctantly, or obtained by other means, all of which would potentially undermine the perception of trustworthiness. In all our relationships we incessantly use (subtle or not so subtle) signs to signal our position. So, if physicians want to overcome patients' mistrust, they will have to send the patient signs signalling their trustworthiness. There are innumerable ways physicians and hospitals can signal to the patient that they are (making every effort to be) trustworthy.

In order, therefore, to start to build a picture as to how it might be possible to improve merit trust, we will first look at how physicians can signal their trustworthiness in the individual patient–physician relationship. Following this, we will consider a few means that might be used to signal trustworthiness at the institutional level.

13.2.1   Demonstrating Trustworthiness at an Individual Level

At the personal level, most of the signs signalling trustworthiness have to do with the physician's behaviour. There are a number of key aspects of behaviour that are most relevant to achieving this, and we think it is worth mentioning the role of just three of them here (availability, genuine shared decision-making, and admitting uncertainty and errors) to

---

[18] Roberts 2017, p. 307. An example of such a consumer report is Rate MDs (accessible via: www.ratemds.com/best-doctors/eng/).

indicate the sorts of behavioural signalling we are suggesting as indicators of trustworthiness. In Section 12.2, we argued that 'availability' is no guarantee for trustworthiness[19] and, of course, it is not. Nevertheless, availability of their doctor in the case of a (true or perceived) emergency is very important for anxious patients, and it often pays-off to prove this availability,[20] for example, by letting the patient have a direct contact phone number.[21] While some might find the likelihood of such a level of access to a physician unlikely to be widely offered, emphasising the quality of general accessibility, such as making sure the patient gets an appointment as and when (he thinks) he needs one and taking one's time during consultations, is something that falls well within a standard professional relationship but when properly implemented can support this perception of trustworthiness.

Although there may be practical difficulties surrounding managing availability at all points, practising genuine *shared decision-making* is perhaps the single most important sign of trustworthiness that can be fully incorporated into daily practice.[22] However, it is important to remember that this is much more than just flooding the patient with information and then letting him decide (or giving him the impression that he has made the decision). What makes shared decision-making *genuine*, as opposed to merely an impression, is that it implies an honest two-way transfer of knowledge. It requires equipoise between what the physician and the patient consider important. On the physician's side this is mostly, although not exclusively, biomedical facts. On the patient's side this can be quite often something the physician would not think of. For example, physicians typically assume that a cancer patient is primarily interested in whether or how he can be cured and in what his chances of success are, whereas in reality his main concern may be whether the disease will make him lose his job and lead him or his family into financial troubles – a consideration that might make him desire a different approach to determining treatment options. Crucially, shared decision-making also means that patient and physician share responsibility. Inviting the patient to share responsibility shows that the physician sees the

---

[19] See page 185.
[20] Larson 2000, p. 12.
[21] Many physicians may be reluctant to do this. However, M.W. has quite often done this in the course of his professional practice and found that it has virtually never been abused.
[22] For a good summary of this, see Kalra et al. 2017, pp. 268–9.

patient as equal and that he trusts him. Just as we have argued earlier, the safest way to make someone trust you is to trust her.[23]

A very good example of a situation in which only open and honest shared decision-making may assure the patient is that of the patient's fear of being overtreated. It is headlines like the following that can make patients question the need for a proposed treatment: "A USA TODAY study found that tens of thousands of times each year, patients undergo surgery they don't need."[24] Overtreatment[25] is not only a concern of patients but also (and perhaps even more so) of health providers and insurance companies (because of the associated costs). However, it is not a simple problem since there is often no agreement as to what constitutes 'overtreatment'. In fact, at the heart of the problem often lies another, equally disputed problem, namely overdiagnosis.[26] Yet, even if we limit the term 'overtreatment' to those cases "in which the diagnosis is correct according current standards, ... the treatment may still have a low probability of benefitting the patient and may instead be harmful",[27] and we do not think that there are any procedural solutions to this problem. A truly trustworthy physician will address the problem directly and, after discussing the pros and cons of the proposed procedure, as well as possible alternatives, will hopefully be able to clear the patient's fears.

Finally, it may come as a surprise to some, but both *admitting uncertainty*[28] and *errors*[29] are important signs of trustworthiness. Conversely, there is hardly anything that signifies untrustworthiness more than (trying) to cover up an error.[30]

These are just three, brief, examples of how physicians can signal their trustworthiness, but we think that, among all the means of restoring trust

---

[23] See page 150.

[24] Published by USA TODAY on June 20, 2013. Retrievable from: www.usatoday.com /story/news/nation/2013/06/18/unnecessary-surgery-usa-today-investigation/2435009/

[25] Overtreatment is probably more of a problem in surgery than in medicine, because, contrary to drugs, surgical interventions do not have to undergo testing for safety and efficacy in trials (Stahel et al. 2017).

[26] By this we mean making a 'diagnosis' where the finding has no disease value. For a good (if somewhat polemical) review of the problem of overdiagnosis, the reader is referred to Welch and Schwartz 2012.

[27] Armstrong 2018. For a discussion of the ethical implications of differentiating between 'what can be done' (but may not benefit, or indeed may even harm the patient) and 'what should be done' (because it unquestionably benefits the patient), see page 134.

[28] William 2007, p. 75.

[29] Shore 2007, p. 15.

[30] As many politicians (and, of course, others too) know 'you don't get in trouble for the deed – you get in trouble for the cover-up' (taken from Shore 2007, p. 15).

we mention in this final chapter, they (and the many more examples that certainly exist) probably offer the highest chance of recovering some of the lost trust because (contrary to the other means) these signals are those that are all readily perceived by the patient. We will now turn our attention from individual physicians to how hospitals (or other health-care institutions) can signal their trustworthiness.

13.2.2 Demonstrating Trustworthiness at the Institutional Level

The biggest fear of many patients (apart from fears directly related to their condition or disease) is probably the fear of grave medical errors, such as 'wrong medication' (or dosage) and 'wrong surgery'.[31] Indeed, wrong surgery scandals have probably raised more fears in patients and thus contributed more to the decline of trust than the 'really big scandals' (such as the Shipman and the Alder Hey cases referred to earlier).[32] Most patients probably do not really fear that their physician may be a killer or a sexual offender, but they do fear that the surgeon might operate on the wrong side (i.e. the wrong limb or organ), or perform the wrong procedure. Unfortunately, all of this happens,[33] and since hospitals fear wrong surgery at least much as their patients, they implement procedural standards to minimise (or better still prevent) such disastrous mistakes. The adoption of error-reducing (or preventing) procedures can certainly help to improve trust, provided patients learn about them and can understand their significance (again, reminding us of the importance not only 'to do good' but also to 'talk about it'). Here, we will confine ourselves to two examples, namely 'time-out procedures' and 'critical incident reporting'. In addition, we will briefly mention two more general means of demonstrating the hospital's competency: case-load (i.e. the number of patients treated by specific units or for a specific disease) and accreditation.

One procedure aimed at preventing 'wrong surgery' which has gained wide acceptance is the so-called *time-out procedure*, which involves introducing a stop in the ongoing workflow. Of course, you can introduce a 'time-out' at any point in the workflow, but some timings may prove more effective, valuable, or easier to manage than others. The most common form is a stop after the patient is anaesthetised and prepared

[31] Such as amputation of the wrong leg.
[32] And, as M.W. can testify, fear of 'wrong surgery' also haunts the dreams of surgeons.
[33] Since this is not a medical text, we will not go into the (rather shocking) statistics of this problem. Anyone interested in this is referred to the paper by Clarke et al. 2007.

for the intended operation. This means that the surgeon, before he gets permission (e.g. by the anaesthesiologist) to start the surgery, has to repeat the name of the patient, the operation he is going to perform, the side of the intervention, etc. Only if all of this corresponds to the notes in the chart (or on the informed consent form) may the surgeon start with the operation.

Other forms include a stop before the patient is brought into the operating room. In this case the patient is asked his name, the surgeon's name, the operation he is about to undergo, and the side. This type of 'time-out' has the advantage of ruling out what is probably even more disastrous than 'wrong surgery', namely 'wrong patient'. Since the patient himself is involved in the checking, this is perceived as a positive, trust-enhancing experience by patients.[34] Given the rarity (in absolute figures) of wrong surgery,[35] it is statistically difficult to prove the efficacy of time-out implementation. However, simply knowing that such procedures are used at a hospital can bolster patients' trust. For hospitals, informing patients about 'time-out' is a good way to signal their interest in improving patient safety and thus demonstrate their trustworthiness. Some hospitals present information about 'time-out' routines on their home-pages. Others opt to leave it to the surgeon to inform the patient. A particularly apt moment is to explain it to the patient on the evening before the surgery and to combine it (whenever feasible) with marking the operation site with an indelible pen on the patient's skin.

Fortunately, not all errors result in catastrophes. Many times, errors are detected in time. In order to learn from such 'near misses'[36] various types of reporting systems have been developed. They are most commonly used in high-risk industries, such as aviation, NASA, petrochemical processing, and the nuclear power industry. More recently, such error reporting systems, often called *'critical incident reporting systems'* (CIRS), have also been introduced in medicine. Since it is not the scope of this book to discuss various types of incident reporting and their inherent problems,[37] suffice it to say that they offer another means to improve patient safety and signal trustworthiness, and thus boost patients' trust.

---

[34] Kozusko et al. 2016, p. 617.
[35] Typical figures cited in the literature vary between 1 in 17,000 and 1 in 100,000 surgical interventions (Clarke et al. 2007).
[36] A 'near miss' is "any event that could have had adverse consequences but did not and was indistinguishable from fully fledged adverse events in all but outcome" (Barach and Small 2000, p. 761).
[37] For an excellent review of the topic, the reader is referred to Barach and Small 2000.

Recall in the second case history presented at the beginning of this book we cited a patient asking her physician 'whether he has performed the proposed operation before'.[38] This points to an important belief many people have, namely that 'numbers count'. And, indeed, there is quite good (although not entirely undisputed) evidence that the outcome is better if the surgeon has performed an operation at least a minimal number of times and also performs the operation a minimal number of times per year. Also, surgical units with larger *case-loads* generally have better outcomes.[39] For this reason, many hospitals present data about their case-load on their home-pages or in their annual reports.

The knowledge about the case-load/outcome relationship is also reflected in the fact that *Accrediting Offices*[40] typically require certain minimal numbers of cases and/or procedures. The observation that hospitals proudly present their Accreditation Diplomas on their home-page points to the fact that they see such diplomas as tokens of their trustworthiness and as a means of bolstering their patients' trust.[41] However, basing one's trust in healthcare institutions on the fact that the institution is 'accredited' really transfers trust from the hospital to the accrediting agency. In other words, we are once more confronted with the problem of transferring trust from a first-order to a second-order object.[42]

Time-out, CIRS, presenting case-load data, and accreditation are four examples of how hospitals can demonstrate their efforts to improve patient safety and signal their trustworthiness. The reverse side of this coin is that the prominent presentation of such measures may also be used or even abused, such as for PR purposes in an increasingly competitive healthcare system. Much the same applies to the publication of

---

[38] See page 5.

[39] For a discussion of the relevant literature, see Reames et al. 2014.

[40] Although we use the term 'accreditation' here, there are variances in usage. For example, in Switzerland and Germany, the term 'certification' is more commonly used. In the United Kingdom, the two most widely used terms are either 'licensing' (given the requirement for NHS service providers to apply for a licence with the NHS independent regulator under the Health and Social Care Act, 2012) or 'registration' (due to the requirements for health and social care service providers, including both NHS and independent hospitals, to be registered with the independent Care Quality Commission (CQC) regulator, which monitors, inspects, and regulates standards and publishes these inspection reports for each individual provider).

[41] Of course, there is a lot more to be said about 'certification' and 'accreditation', which is beyond the scope of this text. We recognise that different countries use different schemes and approaches but that our underlying point remains the same regardless.

[42] See page 154 for a detailed discussion of this dilemma.

standard quality indicators (for example, infection rates, mortality rates, and unplanned readmission rates). Often, the publication of such quality indicators is done under the label of 'transparency', transparency being considered by many as the panacea to demonstrate trustworthiness and boost trust,[43] despite the fact that there is no evidence that transparency increases trust, not least because it does not rule out deception.[44] Last, but not least, we must not forget that measures aimed at signalling trustworthiness can also backfire when it becomes obvious that 'words and reality do not fit',[45] something that would be particularly apparent to an already highly sceptical public armed with freely available data.

In the next and final section, we will go on to analyse the means that physicians and healthcare organisations have to convince patients that 'managed care' and trust are not mutually exclusive.

13.3   Can We Improve Trust in Managed Care?

Now that we have looked at the (rather slim) chances of regaining status trust and discussed some (more promising) means of upping merit trust, we wish to end the book with a brief analysis of whether and, if so, how physicians engaged by managed care[46] organisations can regain some of the lost trust.

One (or perhaps the) principal goal of managed care is reducing the costs of health care. To achieve this, such organisations have to limit access to health care by encouraging their employed physicians to follow cost-reducing strategies with positive or negative incentives. This is, in turn, perceived by the public as rationing and also leads to a re-conceptualisation of physicians as corporate employees rather than as fully autonomous agents. While both of these hold true for managed care, the belief that this is specific only to managed care is based on two illusions: First, even in affluent countries, resources are limited. Unless we are willing to allocate many of our finite resources exclusively to health care – and at the expense of other social goods, such as public safety, education, and defence –

---

[43] Manson and O'Neill 2007, p. 177.
[44] O'Neill 2002b, p. 70.
[45] Manson and O'Neill 2007, p. 161.
[46] We are using the term 'managed care' as an umbrella term for any type health care in which physicians are financially accountable to third parties, and in which (positive or negative) incentives are used to encourage physicians to reduce costs, basically by limiting access to care.

rationing is unavoidable.[47] Rationing can be done in two main ways: "The private sector rations access by charging market prices to patients, with demand driven by a person's ability and willingness to pay. Public systems generally ration care on the basis of a patient's need, for example by covering priority cost-effective treatments."[48] We have already discussed and illustrated regulating access by charging market prices in Section 12.4.[49] Here, we will focus on rationing in public healthcare systems (as exemplified by managed care).

Second, it has always been an illusion to believe "that physicians owe an absolute duty of fidelity to each individual patient'[50] In fact, it is an illusion to think that physicians could act solely in any single patient's interest 'without undue outside influence' (that is, entirely independently) even if they wanted to. Physicians are social agents and so have always acted within society, having to balance the individual patient's interests with those of society or those of other patients. In fact, even physicians in private for-profit hospitals, who, as many people (in particular the physicians themselves) believe act 'solely in their patients' interests, are in reality bound by the hospital board's and the stakeholder's demand to 'maximise profit'.

So far, we have talked of physicians working for 'profit-oriented' hospitals and of physicians engaged by 'cost-oriented' managed care organisations. Somewhere between the two are all those physicians who have their independent practices, are paid by third-party payers, and who are typically considered the paragons of autonomous physicians who have only the interests of their patients at heart. However, even these physicians increasingly come under pressure to reduce costs and have to follow external regulations. So, there probably is not that much difference between the three types of physicians working in the commercialised arms of healthcare provision. As we have seen, all of them have lost status trust, and, in principle, all of them can gain merit trust, although this probably is most difficult for physicians engaged in managed care, since

---

[47] Scheunemann and White 2011, p. 1626. There is a vast body of literature on medical, ethical, legal, and political aspects of rationing. It is not the purpose of this chapter and would not contribute to our arguments to enter into a discussion of the various aspects of rationing.

[48] WHO Health financing for universal coverage, available from: www.who.int/health_finan cing/topics/benefit-package/benefits-and-rationing/en/

[49] See page 194.

[50] Brody 2012, p. 2012.

they are hampered by the suspicion of practising (covert) rationing and being too much at their 'cost-oriented' organisations' bidding.

If managed care physicians and managed care organisations want to appear trustworthy and to regain trust, they must convince their patients that these suspicions are unfounded, because most of the cost reduction is achieved through cutting managerial overhead, reducing unnecessary costly referrals to specialists, avoiding duplicate testing, opting for less expensive but equally effective treatment options, and eschewing over-treatment, all of which do not entail denying patients beneficial care.[51] However, even if all of this is true (and there is a reasonable likelihood that much of it genuinely is correct), it will be difficult to bring this message across.

It is worth briefly mentioning an alternative answer posited by Buchanan, that they will have to convince their patients that whatever is done to reduce costs (including limiting access to care) is legitimate. In other words, managed care physicians will want to merit their patients' trust not (or, preferably, not only) because they are individually perceived as trustworthy but because they work in a trustworthy organisation. The first type of merit trust has been called by Buchanan 'primary merit trust' and the second type 'derivative merit trust'.[52]

For derivative merit trust to be justified it must be grounded in the legitimacy of the managed care organisation. This means that the organisation must have a structure and policies that allow to solve disputes between the organisation's demands and the physician's ethics concerning patient treatment and care. In addition, since ethical rationing requires deliberate choices, it must guarantee procedural justice in determining how this is carried out. Let us unpack this. Even though working for a managed care organisation, a managed care physician will still want to fulfil his fiduciary obligation to act in the patient's interest or to act as the patient's agent. Inevitably, this will occasionally lead to discrepancies between what the organisation's commitment to reducing costs demands and what the physician finds ethically acceptable. In this situation, for a managed care organisation to be legitimised, a number of different factors need to be in place. According to Buchanan, its organisation and structure must (1) empower the physician to voice 'constructive criticism' of organizational policies and decisions and (2) identify

[51] Scheunemann and White 2011, p. 1626.
[52] Buchanan 2000, p. 194.

those individuals within the organisation who are responsible to respond appropriately to this criticism. Moreover, the organization's structure, policies, must (3) recognise the special responsibility of physicians as medical professionals who are assumed to have a non-instrumental commitment to patients' well-being and (4) reflect a proper appreciation of the distinctive technical expertise of physicians. Procedural justice is important because there are no societal standards as to what constitutes adequate care and justified limitations of care. It implies transparency, non-discrimination, impartiality, publicity of the rules applied and of their justification, and, finally, fair and accessible appeal procedures.[53]

This is, as it were, in a nutshell Buchanan's concept of 'derivative merit trust'. It is philosophically very thick. We do not doubt that it explains the conditions under which managed care is trustworthy. We do not quite see, however, what it can do to help managed care organisation and their physicians gain their patients' trust.[54]

13.4 Conclusions

As it is extremely unlikely to ever be a return to the sort of status trust possessed by the medical profession in the past, by far the most likely means of re-establishing trust between physicians and patients will be through advancing merit trust. We have made some observations and tentative suggestions as to how we think this might be achieved. We believe that individual physicians have the best chances of gaining their patients' trust by (1) practising genuine shared decision-making which involves an honest *two-way* transfer of knowledge, (2) inviting the patient to share responsibility, and (3) admitting uncertainty (whether personal or inherent in the available information). Although there is no guarantee that these will be sufficient to restore trust in all cases, from reflecting upon the nature of both trust as a concept and the causes of the decline of trust, these all seem to be extremely important considerations for any attempt to do so.

Medical institutions of any type will most likely find it harder to re-gain trust. This is especially likely to be true for those engaged in

---

[53] Buchanan 2000, pp. 195–7.
[54] It would be exciting to see the results of an empirical study comparing trust levels in managed care organizations which fulfil Buchanan's criteria with organizations which do not fulfil them.

commercialised medicine due to the increased number of factors that can lead to patient concern as to the trustworthiness of their medical practices. For them, it might be best to consider that although

> we still know little empirically about the transfer of trust between personal doctors and managers, consultants, hospitals, and the larger health system, *doctors are the gateway to organisational trust.* Health plans . . . elicit trust through the qualifications and reputations of affiliated doctors.[55]

Therefore, for trust to be restored, it is likely to be most successfully managed by institutions allowing individual physicians the freedom and scope to advance their own trustworthiness in the eyes of patients, allowing at least those with the 'suspended' form of mistrust to perceive the attempt at establishing trustworthiness.

---

[55] Mechanic 2004, p. 1419, our emphasis.

REFERENCES

Ahern MM, Hendryx MS (2003) 'Social Capital and Trust in Providers', *Social Science & Medicine*, vol. 57, pp. 1195–203.

Alaszewski A, Brown P (2007) 'Risk, Uncertainty and Knowledge', *Health Risk & Society*, vol. 9, pp. 1–10.

Alfano M (2016) 'Friendship and the Structure of Trust', in Masala A, Webber J (eds.) *From Personality to Virtue*, Oxford, Oxford University Press, pp. 186–206.

Allsop J (2006) 'Regaining Trust in Medicine: Professional and State', *Current Sociology*, vol. 54, pp. 621–36.

Alston W (1986) 'Epistemic Circularity', *Philosophy and Phenomenological Research*, vol. 47, pp. 1–30.

Amit AA, Nehama H, Rishpon S et al. (2017) 'Parents with High Levels of Communicative and Critical Health Literacy Are Less Likely to Vaccinate Their Children', *Patient Education and Counseling*, vol. 100, pp. 768–75.

Appelbaum PS, Lidz CW, Klitzman R (2009) 'Voluntariness of Consent to Research: A Conceptual Model', *The Hastings Center Report*, vol. 39, pp. 30–9.

Armstrong N (2018) 'Overdiagnosis and Overtreatment as a Quality Problem: Insights from Healthcare Improvement Research', *BMJ Quality and Safety*, vol. 27, pp. 571–575.

Audi R (1993) *The Structure of Justification*, Cambridge, Cambridge University Press.

Audi R (2001) *The Architecture of Reason: The Structure and Substance of Rationality*, Oxford, Oxford University Press.

Ayer A (1936) *Language Truth and Logic*, London, Victor Gollancz Ltd (reprint 1952, Dover Publications, New York).

Badhwar N (1993) *Friendship: A Philosophical Reader*, Ithaca, NY, Cornell University Press.

Baier A (1991) 'Trust – The Tanner Lectures on Human Values'. Available via www .tannerlectures.utah.edu/lectures/documents/baier92.pdf accessed 30 January 2011

Baier A (1986) 'Trust and Antitrust', *Ethics*, vol. 96, pp. 231–60.

Baier A (1994) 'The Possibility of Sustaining Trust', in Pauer-Studer H (ed.) *Norms, Values, and Society*, Dordrecht, Boston, London, Kluwer Academic Publishers, pp. 245–59.

Barach P, Small SD (2000) 'Reporting and Preventing Medical Mishaps: Lessons from Non-medical Near Miss Reporting Systems', *BMJ*, vol. 320, pp. 759–63.

Barrera D (2007) 'The Impact of Negotiated Exchange on Trust and Trustworthiness', *Social Networks*, vol. 29, pp. 508–26.

Baurmann M (2010) 'Collective Knowledge and Epistemic Trust. The Approach of Social Epistemology', *Kölner Zeitschrift für Soziologie und Sozialpsychologie*, vol. 50, pp. 185–201.

Becker LC (1996) 'Trust as Noncognitive Security about Motives', *Ethics*, vol. 107, pp. 43–61.

Belnap N (1993) 'On Rigorous Definitions', *Philosophical Studies*, vol. 72, pp. 115–46.

Bennett O (2011) 'Cultures of Optimism', *Cultural Sociology*, vol. 5, pp. 301–20.

Berghmans R (2011) 'Voluntary Consent, Normativity, and Authenticity', *The American Journal of Bioethics*, vol. 11, pp. 23–4.

Berlin L (2017) 'Medical Errors, Malpractice, and Defensive Medicine: An Ill-fated Triad', *Diagnosis (Berl)*, vol. 4, pp. 133–9.

Bickerton D (2009) *Adam's Tongue – How Humans Made Language, How Language Made Humans*, New York, Hill and Wang.

Birkhauer J, Gaab J, Kossowsky J et al. (2017) 'Trust in the Health Care Professional and Health Outcome: A Meta-Analysis', *PLoS One*, vol. 12, pp. 1–3.

Blendon J (2007) 'Why Americans Don't Trust the Government and Don't Trust Healthcare', in Shore DA (ed.) *The Trust Crisis in Health Care*, Oxford, Oxford University Press, pp. 21–31.

Blum L (1980) *Friendship, Altruism, and Morality*, London, Routledge & Kegan Paul.

Bonds D, Camacho F, Bell R et al. (2004) 'The Association of Patient Trust and Self-Care among Patients with Diabetes Mellitus', *BMC Fam Pract*, vol. 16, pp. 5–26.

Borlotti L (2010) *Delusions and Other Irrational Beliefs*, Oxford, Oxford University Press.

Bradford J, Knott D, Levine D et al. (2011) 'Accounting for the Cost of US Health Care'. Available via healthcare.mckinsey.com/accounting-cost-us-health-care-pre-reform-trends-and-impact-recession–2011.

Brody H (2012) 'From an Ethics of Rationing to an Ethics of Waste Avoidance', *New England Journal of Medicine*, vol. 366, pp. 1949–51.

Brown PR (2008) 'Trusting in the New NHS: Instrumental versus Communicative Action', *Sociology of Health & Illness*, vol. 30, pp. 349–63.

Buchanan A (1988) 'Principal-Agent Theory and Decision Making in Health Care', *Bioethics*, vol. 2, pp. 317–33.

Buchanan A (1991) 'The Physician's Knowledge and the Patient's Best Interest', in Pellegrino D, Veatch RM et al. (eds.) *Ethics, Trust, and the Professions*, Washington, DC, Georgetown University Press, pp. 93–107.

Buchanan A (2000) 'Trust in Managed Care Organizations', *Kennedy Institute of Ethics Journal*, vol. 10, pp. 189–212.

Burge T (1993) 'Content Preservation', *The Philosophical Review*, vol. 102, pp. 457–88.

Burgess J (2008) 'When Is Circularity in Definitions Benign?', *The Philosophical Quarterly*, vol. 58, pp. 214–33.

Cahoone, L (ed.) (2003) *From Modernism to Postmodernism: An Anthology*, Oxford, Blackwell Publishing Ltd.

Calnan M, Sanford E (2004) 'Public Trust in Health Care: the System or the Doctor?', *Quality & Safety in Health Care*, vol. 13, pp. 92–7.

Carnap R (1956) *Meaning and Necessity: A Study in Semantics and Modal Logic*, Chicago, The University of Chicago Press.

Chan CS (2018) '*Mistrust of Physicians in China: Society, Institution, and Interaction as Root Causes*', *Dev.World Bioeth*, vol. 18, pp. 16–25.

Chandratilake M (2010) 'Medical Professionalism: What Does the Public Think?', *Clinical Medicine*, vol. 10, pp. 364–9.

Charlton BG (1992) 'Philosophy of Medicine: Alternative or Scientific', *Journal of the Royal Society of Medicine*, vol. 85, pp. 436–8.

Chief Medical Officer (2006) *Good Doctors, Safer Patients*, London, Department of Health.

Clark CC (2002) 'Trust in Medicine', *Journal of Medicine and Philosophy*, vol. 27, pp. 11–29.

Clarke JR, Johnston J, Finley ED (2007) 'Getting Surgery Right', *Annals of Surgery*, vol. 246, pp. 395–405.

Cobb LA, Thomas GI, Dillard DH et al. (1959) 'An Evaluation of Internal-Mammary-Artery Ligation by a Double-Blind Technic', *New England Journal of Medicine*, vol. 28, pp. 1115–8.

Cohen J (2013) 'Paradox of Hope', *Journal of Palliative Medicine*, vol. 16, pp. 1307–8.

Cohen MA, Dienhart J (2013) 'Moral and Amoral Conceptions of Trust, with an Application in Organizational Ethics', *Journal of Business Ethics*, vol. 112, pp. 1–13.

Collins H, Evans R (2007) *Rethinking Expertise*, Chicago, The University of Chicago Press.

Collins H, Evans R (2010) *Tacit and Explicit Knowledge*, Chicago, The University of Chicago Press.

Corso R (2010) 'Harris Poll Confidence Index 2010'. Available via www .harrisinteractive.com/vault/Harris-Interactive-Poll-Research-Education-Confidence-2010–03.pdf accessed 18 January 2011.

Cruess RL, Cruess SR (2010) 'Professionalism Is a Generic Term: Practicing What We Preach', *Medical Teacher*, vol. 32, pp. 713–4.

Cuccio V, Carapezza M (2015) 'Is Displacement Possible without Language? Evidence from Preverbal Infants and Chimpanzees', *Philosophical Psychology*, vol. 28, pp. 369–86.

Davidoff F (2011) 'Systems of Service: Reflections on the Moral Foundations of Improvement', *BMJ Quality & Safety*, vol. 20, pp. i5–i10.

Davis FD (1997) 'Phronesis, Clinical Reasoning, and Pellegrino's Philosophy of Medicine', *Theoretical Medicine*, vol. 18, pp. 173–95.

Day J (1969) 'Hope', *American Philosophical Quarterly*, vol. 6, pp. 89–102.

De Vries RG, Kim SYH (2008) 'Bioethics and the Sociology of Trust: Introduction to the Theme', *Medicine Health Care and Philosophy*, vol. 11, pp. 377–9.

Deutsch M (1960) 'The Effect of Motivational Orientation upon Trust and Suspicion', *Human Relations*, vol. 13, pp. 123–39.

DeVellis R (2003) *Scale Development – Theory and Applications*, Thousand Oaks, SAGE Publications.

Diethelm P, McKee M (2009) 'Denialism: What Is It and How Should Scientists Respond?', *European Journal of Public Health*, vol. 19, pp. 2–4.

Dixon-Woods M, Yeung K, Bosk CL (2011) 'Why Is UK Medicine No Longer a Self-Regulating Profession? The Role of Scandals Involving "Bad Apple" Doctors', *Social Science and Medicine*, vol. 73, pp. 1452–9.

Dogan M (1998) 'The Decline of Traditional Values in Western Europe – Religion, Nationalism Authority', *International Journal of Comparative Sociology*, vol. 39, pp. 77–90.

Dowie A (2000) 'Phronesis or "Practical Wisdom" in Medical Education', *Medical teacher*, vol. 22, pp. 240–1.

Dunbar R (1996) *Grooming, Gossip, and the Evolution of Language*, London, Faber and Faber.

Dunn J (2000) 'Trust and Political Agency', in Gambetta D (ed.) *Trust – Making and Breaking Cooperative Relations*, New York, Basil Blackwell, pp. 73–92.

Eagly AH, Chaiken S (2007) 'The Advantages of an Inclusive Definition of Attitude', *Social Cognition*, vol. 25, pp. 582–602.

Elgin CZ (2002) 'Take It from Me: The Epistemological Status of Testimony', *Philosophy and Phenomenological Research*, vol. 65, pp. 291–308.

Elliott R (2011) 'Evidence-Based-Medicine and the Integrity of the Medical Profession', *Journal of Clinical Ethics*, vol. 22, pp. 71–3.

Elster J (2007) *Explaining Social Behaviour – More Nuts and Bolts for the Social Sciences*, Cambridge, Cambridge University Press.

Erde EL (2008) 'Professionalism's Facets: Ambiguity, Ambivalence, and Nostalgia', *Journal of Medicine and Philosophy*, vol. 33, pp. 6–26.

Ernst E (2009) 'Complementary/Alternative Medicine: Engulfed by Postmodernism, Anti-Science and Regressive Thinking', *British Journal of General Practice*, vol. 59, pp. 298–301.

Faulkner P (2002) 'On the Rationality of Our Response to Testimony', *Synthese*, vol. 131, pp. 353–70.

Faulkner P (2003) 'The Epistemic Role of Trust', in Falcone R, Barber S et al. (eds.) *Trust, Reputation, and Security: Theories and Practice*, Berlin, Heidelberg, Springer, pp. 30–8.

Fiscella K (1999) 'Does Skepticism towards Medical Care Predict Mortality?', *Medical Care*, vol. 37, pp. 409–14.

Fitzpatrick M (2001) *The Tyranny of Health*, London, Routledge.

Foster K, Bernstein D, Huber P (1999) *Phantom Risk – Scientific Inference and the Law*, Cambridge, MA, MIT Press.

Frank A (2012) 'Reflective Healthcare Practice', in Kinsella EA, Pitman A (eds.) *Phronesis as Professional Knowledge*, Rotterdam, Sense Publishers, pp. 53–60.

Frege G (1892) 'Über Sinn und Bedeutung', in Beaney M (ed.) *The Frege Reader* (1997), Oxford, Wiley Blackwell

Freidson E, Rhea B (1963) 'Processes of Control in a Company of Equals ', *Social Problems*, vol. 11, pp. 119–31.

Freudenburg WR (1993) 'Risk and Recreancy – Weber, the Division of Labor, and the Rationality of Risk Perceptions', *Social Forces*, vol. 71, pp. 909–32.

Freudenburg WR (1996) 'Risky Thinking: Irrational Fears about Risk and Society', *Annals of the American Academy of Political and Social Science*, vol. 545, pp. 44–53.

Fricker E (2006) 'Second-Hand Knowledge', *Philosophy and Phenomenological Research*, vol. 73, pp. 592–618.

Fried C (1974) *Medical Experimentation: Personal Integrity & Social Policy*, New York, Elsevier (reprinted in 2016 by Oxford University Press).

Frost DP (1997) 'Medicine, Postmodernism, and the End of Certainty – Complex Systems Result in a New Kind of Fundamental Uncertainty', *British Medical Journal*, vol. 314, p. 1045.

Gallup (2003) 'Public Rates Nursing as Most Honest and Ethical Profession (Gallup Survey 2003)'. Available via www.gallup.com/poll/9823/Public-Rates-Nursing-Most-Honest-Ethical-Profession.aspx accessed 20 January 2011.

Garrard E, Wrigley A (2009) 'Hope and Terminal Illness: False Hope versus Absolute Hope', *Clinical Ethics*, vol. 4, pp. 38–43.

Gerretsen P, Myers J (2008) 'The Physician: A Secure Base', *Journal of Clinical Oncology*, vol. 26, pp. 5294–6.

Gettier E (1963) 'Is Justified True Belief Knowledge?', *Analysis*, vol. 23, pp. 121–3.

Gillett G (1995) 'Virtue and Truth in Clinical Science', *The Journal of Medicine and Philosophy*, vol. 20, pp. 285–98.

Gilson L (2006) 'Trust in Health Care: Theoretical Perspectives and Research Needs', *Journal of Health Organization and Management*, vol. 20, pp. 359–75.

Glaeser EL, Laibson DI, Scheinkman JA et al. (2000) 'Measuring Trust', *Quarterly Journal of Economics*, vol. 115, pp. 811–46.

Goldberg S (2006) 'Reductionism and the Distinctiveness of Testimonial Knowledge', in Lackey J, Sosa E (eds.) *The Epistemology of Testimony*, Oxford, Oxford University Press, pp. 127–44.

Goldman AI (2001) 'Experts: Which Ones Should You Trust? (Epistemic Considerations)', *Philosophy and Phenomenological Research*, vol. 63, pp. 85–110.

Goldman D (2014) 'Modification of the Reactive Attitudes', *Pacific Philosophical Quarterly*, vol. 95, pp. 1–22.

Goold SD (2001) 'Trust and the Ethics of Health Care Institutions', *Hastings Center Report*, vol. 31, pp. 26–33.

Goold SD (2002) 'Trust, Distrust and Trustworthiness – Lessons from the Field', *Journal of General Internal Medicine*, vol. 17, pp. 79–81.

Govier T (1998) *Dilemmas of Trust*, Montreal, McGill-Queen's University Press.

Gregory A (2002) 'Doctors Often Reluctant to Testify Against Peers', *New Zealand Herald*, edition of Feb. 18.

Hall MA (2006) 'Researching Medical Trust in the United States', *Journal of Health Organization and Management*, vol. 20, pp. 456–67.

Hall MA, Dugan E, Zheng BY et al. (2001) 'Trust in Physicians and Medical Institutions: What Is It, Can It Be Measured, and Does It Matter?', *Milbank Quarterly*, vol. 79, pp. 613–39.

Hardin R (1993) 'The Street-Level Epistemology of Trust', *Politics & Society*, vol. 21, pp. 505–29.

Hardin R (1996) 'Trustworthiness', *Ethics*, vol. 107, pp. 26–42.

Hardin R (2002) *Trust and Trustworthiness*, New York, Russel Sage Foundation.

Hardin R (2006) *Trust*, Cambridge, Polity Press.

Hardwig J (1985) 'Epistemic Dependence', *Journal of Philosophy*, vol. 82, pp. 335–49.

Hardwig J (1991) 'The Role of Trust in Knowledge', *Journal of Philosophy*, vol. 88, pp. 693–708.

Harrison S, Smith C (2004) 'Trust and Moral Motivation: Redundant Resources in Health and Social Care?', *Policy and Politics*, vol. 32, pp. 371–86.

Hawkes N (2017) 'Public's Distrust of Medicines Needs Urgent Action, Says Academy', *BMJ*, vol. 357, p. j2974.

Hawley K (2012) *Trust – A Very Short Introduction*, Oxford, Oxford University Press.

Hawley K (2015) 'Trust and Distrust between Patient and Doctor', *Journal of Evaluation in Clinical Practice*, vol. 21, pp. 798–801.

Helg M (2018) 'Ist der Bankräuber auf der Flucht versichert?', *Folio Neue Zürcher Zeitung*, pp. 54–7.

Helliwell JF, Putnam RD (2004) 'The Social Context of Well-Being', *Philosophical Transactions of the Royal Society of London Series B-Biological Sciences*, vol. 359, pp. 1435–46.

Heritage J (2005) 'Revisiting Authority in Physician-Patient Interaction', *Diagnosis as Cultural Practice*, vol. 16, pp. 83–102.

Hertzberg L (1988) 'On the Attitude of Trust', *Inquiry – An Interdisciplinary Journal of Philosophy*, vol. 31, pp. 307–22.

Hieronymi P (2008) 'The Reasons of Trust', *Australasian Journal of Philosophy*, vol. 86, pp. 213–36.

Hildebrand C (2013) 'Thinking with Your Emotions: A Brief Look at the Role of Attitudes and Emotions in Moral Life', Cognizance. Available via www .cognizancejournal.com/journal.html accessed 4 October 2014.

Hinchliffe G (2002) 'Situating Skills', *Journal of Philosophy of Education*, vol. 36, pp. 187–205.

Hinchman ES (2005) 'Telling as Inviting to Trust', *Philosophy and Phenomenological Research*, vol. 70, pp. 562–87.

Hintikka J, Bachman J (1991) *What If?: Toward Excellence in Reasoning*, London, Mayfield Pub.

Hirschi, C (2014) 'Transparenz ist nur eine andere Form der Intransparenz', Frankfurter Allgemeine Zeitung, Geisteswissenschaften, edition of Jan. 8. page N4.

Hofmann B (2003) 'Medicine as Techne – A Perspective From Antiquity', *The Journal of Medicine and Philosophy*, vol. 28, pp. 403–25.

Hollis M (1998) *Trust within Reason*, Cambridge, Cambridge University Press.

Holtman MC (2008) 'A Theoretical Sketch of Medical Professionalism as a Normative Complex', *Advances in Health Sciences Education*, vol. 13, pp. 233–45.

Holton R (1994) 'Deciding to Trust, Coming to Believe', *Australasian Journal of Philosophy*, vol. 72, pp. 63–76.

Honderich T (2005) *The Oxford Companion of Philosophy*, Oxford, Oxford University Press.

Horton R (2005) 'Doctors in Society. Medical Professionalism in a Changing World (Report of the Working Party of the Royal College of Physicians)', *Clinical Medicine*, vol. 5, pp. S1–S40.

Huang CF (2013) 'Experimental Riskology: A New Discipline for Risk Analysis', *Human and Ecological Risk Assessment*, vol. 19, pp. 389–99.

Hughes J (2010) 'Justice in Research', in Hughes J (ed.) *European Textbook on Ethics in Research*, Brussels, European Commission, pp. 119–42.

Hughes J, Hunter M, Sheehan S et al. (2010) *European Textbook on Ethics in Research*, Luxembourg, Publications Office of the European Union.

Illingworth P (2002) 'Trust: The Scarcest of Medical Resources', *The Journal of Medicine and Philosophy*, vol. 27, pp. 31–46.

Iltis A (2007) 'Trust in Health Care: Reliable and Justifiable Expectations', *Revista Romana de Bioetica*, vol. 5, pp. 47–67.

Imber JB (2008) *Trusting Doctors – The Decline of Moral Authority in American Medicine*, Princeton NJ, Princeton University Press.

Imber JB (2017) 'How Navigating Uncertainty Motivates Trust in Medicine', *AMA.J Ethics*, vol. 19, pp. 391–8.

Ipsos MORI (2007) 'Ipsos MORI: Trust in Professions 2007'. Available via www.ipsos-mori.com/content/trust-in-professions-2007.ashx accessed 16 May 2018.

Ipsos MORI (2009) 'Ipsos MORI: Trust in Professions 2009'. Available via www.ipsos-mori.com/researchpublications/researcharchive/15/Trust-in-Professions.aspx?view=wide accessed 22 April 2011.

Jackson E (2013) *Medical Law: Text, Cases and Materials*, Oxford, Oxford University Press.

Jackson F (2010) 'Conceptual Analysis for Representationalists', *Grazer Philosophische Studien*, pp. 173–88.

Jacobs AK (2005) 'Rebuilding an Enduring Trust in Medicine – A Global Mandate – Presidential Address American Heart Association Scientific Sessions 2004', *Circulation*, vol. 111, pp. 3494–8.

Jacobs LR, Shapiro RY (1994) 'Public Opinion's Tilt against Private Enterprise', *Health Affairs*, vol. 13, pp. 285–98.

Jen MH, Sund ER, Johnston R et al. (2010) 'Trustful Societies, Trustful Individuals, and Health: An Analysis of Self-Rated Health and Social Trust Using the World Value Survey', *Health & Place*, vol. 16, pp. 1022–9.

Johnson D, Grayson K (2005) 'Cognitive and Affective Trust in Service Relationships', *Journal of Business Research*, vol. 58, pp. 500–7.

Jones K (2013) 'Trusting Interpretations', in Mäkelä P, Townley C (eds.) *Trust – Analytic and Applied Perspectives*, Amsterdam, Rodopi, pp. 15–29.

Jones K (1996) 'Trust as an Affective Attitude', *Ethics*, vol. 107, pp. 4–25.

Jones K (2012) 'Trustworthiness', *Ethics*, vol. 123, pp. 61–85.

Kadlac A (2015) 'The Virtue of Hope', *Ethical Theory & Moral Practice*, vol. 18, pp. 337–54.

Kahan DM (1999) 'The Progressive Appropriation of Disgust', in Bandes SA (ed.) *The Passions of Law. Critical America*, New York, New York University Press, pp. 63–79.

Kalra S, Unnikrishnan A, Baruah M (2017) 'Interaction, Information, Involvement: Rebuilding Trust in the Medical Profession', *Indian Journal of Endocrinology and Metabolism*, vol. 21, pp. 268–70.

Kane S, Calnan M (2016) 'Erosion of Trust in the Medical Profession in India: Time for Doctors to Act', *International Journal of Health Policy and Management*, vol. 6, pp. 5–8.

Kant I (1793) 'Religion within the Boundaries of mere Reason', in Wood AW, di Giovanni G (eds.) *Religion within the Boundaries of Mere Reason (1998)*, Cambridge, Cambridge University Press.

Kass LR (1997) 'The Wisdom of Repugnance', *New Republic*, vol. 216, pp. 17–26.

Kassirer J (2007) 'Commercialism and Medicine: an Overview', *Cambridge Quarterly of Healthcare Ethics;* vol. 16, pp. 377–86.

Keefe R (2002) 'When Does Circularity Matter?', *Proceedings of the Aristotelian Society*, vol. 102, pp. 275–92.

Kegan R, Lahey L (2001) *How the Way We Talk Can Change the Way We Work*, San Francisco, John Wiley.

Kelly D, Morar N (2014) 'Against the Yuck Factor: On the Ideal Role of Disgust in Society', *Utilitas*, vol. 26, pp. 153–77.

Kinsella E, Pitman A (2012) 'Engaging Phronesis in Professional Practice and Education', in Kinsella E, Pitman A (eds.) *Phronesis as Professional Knowledge*, Rotterdam, Sense Publishers, pp. 1–11.

Kirchin S (2013) *Thick Concepts*, Oxford, Oxford University Press.

Kitcher P, Schacht R (2004) *Finding an Ending – Reflections on Wagner's Ring*, Oxford, Oxford University Press.

Kiyonari T, Yamagishi T, Cook KS et al. (2006) 'Does Trust Beget Trustworthiness? Trust and Trustworthiness in Two Games and Two Cultures: A Research Note', *Social Psychology Quarterly*, vol. 69, pp. 270–83.

Knottnerus JA (1997) 'Medicine Based Evidence, a Prerequisite for Evidence Based Medicine', *British Medical Journal*, vol. 315, pp. 1109–10.

Koballa T (1988) 'Attitude and Related Concepts in Science Education', *Science Education*, vol. 72, pp. 115–26.

Kohn M (2008) *Trust – Self-Interest and the Common Good*, Oxford, Oxford University Press.

Kozusko SD, Elkwood L, Gaynor D et al. (2016) 'An Innovative Approach to the Surgical Time Out: A Patient-Focused Model', *AORN Journal*, vol. 103, pp. 617–22.

Kusch M (2007) 'Towards a Political Philosophy of Risk', in Lewens T (ed.) *Risk – Philosophical Perspectives*, London, Routledge, pp. 131–55.

Lackey J, Sosa E. (eds.) (2006) *The Epistemology of Testimony*, Oxford, Oxford University Press.

Lagerspetz, O, Hertzberg L (2013) 'Trust in Wittgenstein', in Mäkelä P, Townley C (eds.) *Trust – Analytic and Applied Perspectives*, Amsterdam, Rodopi, pp. 31–51.

Larson L (2000) 'Rebuilding Patient Trust. Jump in', *Trustee*, vol. 53, pp. 10–5, 1.

Lazarus R (1991) *Emotion and Adaptation*, New York, Oxford University Press.

Le Fanu J (2011) *The Rise and Fall of Modern Medicine*, London, Abacus.

Lee YY, Lin JL (2008) 'Linking Patients' Trust in Physicians to Health Outcomes', *British Journal of Hospital Medicine*, vol. 69, pp. 42–6.

Lind G (1984) 'Dynamic-Structural Attitude Unit: Concept and Measurement'. Available via www.uni-konstanz.de/ag-moral/pdf/Lind-1984_Attitude-structure_Rom-vortrag.pdf accessed 20 November 2016.

Locke J (1690) 'An Essay Concerning Human Understanding'. Available via http://enlightenment.supersaturated.com/johnlocke/preamble.html.

Lopez-Escamez JA, Carey J, Chung WH et al. (2015) 'Diagnostic Criteria for Meniere's Disease', *Journal of Vestibular Research*, vol. 25, pp. 1–7.

Lorian CN, Grisham JR (2010) 'The Safety Bias: Risk-Avoidance and Social Anxiety Pathology', *Behaviour Change*, vol. 27, pp. 29–41.

Luhmann N (2000) 'Familiarity, Confidence, Trust: Problems and Alternatives', in Gambetta D (ed.) *Trust: Making and Breaking Cooperative Relations*, New York, Basil Blackwell, pp. 94–107.

Lull J, Hinerman S (1997) *Media Scandals*, New York, Columbia University Press.

Mainous AG, Kern D, Hainer B et al. (2004) 'The Relationship between Continuity of Care and Trust with Stage of Cancer at Diagnosis', *Family Medicine*, vol. 36, pp. 35–9.

Manson N, O'Neill O (2007) *Rethinking Informed Consent in Bioethics*, Cambridge, Cambridge University Press.

McCullough LB (2009) 'Tracking the Variability of Authority and Power in the Physician-Patient Relationship', *Journal of Medicine and Philosophy*, vol. 34, pp. 1–5.

McGeer V (2008) 'Trust, Hope and Empowerment', *Australasian Journal of Philosophy*, vol. 86, pp. 237–54.

McKeown T (1976) *The Role of Medicine: Dream, Mirage, or Nemesis?*, London, Nuffield Provincial Hospitals Trust.

McKinlay JB, Marceau LD (2002) 'The End of the Golden Age of Doctoring', *International Journal of Health Services*, vol. 32, pp. 379–416.

McKnight DH, Chervany N (2001) 'Trust and Distrust Definitions: One Bite at a Time', *Lecture Notes in Computer Science*, vol. 2246, pp. 27–54.

Mcmyler B (2007) 'Knowing at Second Hand', *Inquiry*, vol. 50, pp. 511–40.

Mechanic D (1998) 'The Functions and Limitations of Trust in the Provision of Medical Care', *Journal of Health Politics, Policy and Law*, vol. 23, pp. 661–86.

Mechanic D (2004) 'In My Chosen Doctor I Trust', *British Medical Journal*, vol. 329, pp. 1418–9.

Mechanic D, Meyer S (2000) 'Concepts of Trust among Patients with Serious Illness', *Social Science & Medicine*, vol. 51, pp. 657–68.

Meirav A (2009) 'The Nature of Hope', *Ratio*, vol. 22, pp. 216–33.

Merrick A (2016) 'A Paradox of Hope?: Towards a Feminist Approach to Palliation', *International Journal of Feminist Approaches to Bioethics*, vol. 9, pp. 104–12.

Miller A (2003) *Contemporary Metaethics: An Introduction*, Cambridge, Polity Press.

Miller A (2006) 'Realism and Antirealism', in Lepore E, Smith B (eds.) *A Handbook of Philosophy of Language*, Oxford, Oxford University Press, pp. 983–1005.

Miller J (2000) 'Trust: The Moral Importance of an Emotional Attitude', *Practical Philosophy*, vol. 3, pp. 45–54.

Miller J (2007) 'The Other Side of Trust in Health Care: Prescribing Drugs with the Potential for Abuse', *Bioethics*, vol. 21, pp. 51–60.

Miller VA, Reynolds WW, Ittenbach RF et al. (2009) 'Challenges in Measuring a New Construct: A New Perception of Voluntariness for Research and Treatment Decision Making', *Journal of Empirical Research on Human Research Ethics*, vol. 4, pp. 21–31.

Millstone E, van Zwanenberg P (2000) 'A Crisis of Trust: for Science, Scientists or for Institutions?', *Nature Medicine*, vol. 6, pp. 1307–8.

Misztal BA (1996) *Trust in Modern Societies*, Cambridge, Polity Press.

Montgomery K (2009) 'Thinking about Thinking: Implications for Patient Safety', *Healthcare Quarterly*, vol. 12, pp. e191–e194.

Moore J (2009) *'The Logic of Definition'*, Toronto, Defense R&D Canada, pp. 1–13.

Mossialos E, McKee M (2003) 'Rationing Treatment on the NHS – Still a Political Issue', *Journal of the Royal Society of Medicine*, vol. 96, pp. 372–3.

Nelson RM, Beauchamp T, Miller VA et al. (2011) 'The Concept of Voluntary Consent', *The American Journal of Bioethics*, vol. 11, pp. 6–16.

Newson A, Wrigley A (2016) 'Being Human: The Ethics, Law, and Scientific Progress of Genome Editing', *Australian Quarterly, the Australian Institute of Policy and Science*, vol. 87, pp. 3–8.

Nichols T (2017) *The Death of Expertise: The Campaign against Established Knowledge and Why It Matters*, New York, Oxford University Press.

Nickel PJ (2007) 'Trust and Obligation-Ascription', *Ethical Theory and Moral Practice*, vol. 10, pp. 309–19.

Nickel PJ (2009) 'Trust, Staking, and Expectations', *Journal for the Theory of Social Behaviour*, vol. 39, pp. 345–62.

Nie JB, Cheng Y, Zou X et al. (2017) 'The Vicious Circle of Patient-Physician Mistrust in China: Health Professionals' Perspectives, Institutional Conflict of Interest, and Building Trust through Medical Professionalism', *Developing World Bioethics*, vol. 18, pp. 26–36.

Norris P (2009) 'Skeptical Patients: Performance, Social Capital, and Culture', in Shore DA (ed.) *The Trust Crisis in Health Care*, Oxford, Oxford University Press, pp. 32–46.

Nozick R (1993) *The Nature of Rationality*, Princeton, NJ, Princeton University Press.

O'Brien W (2014) 'The Meaning of Life: Early Continental and Analytic Perspectives'. Available via www.iep.utm.edu/2014/ accessed 16 May 2018.

O'Neill J (1992) 'The Varieties of Intrinsic Value', in Keller DR (ed.) *Environmental Ethics - the Big Questions*, Chichester, Wiley-Blackwell (Reprint 2010), pp. 120–9.

O'Neill O (2002a) *Autonomy and Trust in Bioethics*, Cambridge, Cambridge University Press.

O'Neill O (2002b) *A Question of Trust*, Cambridge, Cambridge University Press.

Omodei M (2000) 'Conceptualizing and Measuring Global Interpersonal Mistrust-Trust', *The Journal of Social Psychology*, vol. 140, pp. 279–94.

Origgi G (2004) 'Is Trust an Epistemological Notion?', *Episteme*, vol. 1, pp. 61–72.

Origgi G (2008) 'Trust, Authority and Epistemic Responsibility', *Theoria*, vol. 23, pp. 35–44.

Pellegrino ED (1991) 'Trust and Distrust in Professional Ethics', in Pellegrino D, Veatch RM et al. (eds.) *Ethics, Trust, and the Professions*, Washington, DC, Georgetown University Press, pp. 69–89.

Peterson C (2000) 'The Future of Optimism', *American Psychologist*, vol. 55, pp. 44–55.

Pettit P (2004) 'Hope and Its Place in Mind', *The Annals of the American Academy of Political and Social Science*, vol. 592, pp. 152–65.

Pettit P (1995) 'The Cunning of Trust', *Philosophy & Public Affairs*, vol. 24, pp. 202–25.

Pieters W (2006) 'Acceptance of Voting Technology: Between Confidence and Trust', in Stoelen K, Winsborough WH et al. (eds.) *Trust Management*, Berlin, Springer-Verlag, pp. 283–97.

Pitman A (2012) 'Professionalism and Professionalisation – Hostile Ground for Growing Phronesis?', in Kinsella EA, Pitman A (eds.) *Phronesis as Professional Knowledge*, Rotterdam, Sense Publishers, pp. 131–46.

Priaulx N, Weinel M, Wrigley A (2016) 'Rethinking Moral Expertise', *Health Care Analysis*, vol. 24, pp. 393–406.

Quill T (1983) 'Partnerships in Patient Care: A Contractual Approach', *Annals of Internal Medicine*, vol. 98, pp. 228–34.

Quine W (1951) 'Two Dogmas of Empiricism', *The Philosophical Review*, vol. 60, pp. 20–43.

Rawls J (1971) *A Theory of Justice*, Cambridge, MA, Harvard University Press (revised edition 1999).

Reames BN, Ghaferi AA, Birkmeyer JD et al. (2014) 'Hospital Volume and Operative Mortality in the Modern Era', *Annals of Surgery*, vol. 260, pp. 244–51.

Rhodes R (2000) 'Trust and Transforming Medical Institutions', *Cambridge Quarterly of Healthcare Ethics*, vol. 9, pp. 205–17.

Rhodes R (2001) 'Understanding the Trusted Doctor and Constructing a Theory of Bioethics', *Theoretical Medicine and Bioethics*, vol. 22, pp. 493–504.

Roberts LW (2017) 'Is a Doctor Like a Toaster? Earning Trust in the Profession of Medicine', *Academic Psychiatry*, vol. 41, pp. 305–8.

Rodwin MA (1994) 'Patient Accountability and Quality of Care: Lessons from Medical Consumerism and the Patients' Rights, Women's Health and Disability Rights Movements', *American Journal of Law & Medicine*, vol. 20, pp. 147-67.

Rokeach M, Smith M (1968) 'Attitudes'. Available via www.encyclopedia.com accessed 14 January 2014.

Rose A, Peters N, Shea JA et al. (2004) 'Development and Testing of the Health Care System Distrust Scale', *Journal of General Internal Medicine*, vol. 19, pp. 57-63.

Rowe R, Calnan M (2006) 'Trust Relations in Health Care–The New Agenda', *European Journal of Public Health*, vol. 16, pp. 4-6.

Ruokonen F (2013) 'Trust, Trustworthiness, and Responsibility', in Mäkelä P, Townley C (eds.) *Trust – Analytic and Applied Perspectives*, Amsterdam, Rodopi, pp. 1-14.

Sackett DL, Rosenberg WMC, Gray JAM et al. (1996) 'Evidence Based Medicine: What It Is and What It Isn't – It's about Integrating Individual Clinical Expertise and the Best External Evidence', *British Medical Journal*, vol. 312, pp. 71-2.

Sampson W (1996) 'Antiscience Trends in the Rise of the "Alternative Medicine" Movement', *Annals of the New York Academy of Science*, vol. 775, pp. 188-97.

Sandel M (2012) *What Money Can't Buy – The Moral Limits of Markets*, London, Allen Lane.

Schermer M (2002) *The Different Faces of Autonomy*, Dordrecht, Boston, London, Kluwer Academic Publishers.

Scheunemann LP, White DB (2011) 'The Ethics and Reality of Rationing in Medicine', *CHEST*, vol. 140, pp. 1625-32.

Schiltz, C (2008) 'Ärzte pfuschen bei jedem zehnten Patienten', *DIE WELT*, edition of Nov. 24.

Schlesinger M (2002) 'A Loss of Faith: The Sources of Reduced Political Legitimacy for the American Medical Profession', *The Milbank Quarterly*, vol. 80, p. 185.

Schmitt F (2004) 'What Is Wrong with Epistemic Circularity?', *Philosophical Issues*, vol. 14, pp. 379-402.

Schwab AP (2008) 'Epistemic Trust, Epistemic Responsibility, and Medical Practice', *Journal of Medicine and Philosophy*, vol. 33, pp. 302-20.

Schwartz J, Chapman G, Brewer N et al. (2004) 'The Effects of Accountability on Bias in Physician Decision Making: Going from Bad to Worse', *Psychonomic Bulletin & Review*, vol. 11, pp. 173-8.

Schwarz N, Bohner G (2001) 'The Construction of Attitudes', in Tesser A, Schwarz N (eds.) *Intraindividual Processes (Blackwell Handbook of Social Psychology)*, Oxford, Oxford University Press, pp. 436-57.

Schwitzgebel E (2011) 'Belief', in Zalta E (ed.) *The Stanford Encyclopedia of Philosophy (Winter 2011 Edition)*.

Searle J (1969) *Speech Acts*, Cambridge, Cambridge University Press.

Seemungal B, Kaski D, Lopez-Escamez JA (2015) 'Early Diagnosis and Management of Acute Vertigo from Vestibular Migraine and Meniere's Disease', *Neurologic Clinics*, vol. 33, pp. 619–28.

Sellman D (2012) 'Reclaiming Competence for Professional Phronesis', in Kinsella EA, Pitman A (eds.) *Phronesis as Professional Knowledge*, Rotterdam, Sense Publishers, pp. 115–30.

Sharlin HI (1989) 'Risk Perception – Changing the Terms of the Debate', *Journal of Hazardous Materials*, vol. 21, pp. 261–72.

Shea J, Micco E, Dean L et al. (2008) 'Development of a Revised Health Care System Distrust Scale', *Journal of General Internal Medicine*, vol. 23, pp. 727–32.

Shore D (2007) 'The (Sorry) State of Trust in the American Healthcare Enterprise', in Shore DA (ed.) *The Trust Crisis in Health Care*, Oxford, Oxford University Press, pp. 3–20.

Sierpina VS (2006) 'The History of Complementary and Integrative Medicine', *Southern Medical Journal*, vol. 99, pp. 906–7.

Simpson T (2012) 'What Is Trust?', *Pacific Philosophical Quarterly*, vol. 93, pp. 550–69.

Smith C (2005) 'Understanding Trust and Confidence: Two Paradigms and Their Significance for Health and Social Care', *Journal of Applied Philosophy*, vol. 22.

Specter M (2009) *Denialism: How Irrational Thinking Hinders Scientific Progress, Harms the Planet, and Threatens Our Lives*, New York, Penguin Press.

Stahel PF, VanderHeiden TF, Kim FJ (2017) 'Why Do Surgeons Continue to Perform Unnecessary Surgery?', *Patient Safety in Surgery*, vol. 11, p. 1

Starr P (1984) *The Social Transformation of American Medicine*, New York, Basic Books.

Stirrat GM, Gill R (2005) 'Autonomy in Medical Ethics after O'Neill', *Journal of Medical Ethics*, vol. 31, pp. 127–30.

Strawson PF (1992) *Analysis and Metaphysics – An Introduction to Philosophy*, Oxford, Oxford University Press.

Strawson P (1962) 'Freedom and Resentment', *Reprinted in Freedom and Resentment and Other Essays*, Oxford, Routledge, 2008, pp. 1–28.

Sturmberg JP (2015) 'Rebuilding Trust – the Real Challenge for Health System Improvement', *European Journal of Clinical Investigation*, vol. 45, pp. 441–2.

Sulmasy DP (1993) 'What's So Special about Medicine?', *Theoretical Medicine*, vol. 14, pp. 27–42.

Sunstein C (2007) 'Moral Heuristics and Risk', in Lewens T (ed.) *Risk – Philosophical Perspectives*, London, Routledge, pp. 156–70.

Swartz N (2010) 'Definitions, Dictionaries, and Meanings'. Available via www .sfu.ca/~swartz/definitions.htm accessed 2 June 2015.

Sweeney K (2002) 'Clinical Evaluation: Constructing a New Model for Post-Normal Medicine', *Journal of Evaluation in Clinical Practice*, vol. 8, pp. 131–8.

Sztompka P (1999) *Trust: A Sociological Theory*, Cambridge, Cambridge University Press.

Tanis S, DiNapoli P (2008) 'Paradox of Hope in Patients Receiving Palliative Care: A Concept Analysis', *International Journal for Human Caring*, vol. 12, pp. 50–4.

Thom DH (2001) 'Physician Behaviors that Predict Patient Trust', *Journal of Family Practice*, vol. 50, pp. 323–8.

Tuomela M, Hofmann S (2003) 'Simulating Rational Social Normative Trust, Predictive Trust, and Predictive Reliance between Agents', *Ethics and Information Technology*, vol. 5, pp. 163–76.

Tyreman S (2000) 'Promoting Critical Thinking in Health Care: Phronesis and Criticality', *Medicine, Health Care and Philosophy*, vol. 3, pp. 117–24.

Veatch R (1991) 'Is Trust of Professionals a Coherent Concept?', in Pellegrino D, Veatch RM et al. (eds.) *Ethics, Trust, and the Professions*, Washington, DC, Georgetown University Press, pp. 159–73.

Wall E (2001) 'Voluntary Action', *Philosophia*, vol. 28, pp. 127–36.

Wallace R (2008) 'Emotions, Expectations, and Responsibility', in McKenna M, Russel P (eds.) *Free Will and Reactive Attitudes*, Farnham, Ashgate, pp. 157–85.

Ward NS, Teno JM, Curtis JR et al. (2008) 'Perceptions of Cost Constraints, Resource Limitations, and Rationing in United States Intensive Care Units: Results of a National Survey', *Critical Care Medicine*, vol. 36, pp. 471–6.

Welch G, Schwartz L (2012) *Overdiagnosed: Making People Sick in the Pursuit of Health*, Boston, Beacon Press.

Wertheimer A (2012) 'Voluntary Consent: Why a Value-Neutral Concept Won't Work', *Journal of Medicine and Philosophy*, vol. 37, pp. 226–54.

Wiedemann PM, Thalmann AT, Grutsch MA et al. (2006) 'The Impacts of Precautionary Measures and the Disclosure of Scientific Uncertainty on EMF Risk Perception and Trust', *Journal of Risk Research*, vol. 9, pp. 361–72.

Wildavsky A (1989) 'The Secret of Safety Lies in Danger', *Society*, vol. 27, pp. 4–5.

Wildavsky A (1994) 'Exaggerated Danger', *Nature*, vol. 367, pp. 227–8.

Wildavsky A, Wildavsky A (2014) 'Risk and Safety'. Available via www.econlib.org /library/Enc/RiskandSafety.html accessed 24 April 2014.

Wilkinson S (2013) *Bodies for Sale*, New York, Routledge.

William CG (2007) 'Assessing Quality: Today's Data and a Research Agenda', in Shore DA (ed.) *The Trust Crisis in Health Care*, Oxford, Oxford University Press, pp. 70–6.

Wilson E (1998) *Consilience: The Unity of Knowledge*, New York, Vintage (reprint 1999).

Wittgenstein L (1953) *Philosophical Investigations*, Oxford, Basil Blackwell (Translation by G.E.M. Anscombe, 1998).

WMA (2009) 'WMA Declaration of Madrid on Professionally-led Regulation'. Available via www.wma.net/en/30publications/10policies/r4/index.html accessed 7 November 2013.

Wolfensberger M (1992) 'Using Cox's Proportional Hazards Model for Prognostication in Carcinoma of the Upper Aerodigestive Tract', *Acta Oto-Laryngologica*, vol. 112, pp. 376–82.

Wolfensberger M, Arnoux A, Zbären Pet al. (2002) 'Empfehlungen für die Abklärung, Behandlung und Nachsorge von Patienten mit Karzinomen des Kopf-Hals-Bereiches (published 2002, last up-date 2011)'. Available via www .orl-hno.ch.

Wright C (1992) *Truth and Objectivity*, Cambridge, MA, Harvard University Press.

Wrigley A (2006) 'Genetic Selection and Modal Harms', *The Monist*, vol. 89, pp. 505–25.

Wrigley A (2007a) 'Proxy Consent: Moral Authority Misconceived', *The Journal of Medical Ethics*, vol. 33, pp. 527–31.

Wrigley A (2007b) 'Personal Identity, Autonomy and Advance Statements', *The Journal of Applied Philosophy*, vol. 24, pp. 381–96.

Wrigley A (2012) 'Harm to Future Persons: Non-Identity Problems and Counterpart Solutions', *Ethical Theory and Moral Practice*, vol. 15, pp. 175–90.

Wrigley A (2015) 'An Eliminativist Approach to Vulnerability', Bioethics, vol. 29, pp. 478–87.

Xin Z, Xin S (2017) 'Marketization Process Predicts Trust Decline in China', *Journal of Economic Psychology*, vol. 62, pp. 120–9.

Yan Y (2017) 'The Ethics and Politics of Patient-Physician Mistrust in Contemporary China', *Developing World Bioethics*, vol. 8, pp. 7–15.

INDEX

Books in the Series

Marcus Radetzki, Marian Radetzki and Niklas Juth
Genes and Insurance: Ethical, Legal and Economic Issues

Ruth Macklin
Double Standards in Medical Research in Developing Countries

Donna Dickenson
Property in the Body: Feminist Perspectives

Matti Häyry, Ruth Chadwick, Vilhjálmur Árnason and Gardar Árnason
The Ethics and Governance of Human Genetic Databases: European Perspectives

Ken Mason
The Troubled Pregnancy: Legal Wrongs and Rights in Reproduction

Daniel Sperling
Posthumous Interests: Legal and Ethical Perspectives

Keith Syrett
Law, Legitimacy and the Rationing of Health Care

Alastair Maclean
Autonomy, Informed Consent and the Law: A Relational Change

Heather Widdows and Caroline Mullen
The Governance of Genetic Information: Who Decides?

David Price
Human Tissue in Transplantation and Research

Matti Häyry
Rationality and the Genetic Challenge: Making People Better?

Mary Donnelly
Healthcare Decision-Making and the Law: Autonomy, Capacity and the Limits of Liberalism

Anne-Maree Farrell, David Price and Muireann Quigley
Organ Shortage: Ethics, Law and Pragmatism

Sara Fovargue
Xenotransplantation and Risk: Regulating a Developing Biotechnology

John Coggon
What Makes Health Public? A Critical Evaluation of Moral, Legal, and Political Claims in Public Health

Mark Taylor
Genetic Data and the Law: A Critical Perspective on Privacy Protection

Anne-Maree Farrell
The Politics of Blood: Ethics, Innovation and the Regulation of Risk

Stephen Smith
End-of-Life Decisions in Medical Care: Principles and Policies for Regulating the Dying Process

Michael Parker
Ethical Problems and Genetics Practice

William W. Lowrance
Privacy, Confidentiality, and Health Research

Kerry Lynn Macintosh
Human Cloning: Four Fallacies and Their Legal Consequence

Heather Widdows
The Connected Self: The Ethics and Governance of the Genetic Individual

Amel Alghrani, Rebecca Bennett and Suzanne Ost
Bioethics, Medicine and the Criminal Law Volume I: The Criminal Law and Bioethical Conflict: Walking the Tightrope

Danielle Griffiths and Andrew Sanders
Bioethics, Medicine and the Criminal Law Volume II: Medicine, Crime and Society

Margaret Brazier and Suzanne Ost
Bioethics, Medicine and the Criminal Law Volume III: Medicine and Bioethics in the Theatre of the Criminal Process

Sigrid Sterckx, Kasper Raus and Freddy Mortier
Continuous Sedation at the End of Life: Ethical, Clinical and Legal Perspectives

A. M. Viens, John Coggon and Anthony S. Kessel
Criminal Law, Philosophy and Public Health Practice

Ruth Chadwick, Mairi Levitt and Darren Shickle
The Right to Know and the Right Not to Know: Genetic Privacy and Responsibility

Eleanor D. Kinney
The Affordable Care Act and Medicare in Comparative Context

Katri Lõhmus
Caring Autonomy: European Human Rights Law and the Challenge of Individualism

Catherine Stanton and Hannah Quirk
Criminalising Contagion: Legal and Ethical Challenges of Disease Transmission and the Criminal Law

Sharona Hoffman
Electronic Health Records and Medical Big Data: Law and Policy

Barbara Prainsack and Alena Buyx
Solidarity in Biomedicine and Beyond

Camillia Kong
Mental Capacity in Relationship

Oliver Quick
Regulating Patient Safety: The End of Professional Dominance?

Thana C. de Campos
The Global Health Crisis: Ethical Responsibilities

Jonathan Ives, Michael Dunn and Alan Cribb
Empirical Bioethics: Theoretical and Practical Perspectives

Alan Merry and Warren Brookbanks
Merry and McCall Smith's Errors, Medicine and the Law (second edition)

Donna Dickenson
Property in the Body: Feminist Perspectives (second edition)

Rosie Harding
Duties to Care: Dementia, Relationality and Law

Ruud ter Meulen
Solidarity and Justice in Health and Social Care

David Albert Jones, Chris Gastmans and Calum MacKellar
Euthanasia and Assisted Suicide: Lessons from Belgium

Muireann Quigley
Self-Ownership, Property Rights, and the Human Body

Françoise Baylis and Alice Dreger
Bioethics in Action

John Keown
Euthanasia, Ethics and Public Policy: An Argument against Legislation (second edition)

Amel Alghrani
Regulating Assisted Reproductive Technologies: New Horizons

Britta van Beers, Sigrid Sterckx and Donna Dickenson
Personalized Medicine, Individual Choice and the Common Good

David G. Kirchhoffer and Bernadette J. Richards
Beyond Autonomy: Limits and Alternatives to Informed Consent in Research Ethics and Law

Markus Wolfensberger and Anthony Wrigley
Trust in Medicine: Its Nature, Justification, Significance, and Decline

Printed in Great Britain
by Amazon